How to Be Safe in an Unsafe World

Also by Harold H. Bloomfield, M.D.

HOW TO BE SAFE
IN AN UNSAFE WORLD

Harold H. Bloomfield, M.D.
and Robert K. Cooper, Ph.D.

CROWN PUBLISHERS, INC.
New York

Every effort has been made to obtain permission from the appropriate parties to include the cited works, but if any errors have been made we will be happy to correct them. We gratefully acknowledge the following permissions: Excerpts and adaptations from *Options for Avoiding Assault* by Mary Tesoro. Copyright 1994. Reprinted with permission of Mary Tesoro and SDE News, San Luis Obispo, California. Excerpts from *Aikido in Everyday Life: Giving In to Get Your Way* by Terry Dobson and Victor Miller. Copyright 1978 and 1993. Reprinted by permission of North Atlantic Books, Berkeley, California. Excerpts from *Fist Stick Knife Gun* by Geoffrey Canada. Copyright 1995. Reprinted with permission of Beacon Press, Boston.

Published by Crown Publishers, Inc., 201 East 50th Street, New York, New York 10022. Member of the Crown Publishing Group.

Random House, Inc. New York, Toronto, London, Sydney, Auckland
http://www.randomhouse.com/

CROWN and colophon are trademarks of Crown Publishers, Inc.

Printed in the United States of America

Design by Susan Hood

Library of Congress Cataloging-in-Publication Data is available upon request.

ISBN 0-517-70308-4

10   9   8   7   6   5   4   3   2   1

First Edition

We dedicate this book to those
who value Safety
not as an end in itself
but as a Way through which
the heart, mind, and spirit can grow
and, in growing, help to create
a more peaceful and enlightened world
through everyday acts of
conscious caring and courage.

Contents

DISCOVERING INNER SAFETY

It is a great joy to introduce this book, which is a milestone achievement—a compassionate, scientifically referenced, and immediately empowering guide to one of the most vital yet misunderstood issues of our era: safety. It is urgently clear that outer security and inner safety are absolutely essential to personal health, loving relationships, and spiritual growth. I would like to tell you about two instances in my life when my safety was threatened.

The first was in 1971 when my daughter Malika was about six weeks old. My wife, Rita, had gone shopping leaving me alone with Malika, who was asleep in her crib. At the time, I was earning about $500 a month as a medical intern, so we lived in a poor area of Boston. When the doorbell rang, I thought it must be Rita.

I opened the door and there was a man who must have been six feet four inches tall. He was large and muscular and was hiding his hands behind his back. I said, "Could I help you?" He said nothing, but his look was terribly menacing as he pushed his way inside and brandished a baseball bat. Though I felt only half his size, my only safety instinct at that moment was to protect my daughter. I let out a bloodcurdling scream, and at the same time I leaped to the side. He seemed completely stunned at my sudden response, and the baseball bat dropped from his hands. I jumped forward and picked it up, swinging it with all my might and striking him on the neck and back of the head. The next thing I knew he was sprawled on the floor, bleeding. My scream had been so loud that three of my neighbors opened their windows and one of them called the police. Soon, I heard the sirens and police cars screeching to a halt outside the apartment building. Miraculously, Malika was still blissfully asleep in her crib and didn't seem to have heard or seen any of the commotion. When the police identified my intruder, he turned out to be one of their "most wanted" criminals for multiple murders and armed robbery. Everyone took my photograph and wanted my autograph. This was the real reason I became famous!

The second attack happened in Louisville, Kentucky, in 1994. I was feeling great after giving an evening lecture at a downtown auditorium where about twelve hundred people had assembled to hear me talk about spirituality. By about 10:30 P.M., I had finished signing books and going through the crowd. My hotel was two blocks away. I thought I'd take the back alley from the theater to my hotel because I didn't want the crowd to follow me. I was finished for the day!

As I stepped out into the alley and the heavy metal door slammed closed, two people immediately appeared out of the shadows and cornered me, blocking my path. I could see they were young, about eighteen to twenty years old. They each had a gun, which they put to my temples. At once, I sensed their fear and nervousness. My response to them was, "Relax. Really . . . relax. I'll give you my wallet. Don't be nervous. Take my wallet and run." They had their guns to my head all the while I was saying this. I slowly took out my wallet and gave them all my money, about $700, and told them to run, which they did. They sprinted away down the alley. Finally, I reached my hotel but did not report the incident to the police and actually had a sound night's sleep. I had to borrow some cash the next day and flew home to San Diego as if nothing had happened. Yet something certainly had!

In hindsight, I believe that if you feel safe in your heart, your inner intelligence can compute the best response to make. In the first attack, my quantum intelligence made an evaluation: "This man is hostile and dangerous," so I had to act suddenly and use surprise to unnerve him and take control. That's what happened. In the second attack, my quantum intelligence computed something else: "These muggers seem nervous and afraid, and if I respond aggressively, they may become violent and shoot me." And that would have been the end of the story. So I tried to remain calm and allay their anxiety, not to threaten them or demean them in any way, handing over my money and encouraging them to run.

Once developed, a keen sense of inner safety can be far more precise and accurate than the rigid limits of rational thought. I believe in placing *intention* and *attention* on the principle "Safety first." Using simple mind-body exercises, almost anyone can learn to convert the racing heartbeat of free-floating fear, anger, or anxiety into the calm-alertness of inner safety. What seems out of control when you feel unsafe can be brought back into control with the proper technique.

In harmony, there is no violence. It is fear that inevitably brings violence in its wake. Instead of futilely trying to control the uncontrollable, a person in unity learns to acknowledge reality, not because he has to but because there is actually peace and inner safety in calmly facing whatever is happening. The involuntary centers of the brain can be programmed to automatically be alert for danger, poised to activate the safety response at a moment's notice and to use your *safety intelligence*—one of the key foundations of this book—to avoid or cope with any danger or threat.

Inner safety is characterized by the following:

I am calm, present, and relaxed within my body.
I am fully aware, and I am secure.

My breathing is smooth and deep, approaching stillness.
Self-acceptance flows through me to others.

I recommend experiencing and renewing your inner safety
with a short period of meditation each day in the morning before
you go to work and again just after you arrive home in the
evening. In a world gone more than slightly violent and mad,
finding your core of safety is like recapturing the fort of silence,
sanity, and peace. The mind replenishes itself in silence and
peace, the quantum source for all activity. The release of emotional burdens and negative energies during these inner "safety
meditations" can be quite dramatic and invigorating. Most important, you will begin to live each moment with a foundation of
inner safety, which is the most natural and healthful way to face
life, no matter how hectic or threatening.

Drs. Bloomfield and Cooper can help each of us develop one
of the greatest gifts of all, safety within ourselves and in the
world. This brilliant book belongs on every coffee table, night-
stand, and office desk in America!

> DEEPAK CHOPRA,
> best-selling author of *The Seven Spiritual
> Laws of Success; Ageless Body, Timeless Mind;*
> and *The Path to Love*

OUR NEED TO BE SAFE

My father's death serves as a symbol of the need for physical and emotional safety. He was a generous, compassionate man who was robbed by a hitchhiker and then left locked in the trunk of his car. After spending several desperate hours struggling to get out, he died of heat asphyxiation. Twice while he was struggling to survive, nearby residents called the police to report an abandoned car. Twice, the police responded but, because of vague directions from the callers, could not locate the car. On the third call, they found my father's car, but it was too late.

Returning home from the funeral, I went to the car to see how my father had died, to feel what it must have been like. I climbed into the trunk and pulled shut the trunk lid, running my fingers over the dents where he had repeatedly pounded to get help or to break out. I felt his aloneness and terror. Still in the trunk, I noticed where he had broken out the back light trying to get air. Instinctively, I stretched my arm and extended my hand through the hole he had made. One of my brothers, who had been standing outside the car, said, "See if you can reach the button and pop the trunk." I reached my hand out a little farther and released the trunk lid. If my dad had thought to open the trunk with his hand, he might have lived. I, too, being inside the trunk and struggling to get out, did not think to reach for the trunk button and release it from the outside.

How to Be Safe in an Unsafe World is a vital, practical book that points to many of the "buttons" by which we can free ourselves from the tyranny of fear and violence in our personal lives, relationships, at work, and in our neighborhoods and communities.

While growing up, nearly all of us are taught in various direct and indirect ways to manage, or control, our feelings. Little boys are taught: "Big boys don't cry—be strong." The message is that they don't have permission to show their vulnerable feelings. They are given implicit or overt permission to be aggressive because this is supposedly a "natural" and inherently masculine trait. In many cases, boys are taught that they can show their anger and rage, but that it isn't safe for them ever to show hurt or fear, because that might make other boys ridicule them or beat them up.

Most violent crimes are perpetrated by men because they are stuck on the level of anger and rage and driven to be more action-oriented. When a typical adult male has a strong emotional reaction, he may tend to flare into anger or turn to blame, since it isn't safe for him to explore or express other emotions and feelings of vulnerability. Sometimes, men will stay stuck in their angry feelings until they get even or until they repress their emotions entirely and shut down, becoming numb and unreachable. I have worked with many men who, when given permission to express their hurt, fear, and guilt, have experienced a tremendous emotional and physical release and sense of healing, letting go of chronic free-floating anger and beginning to feel love again.

I believe that, to some degree, all family violence is the result of unresolved anger. Unfortunately, if a man feels threatened, the last thing he feels safe doing is admitting that he is vulnerable and feels hurt or fear. So he will probably just pretend he doesn't care or pretend he "can handle it," which causes him to stay stuck in feeling angry or frustrated. Staying angry is one of the most common ways of resisting our hurt, anxieties, and sadness. The angriest people I know don't feel safe accepting or expressing the true feelings of hurt they have inside. The louder they scream and yell, the more confrontational they become, the more out of touch with their true feelings they become, and the worse things get in their life, relationships, and work. This has become a national crisis of epidemic proportions.

For many women, the situation is the reverse. Little girls are often taught never to express anger or hostility. It's not "nice" to become upset, get angry, or scream—Daddy won't like it and neither will other men. However, many girls are taught that it is just fine to display their feelings of vulnerability, hurt, and sadness. They can cry all they want to and are even programmed by the dangers in our male-violence-centered society, and the experiences girls have in life, television, and news headlines, to feel afraid for their safety much of the time. So, as an adult, when a woman has something frightening or painful happen to her, she will tend to cry and feel afraid but probably will not openly and consistently express her inner anger. Criticism, crying, or sulking can become a cover-up for anger, mistrust, and rage. The woman becomes stuck in sadness and despair and may eventually, in this trap, become hysterical. I've worked with many women who felt stuck in grief and hurt. After teaching them how to safely express anger, I've watched them miraculously recover and feel safer and more alive, loving, and less critical of others.

When you numb yourself to so-called undesirable emotions, you are in truth numbing your ability to feel strong positive emotions—enthusiasm, joy, and intimacy, for example—as well. Every time you suppress a feeling you don't feel safe with, you are systematically destroying your ability to feel, and with it the passion and closeness in your relationships. And in this state of repression and numbness, you are, paradoxically, even *more* vulnerable to being a victim of crime or hurt in other ways by the words or actions of others.

Down through the centuries, women have looked to men for protection because it was crucial to their family's survival. This

protector role carries over into the present day and our relationships. Emotional security ensures that a woman is safe to share
her feelings without an invalidating argument, rejection, or interruption from her man. It means that she can talk openly and honestly without worrying about hurting him or reprisal. It means
she can be in a bad mood from time to time without her mate
holding it against her or ignoring or condemning her for it. Emotional security frees her to be herself.

When a man counters a woman's feelings with his own free-
floating anger, it is much harder, even impossible, for her to feel
heard and valued. In many cases, it is okay if he is upset with her
about something, or angry about a difficult day, but it is not okay
when anger is set loose against her simply because she's a conve-
nient target, or when a man "tunes out" what a woman is trying to
express and escalates to arguments and put-downs, which can
result in a woman's legitimate fear of violence. When a woman
truly feels safe in a relationship and can openly and emotionally
"be herself," then the intensity of her feelings eases, making it easier for a man to defuse his need to ignore, deny, or argue.

I'm giving copies of this book to each and every member of my
family and to all of my closest friends. My friend and mentor
Harold H. Bloomfield, M.D., and his colleague Robert K. Cooper, Ph.D., have written a groundbreaking, must-read book. Feeling unsafe blocks millions of Americans from achieving their
goals and dreams and creates a hidden barrier to fulfilling relationships and success in life. At last, we're beginning to discover
some of the answers—and you'll find them in this book. Brilliant!

JOHN GRAY, PH.D.,
best-selling author of *Men Are
from Mars, Women Are from Venus*
and *What You Feel, You Can Heal*

Chapter 1

SAFETY IS THE #1 HUMAN NEED

The need for safety is even deeper than the need to love
and be loved.

ABRAHAM MASLOW, PH.D.,
founder of humanistic psychology

The most essential human need—beyond the necessity for air,
water, and food—is to be *safe*. It is even more essential to life than
to be loved. Unfortunately, all across America the feeling of being
*un*safe has been growing in the hearts and minds of people in
every family, in every neighborhood.

The reasons for this are many. But central to all of them is the
fact that we live in an unsafe world, and we need to make the best
of it. Although we inhabit a planet that, by many accounts, offers
unprecedented opportunities and a dreamscape of dazzling
potential, it's also a place of expanding peril and numbing incivil-
ity. As our population grows, in large cities and small country
towns alike, tens of millions of men, women, and children now
feel trapped in a struggle for safety and survival. No matter who
you are, no matter where you live, personal safety is a legitimate
concern at work, at home, and when traveling.

As health professionals, who for years have been involved in
the war against the premature breakdown of human minds and
bodies, we have come to realize that major causes of health
deterioration go beyond a poor diet, cigarette smoke, or lack of

exercise—and include a *chronic sense of lack of safety.* Unfortunately, health professionals have made few attempts to face this issue head-on. And that is our purpose in researching and writing a book that will teach you ways to be safer in an unsafe world.

THE SAFETY CRISIS

At times, the world can be a dangerous place. We encounter all kinds of strangers. Sometimes they are kind but sometimes they are not, and it pays to be ready . . . for those laying traps for us.

    WILLIAM J. BENNETT, *The Book of Virtues*

"Violence in America has become 'a public health emergency,'" according to the American Medical Association's recent first annual National Report Card on Violence.[1] "Discouraging as it is," AMA president Robert E. McAfee told a news conference in Chicago, "the overall grade is D. And in 'public violence,' which includes firearms crimes, the U.S. receives a grade of F on our report card." "Violence," he said, "is the AMA's number one public health issue." For many reasons it seems that a sense of free-floating anger, powerlessness, depression, anxiety, and hair-trigger rage have become so common as to seem epidemic among us. *The Figgie Report, a national survey on fear of crime, indicates that four out of five Americans "are afraid of being assaulted, robbed, raped, or murdered."*[2] *In a 1995 survey, more than one in three Americans reported feeling "truly desperate" about rising violence.*[3]

Trapped in this new architecture of fear, many people are trying to find a renewed sense of safety behind locked doors and alarm systems. At best, though, these measures are a very limited part of being and feeling *safe;* in fact, they can make us prisoners in our own homes.

According to sociologist Dane Archer of the University of California, Santa Cruz: "If you're afraid, you're already a victim of violent crime."[4] And, the truth is, *feeling safe also matters because being constantly afraid may kill you faster than violence itself.* With deadly precision, an ongoing fear for personal safety can systematically destroy brain cells and the muscle fibers of your heart,[5] undermine your career, erode your love relationships, and accelerate the aging of your mind.[6] Easily the worst mistake many of us make is how we deal with the fear for our safety. Beyond your health, chronic fear for personal and family safety can also damage your career, relationships, and spirit.

The erosion of *inner safety* is actually more than a fear of being mugged or robbed or sexually violated; it's the fear of losing your heart's "safe place," your essential inner sanctuary of security and spiritual well-being. Or it's the vague, haunting threat of living at the edge of a nightmare where, at any moment, even in your own home, you may be assaulted, maimed, or even slain in some unforeseeable act of terror. This pervasive fear of *private danger* is just as detrimental as a fear of *public crime*. When mismanaged or unmanaged, these fears grow, creating what Prof. Robert Agnew from Emory University calls "general strain," a weakening of the physiology and psychology by constant stress and fatigue. Professor Agnew reports that the emotions produced by different "strains" in life can be "a predisposing factor in [violence and crime] when it is chronic and repetitive and creates a hostile, suspicious, and aggressive attitude."[7] In potential victims, this internal stress-and-strain imbalance can contribute to the everyday sense of feeling *emotionally unsafe*. Worries begin to dominate the mind, numb or paralyze the emotions, intimating that on every sidewalk and office doorway are lurking rapists or muggers, or that disaster to your career, hopes, or relationships waits around every corner.

Of course, a small dose of fear can be healthy, even life-saving, if it comes at the right time. Noticing and avoiding a hostile person or a dangerous area of a city makes good sense. On the other hand, a constant, nagging sense of danger or fear for safety— fueled by constant media reports of violence and terror, or witnessing or experiencing it yourself—can overload you with tension and silently erode your mind and body in a number of ways, including:

• Repeatedly shocking your brain chemistry into what is known as *hyperarousal* or *hypervigilance*—or, the opposite, a *numbness or apathy to the danger or violence* that may be occurring all around you.

• Stimulating high levels of internal stress hormones that trigger escalating anxiety, anger, despair, exhaustion, or paranoia—which, over the long term, can disable you (and, in aggressive individuals, low levels of the neurotransmitter serotonin and high levels of the hormone cortisol have each been linked to anxiety, despair, and hostility).

• Draining your energy, thereby numbing your power of perception, narrowing the mind's focus, and inadvertently making you *more* vulnerable to danger.

• Producing feelings of hostility and rage—or of powerlessness and helplessness as we confront a seemingly endless array of social issues: crime, urban decay, inequality, war, AIDS, rampant consumerism, inadequate health care, homelessness, poverty, national and personal debt, and many more.

• Leaving invisible emotional hurts such as shame, humiliation, and resentment.

• Harming children's brains and, in some cases, triggering adult brain dysfunction.[8]

• Damaging the cardiac muscle fibers and functioning of your heart, promoting disease and shortening life.[9]

• Interfering with your creative potential and ability to advance in a career.

• Prompting your memory to become deeply imprinted with the traces of dark or hurtful emotions.

• Eroding your spirit, thereby leaving you feeling increasingly off-balance, reactive, irritable, and frustrated with the uncertainties and difficulties of life, love, and work.

Something deeply human and profoundly social, even spiritual, is at the heart of the safety issue. Inner safety is essential to living a productive and meaningful life. And we, the authors, have our own personal safety issues, too. Harold's mother had both her parents murdered in the Nazi death camps. She had to flee with her daughter, Nora, Harold's sister, to escape the Holocaust. This shadow of violence has led her into a lifetime of hypervigilance and all-encompassing fear for her safety. Harold grew up coping with his mother's brutally disintegrated sense of safety "after the Nazis came." This was one reason he dedicated his career to medicine and psychiatry—to help heal and guard inner safety.

Robert has spent time in Tibet, and has witnessed incidents of, and has heard extensive first-hand reports about, the reign of terror and attempted genocide that has been going on there since the illegal invasion by the occupying army and government of the People's Republic of China. To date, approximately 1.2 million Tibetans have died, countless others have been raped, tortured, or sent to slave labor camps, and many thousands of Tibetan women have been subjected to forced sterilization.[10]

We have learned much from these victims of violence, and from many others who suffer every single day from more subtle but no less devastating feelings of danger and violations of safety. This is a pivotal issue of the human spirit and psyche—its woundings, its mournings, and ultimately its healing. We have found, even in people whose lives have been permanently altered—and who carry a grieving heart, tortured mind, or devastated spirit— a remarkable ability to engage in small daily acts of caring and dignity, of conscience and courage, undertaken to help keep alive the last hopes and dreams for restoring inner safety to their communities.

It is time not only to focus our attention on *preventing crime* but also on *preventing everyday danger and fear,* wherever it occurs. All across America the fear of violence has become the fear of the Other. Private, self-centered security interests threaten to obliterate the common good. More than a century ago, Alexis de Tocqueville worried that America was vulnerable to passing beyond healthy self-interest into a selfish individualism "which disposes each member of the community to sever himself from the mass of his fellows" and to "feel no longer bound by a common interest."[11] And this, "in the long run," might "attack and destroy" society itself.

Today, many Americans are racing in pursuit of divisive, selfish, and increasingly unattainable goals that cannot satisfy the inner desire we all have for respect, trust, love, and justice. Violent crime, pronounced inequalities, and bitter social frustration threaten the bonds of family and community, and appear to be unraveling the fabric of our world. These problems point to the need for all of us to become practitioners of *emotional and social healing* and what we call *safety intelligence.*

THE HEALTH COSTS OF FEELING UNSAFE

Fear is the malignant thing that has plagued mankind since time
began, the thing that mauls and mutilates us, not killing us
outright but letting us live on half a heart and half a lung.

RAY BRADBURY AND JOHN HUSTON,
script, *Moby Dick* (1956)

Medical researchers suggest that a constant *inner sense of fear* or the resulting *chronic hostility* may—by damaging the heart, immune system, or brain—actually end your life sooner than an assailant's bullet, bomb, or blade. In truth, dealing with predatory stares or frequent barrages of hostile words may end up being just as hurtful as getting grabbed or hit. Profanity, "eye rape," and rude, threatening criticisms may be nearly as daunting or violating as a physical attack on the subway, in a dark corridor, or at a parking lot.

Even when everything seems to be going just fine, *fear or hostility*—including the fight-or-flight response—can hit without warning. One moment you're feeling okay and the next your mind is racing wildly, your muscles are defensively braced up, your heart is pounding furiously, and the world around you is narrowing dangerously. This loss of control, caused by the unpredictability of determining *when, where,* and *how* threats of violence or conflict will arise in your life, is a potent cause of chronic fear and anger. What's vitally missing is a core of *inner safety,* and that's a primary focus of this book.

In public health and disease prevention, one of the greatest achievements has been the discovery of vaccines, which work by stimulating the body's natural protective mechanisms to strengthen immune function and fight off invading infections. In this process, nature is the champion. There is far more scientific evidence—and it is growing every day—that certain physiological approaches help create an effective "crime vaccine," both dramatically reducing biological abnormalities that prompt violence and criminal behavior in perpetrators themselves and, at the same time, improving the safety of the general public at large.[12] In fact, some evidence suggests that if just *one percent* of the population regularly practices the TM meditation technique, for example, it may have a dramatic effect on local crime rates. These alternative measures will be reviewed in later chapters of this book, and in some cases they have significantly more research to support them than the currently popular—and, for the most part, ineffective—crime-reduction strategies, yet most people are unaware of them.

THE CALL FOR *INNER* SAFETY

How widespread is the fear for personal safety? There's evidence that nearly all of us have it to a degree. Rather than remaining trapped in a state of hypervigilance or denial, safety fears are an essential thing to face, but not easy. To explore these fears is to come face-to-face with human vulnerability in the natural world and with the capacity for evil in human nature. One of the most difficult challenges confronting us all, especially women and children, is the ever-increasing threat of hostility and the lack of safety. The world *is* getting less and less safe, say crime statisticians. The National Crime Survey indicates that you have an 80 percent chance of experiencing at least one physical attack in your lifetime; in other words, you have only a one in five chance of *not* being attacked and will likely experience many, perhaps hundreds or even thousands, of verbal assaults. In light of this, the fear and pressure we feel in response are to be expected: "They," the Others in the world, do it to us, don't they? Actually, only partially.

Most of the time, we do it to ourselves. We lose our *inner safety.* If crime is only defined as behavior that under the law is punishable by imprisonment or fine, then obviously the physiological imbalances most of us experience do not lead to criminal behavior. However, if crime is more broadly viewed as a display of hostility or aggression in such ways as "losing it" in anger and "flying off the handle" at your partner, children, coworkers, or even strangers in the supermarket line or traffic, or excessive drinking or other forms of substance abuse, or insulting or demeaning behaviors, or infidelity, or "minor" acts of revenge or sabotage at work, then physiological stresses and strains may actually be prompting most of us to engage in these "crimes" of dissocial behavior.

Therefore, we can't just hold our nation's youth, or even criminals, wholly responsible for creating an unsafe world. Daily emotional strains from stressful personal and family experiences and other painful life conditions reinforce the chronic stress cycle. There are some proven approaches to turning this around, several tested in as many as five hundred research studies at more than two hundred independent research institutions in twenty-seven countries.[13] One of the conclusions is *the more we each develop a personal sense of inner safety, the better the results for everyone.*

In truth, how you feel, think, and live depends less on what's going on around you and far more on what's going on *inside* you. Physical protection skills alone—without *inner* development—are, as you will see, not sufficient for dealing with threats of potential violence or with the innumerable situations in risk, conflict, and attack in everyday life.

IT'S TIME FOR NEW SAFETY OPTIONS

If the people of the United States really want to conquer the mounting problem of crime, we cannot continue to use the same failing methods.

> JOSEPH DREW, PH.D., professor, University of the District of Columbia; vice chair, Mayor's Advisory Committee on Drug Abuse; director, Safe Streets Project, Washington, D.C.

Many of us assume there are few options between the extremes of more police/more prisons and a defensive-barricade mentality of personal safety, and the careless "repeat these positive affirmations and you'll be protected" naïveté at the other end of the spectrum.

We don't believe the answer to increased individual safety is in minimizing time out in public places, in constructing alarm-scanned, prisonlike homes, walking along the sidewalk in a defensive stance with chemical Mace spray in hand, turning an attack dog loose in your yard, or creating a larger judicial and prison system. Ask yourself, has any of this reduced our inner fear for personal safety? Probably not. As Friedrich Nietzsche said, "Whoever fights monsters should see to it that in the process he does not become a monster. When you look into an abyss, the abyss also looks into you." A fine line divides vigilantism from predatory crime. On the other hand, we also believe that the ostrichlike habit among educated adults of pretending the problem doesn't even exist is, in fact, one of the very reasons the problems keep spreading and growing worse.

So what do we do now? In America, we are a pragmatic people and want down-to-earth observations and answers. Although there are no perfect solutions, one place to begin is by paying more attention to the flip side of violence. During the 1930s and 1940s, persecuted Jews were chronically fearful for their safety and many of them reportedly had great difficulty passing for non-Jews, regardless of their features or manner of dress.[14] Apparently, the look of constant anxiety or dread made them recognizable, even from afar. What do others see in *your* gaze? Is it tension and fear? Or a calm sense of awareness, confidence, and dignity?

Even though stories of violence make sensational headlines daily and seem to fill the media, plenty of stories also still attest to what de Tocqueville called the American heart that "readily leans toward kindness." In the *New York Times*, next to a story about the drug-related murder of an entire family, was a far different story, of Jackie Knight, a thirty-one-year-old woman who fell six stories to her death while trying to rescue a friend's child. To reach the child, trapped in an upper story of a West Side hotel, the woman had secured what she thought was a sturdy television cable around her waist and tied the other end to a pipe before trying to lower herself from the roof. The cable broke and she fell sixty feet. She was a former foster child with a child of her own.[15] Why do such stories of courage as this one, and hundreds more that we are aware of, stories of one human being taking risks to protect the safety of another, generally get such minimal attention in the media? To listen to the news, it would seem we live in an age of vanishing compassion and heroism. But do we?

There is no magic formula or panacea for personal safety. It's part awareness, part skill, part ingenuity, and in some cases part luck.

Later on, we will address such topics as *emotional safety* (protecting yourself from the *inner violence* of hostile thoughts and panicky feelings), community safety and civility, workplace violence, and more. You'll discover that, instead of just building more prisons, we advocate *deglorifying violence.* Cartoons, for example, teach children to laugh at cruelty and violent acts. Superhero movies teach children to admire violent people, since the brutal actions lead to success. This is now true for girls as well as for boys.[16] If we don't start honoring nonviolence and teaching effective conflict-resolution methods, our children—society's children—may soon fail to believe in it altogether. In fact, it already seems to be happening.[17]

As with health care, we need to take a predominantly preventive, rather than emergency triage or purely punitive, approach to violence. According to Dr. Deborah Prothrow-Stith, dean of the Harvard School of Public Health and author of *Deadly Consequences*, "One way or another, the children in our community will get my time, my attention, my money, and my resources."[18] Prothrow-Stith tells the story of a teenager who had been convicted of a brutal double murder and sentenced to seventy-three years in jail. The mayor of the city told her there weren't enough funds to support summer job programs for teenagers in the city. "We are a society," warns Prothrow-Stith, "willing to spend $35,000 per year for seventy-three years on the same kid we won't give a $2,000 summer job." All around us are emergencies in the provision of affordable housing, jobs at a livable wage, basic health care, education, and social services. It is time not only for increased personal safety but, at the same time and as a result of this safety, for a reawakening of the American sense of community and solidarity, for these are preconditions if a civil society is to thrive, or even survive.

An injury to one is the concern of all.

    Motto of the Knights of Labor

It is worth considering that one of the worst effects of spreading violence, as Mahatma Gandhi taught, is the destruction of compassion. It can also be argued that, above all else, it is compassion—the ability to see ourselves in others and others in ourselves, the ability to *care* deeply—that makes us wholly alive and civilized.

All across America, from the halls of government to the corporate landscape and neighborhood streets, the spread of "wilding" behavior—self-centered acts of violence against others in which the perpetrator takes pleasure in inflicting pain and shows complete indifference to the feelings and humanity of the victim—is poisoning our neighborhoods and society. As this epidemic grows, selfish individual interests—"I will do absolutely anything to have fun, get ahead, and not be left behind"—increasingly obliterate common purposes. For the potential targets of violence—which now include every one of us—the message seems to be to become hypervigilant and assume everyone is a potential threat. Yet *how can we care about others when we feel they are making us unsafe?* How can we devote attention to other children outside our immediate family when we feel unable to protect our own children? Yet, as a U.S. Senate report indicates, "only 6 percent of black children and 30 percent of white children will grow up with both parents."[19] All of us have a responsibility to be mentors in our own neighborhoods and communities, yet the attitude and actions of mentoring require a foundation of safety.

A national poll found a growing and pervasive fear of violence and early death among children ages seven to ten, and widespread experiences of crime and violence among teens.[20] These findings "stunned even veteran children's advocates," says Lois Salisbury, executive director of Children Now, an advocacy group that released the poll with health-care provider Kaiser Permanente. "Kids see too much violence around them," says child psychiatrist Lenore Terr, M.D., of San Francisco, an expert on childhood violence. "In studies of children who have been traumatized, the most striking finding is that they lose their optimism for the future." Salisbury recalls that when she was a youngster, "my fear was of nuclear war . . . but that bomb never went off. These kids [today] fear violence and harm. And *those* bombs are going off all around them."

According to Justice Department statistics, over the next six weeks, 115,000 children will disappear in the United States. About 45 percent will be runaways, 35 percent will be abducted by a family member, 13 percent will be cast out by their own families as "throwaways," and almost 7 percent will wind up missing or lost for many other reasons. Another 14,000 children will experience *failed* kidnapping attempts in the next six weeks, and

35 will be abducted by strangers. More than half of those kid-
napped will end up dead.[21] With crimes of all kinds rising against
children, child advocates are urging more safeguards.

We are hopeful that current trends—including those of escalating violence, and the spiritual decay of civilized life—can be
reversed. We point out changes in attitude that have occurred
over time with regard to slavery, smoking, and eating red meat,
all of which were once seen by some people as positive. *Whatever*
fears and dangers you face, our focus is to give you a variety of
questions, insights, and options to consider, so you may better
handle difficult situations and become healthier while doing it.
You'll learn ways to begin moving from a place characterized by
distress, tension, and pain to one of increased vision, calm energy, and power. We call this *safety intelligence* and have organized the
book around a basic core structure:

SAFETY INTELLIGENCE

I. Safety in Everyday Life
   A. *Calm-Alertness* with Natural, Confident Movements
   B. *Safekeeping*, including *safer spaces* to live and work
   C. *Emotional Safety* to more effectively manage boundaries and
      such feelings as fear, hurt, anger, and rage

II. If Danger Appears . . .
   A. *Split-second PAUSE*
   B. *Focused Emotional Energy*
   C. *TWO+ Responses:*
      • Use two or more *de-escalating phrases*
      • Take two or more *unexpected physical actions*

These choices, as you will see, are simple to learn and, with
some practice, may be applied effectively. But perhaps you're
wondering to yourself, "It sounds like such effort. Will the energy I receive in return be worth it?" Yes. We believe you will get
more back than you spend. A greater reward, however, is that the

quality of your energy will change and you will notice that in many areas of your life you feel more alive, responsive, and confident. Nearly all of us must undergo some form of personal transformation if we are to prosper peacefully—and even survive—in the years ahead.

BECOMING SAFER—ONE STEP AT A TIME—FROM THE INSIDE OUT

In a dark time, the eye begins to see.

THEODORE ROETHKE

| *It is our belief that, above all, awareness, compassion, and cooperation are forces more powerful than hatred and fear.*

In this book, we have approached the issues of violence, fear, safety, and health by investigating the research literature and interviewing experts and specialists across a wide spectrum of safety and security issues. We set a goal to draw together the simplest and most sensible information *we* could find—the insights we wanted to know for ourselves and wanted to share with our loved ones. While we focus on the issues of violence, safety, and human health, we want to remind the reader to keep in mind other important health-safety issues, too. For example, a new follow-up study in the *Journal of the American Medical Association* links lead poisoning in children to increased violence and antisocial behavior. In addition, *seven times as many children die from household accidents as from murder;* 72,000 injuries could be prevented annually if parents used child safety seats properly; and if young bike riders all wore helmets, we could prevent some 40,000 head injuries every year. These health issues warrant concerted preventive action and are rightfully the target of national health education and safety campaigns.

Contrary to popular belief, *physical security and forceful self-protection measures* should be your *last* line of defense, not the *first.*

Many threatening situations can be avoided or de-escalated before they ever reach physical violence. When you learn to *increase your inner safety*, you actually change your brain chemistry and feelings, heightening your awareness. This elevates your vantage point and enables you to live from a calm-yet-alert place in the turbulent everyday world.

To be safe, we must begin with *inner safety*—what it is, how to develop it, how to keep it strong—then add specific strategies for improving *outer security*. You need *both* and that's the unique message of this book. In many situations, when you have a deep sense of *inner safety*, you'll automatically notice more of the appropriate options available to you, and you'll have a better chance of responding instantly—and more effectively—if threatened.

TO BE *SAFE* IS:

90%:
> Awareness
> Knowledge
> Self-esteem
> Attitude
> Choice

10%:
> Strategy
> De-escalating language
> Physical defense tactics
> Protective tools & technology

SAFETY CHOICES ARE SOMETIMES COUNTERINTUITIVE

Taken together, several of the principles in this book are a bit like turning the wheels of your car into a skid on an icy road. Such a response is, without awareness and skills, counterintuitive: Turn *into* the skid? Yet, as you probably know if you've ever driven on ice, such knowledge can indeed be lifesaving. As feelings of fear or danger rise up inside you, your brain is programmed to respond with a rigid, limited set of reactions, including freezing in panic, fuming in rage, or lashing out at the real or imagined attacker. Yet in many cases, these are precisely the reactions that *increase* your risks of being victimized or hurting yourself.

If, instead, as you'll learn in chapters 2 through 5, you maintain what we call "sphere of power, peaceful heart"—which is centered on a state of calm-alertness—you are far better positioned to implement simple, effective responses that put *you* in control of fear or anger and can *automatically* help you deflect or neutralize an attack pattern. We'll provide examples to demonstrate how this works to give you more safety options.

Most of us would agree that we live in an unsafe world. Yet we need to do whatever we can to make the most of it, and to leave it a better place for our having lived here. To one degree or another, all of us carry the memory of frustration, pain, or regret that comes from *reacting* to confrontations rather than *responding*. The right to *inner safety*—to *feeling* safe—is more than a birthright. It is a quality of mind, body, emotions, and spirit that is essential to being fully human.

Chapter 2

THE MOMENT OF CHOICE

We cannot teach people anything; we can only help them
discover it within themselves.

GALILEO GALILEI (1564–1642),
Italian astronomer and physicist

At the beginning of every conflict there is a moment of choice. A
split second when a different decision can be made—the precise
time when what you do or don't do may dramatically change what
happens next. Unfortunately, it's rare when we recognize and
seize this *moment of choice*. It is usually after conflicts and confrontations are over that we say to ourselves, "I wish I'd done something
different . . ." "Damn, if I just hadn't raised my voice . . ." "If only I
hadn't gotten out of the car . . ." "If I just hadn't panicked . . ." "If
only I'd thought to *do something different* . . ." Sound familiar? These
thoughts, these regrets, haunt us all.

In this chapter, we're going to begin exploring a variety of ways
to make better split-second decisions when your emotional, mental, or physical safety is threatened. In many situations, you don't
have to be or *feel* like a victim anymore. Whether the purpose is
to avoid unnecessary dangers and protect yourself from predatory stares, hostile words, escalating arguments, and everyday criticism, or to increase your chances to prevail against a rape
attempt or street attack, according to brain science and security
research the most important skill you can learn is this: *Catch the*

conflict early on—at the very first moment. Chemical and hormonal changes in the brain and body can tighten muscles and unleash negative emotions so quickly that it's much more difficult and time-consuming—and, often, just plain impossible—to reverse these harm-escalating reactions.

As you'll discover through practical examples and scientific insights on the pages ahead, in *every moment of conflict the strongest habit always wins.* Your mind, emotions, body, and spirit will follow, in split seconds, the brain and nervous system pathways that are most facilitated, most developed by *choice* and *rehearsal.* In the absence of such *learned-response pathways,* under conflict the brain will revert to ancient, fear-driven reactions that incapacitate you or plunge you into counterproductive, even life-threatening, outcomes.

This is a vital time to increase your skills in dealing with conflicts that threaten personal safety. That's because conflict itself is, in many cases, unavoidable; it is nature's primary driving force for growth and change. It is a dance of energy, an interaction of differing needs and viewpoints and divergent feelings. Although it takes two people to produce a conflict or confrontation, in truth it only takes one to end it. Not by giving up or giving in but by understanding enough about the nature of conflict to know the part you play in it and the hidden power you have to dramatically influence the outcome of many situations.

There is perhaps no clearer example of how at the very onset of conflict we can be our own worst enemy than to examine what happens in an argument. It is while we are tired or afraid or flushed with anger that we say and do things that clearly work against us, even while we *know* we are making the wrong choices *even while we are making them,* yet feel powerless to stop. Have you ever crossed the "line" in a moment of conflict—and with clenched fists or locked jaw—become paralyzed with fear or shouted obscenities, gone "nuclear" and thrown things, burst into tears, or fumed silently, as you lost, in a single instant, your objectivity, common sense, and inner balance just because someone did or said something that made you angry, resentful, or afraid? We all have. Every one of us.

At the beginning of every conflict there is a moment of choice.

The most dangerous conflicts are those that threaten your personal safety—whether it is *emotional* safety or *physical* safety. In truth, there may ultimately be little difference whether the danger comes on the subway or in an office, or from an angry outburst, a physical blow, or a damaging thought. It's the *feeling* of being unsafe that, more than any other factor, determines the victor and the victim. That's because every single violation of your sense of inner safety exacts a price.

To prove this to yourself, look around you. Look inside yourself. Each time you're the victim of a hateful thought or self-attack, for example, or of a predatory stare on the sidewalk or subway, in the darkness or daylight, a small part of you locks up or seeps away. Every time you are watched or propositioned, followed or hassled, threatened or stalked, in an office hallway or supermarket aisle, in a neighborhood park or suburban mall, a piece of your confidence is torn away, a part of your spirit is lost, a slice of your civility disappears. We know that, like us, you, too, have experienced these things or someone you care about has experienced them—from predatory stares to fear for your life.

The twentieth century has witnessed bloody wars, revolutions, and genocides leaving hundreds of millions dead or injured. Some would argue that this proves we humans are an incredibly vicious breed of predators who find assailing and killing are easy. Yet research shows that the vast majority of us are loathe to attack or harm other people. We recoil from personal violence; however, to a large extent, we also feel powerless to stop it. Worst of all, we have entered an era when the inflicting of pain and suffering has become a source of entertainment, providing millions of people with vicarious pleasure rather than revulsion.

Tragically, recent studies indicate that rifts in our society combine with violence in the media and in interactive video games to indiscriminately condition our nation's children to attack and kill.[1] It is, in fact, a method similar to the way the military desensitized and conditioned our soldiers to overcome their resistance to killing in Vietnam. But, in the case of our children, their conditioning is happening without any safeguards. And we are already paying a terribly high toll for this. Add to this the dissolution of the American family, and we may find ourselves heading toward disasters. Today children from every economic stratum are without an attentive parent, mentor, counselor, or other constructive role model. So they turn to their peers as authority figures and revere the media as the sole connecting point in their world. The media, in turn, feeds them violent stereotypes that often foster our deepest fears. Is this the road to ruin? If so, we must find another way home from this dark and fearful place we now find ourselves trapped in.

As parents, it is our aim to improve your chances for safety and, at the same time, to deglorify violence. Bruno Bettelheim, a noted psychologist and survivor of the Nazi death camps, argued that the root of our failure to deal effectively with violence lies in our refusal to face up to it. We deny our fascination with the "dark beauty of violence," he says, and we condemn aggression and attempt to repress it rather than look at it squarely and try to understand and manage it.[2] Even the law cannot save us from ourselves. Waking up each day, we must face the world and attempt to advance in the direction of our dreams and handle disappointments and resolve conflicts along the way. Our energy and resourcefulness are the key, not hundreds of new laws or a million more attorneys and police officers.

Few would argue that bullying, drugs, gangs, racism, poverty, and guns aren't vital ingredients in the escalating rates of violence and, in particular, aggravated assault in our society. But something else, something deeper, seems at work here. That's because when you attempt to analyze the underlying causes of fear and violence in America, you realize that bullying is an ever-present phenomenon, and we have always had problems with drugs and alcohol. Gangs of one form or another have always been part of most communities, just as warfare has taken place in organized armies.

And guns have always been present in American society. In addition to all of these factors, a serious erosion of *inner safety* has occurred in the hearts and minds of Americans. *This* is what is placing us at the greatest risk of all.

How simple it now seems for our ancestors to have stood
outside their cave guarding against the fang and claw of
predators. The evil we must stand vigilant against is like a virus,
starting from deep inside us, eating its way out.

RICHARD HECKLER, PH.D., *In Search of the Warrior Spirit*

This book discusses the difference between appropriate safety *concerns* and needless safety *worrying*—or even about protecting yourself from violent physical attack. Instead, it is our goal to present to you some of the simplest skills to create a *strong inner sense of personal safety that, according to research, actually empowers you—without needing to raise your hand or voice—to deter or defuse many types of attack. Our foremost aim is to provide you with specific ways to readjust your thinking and guide your emotional energy so you can start feeling safe, living more of your life in a state we have come to call sphere of power, peaceful heart.*

Conflict-resolution methods are well-proven in situations where a person is in a reasonable, rational state of mind. Yet they are largely futile when dealing with highly charged, emotional, even violent circumstances. Because of this, we each need to *create a strong inner reserve of calm, confidence, and "mental shielding" from hostility,* and balance this with *the simplest, most effective skills to remain safe and in control when faced with potentially violent situations.*

Let's look into the heart of the matter. If you review recent arguments and confrontations in your life and work, you can probably ascertain where your reactions tend to lead if undeterred. The challenge is to *recognize* the moment of conflict and *respond* instead of *react,* so that you now have a very real moment of choice—and can influence the outcome. In fact, observes Jon Kabat-Zinn, Ph.D., founder and director of the Stress Reduction Clinic at the University of Massachusetts Medical Center and associate professor of medicine at the University of Massachusetts Medical School, "as soon as you bring your awareness to what is going on in a conflict situation, you have already changed that situation dramatically, just by virtue of *not* being unconscious and on automatic pilot anymore. *And since* you *are an* integral part of the whole *situation*, by increasing your level of awareness, you are actually changing the entire situation even before you do anything."[3]

This instant inner change is extremely important because it *gives you the widest range of options for influencing what happens next.* And, even when you "blow it" by getting angry or upset over something that, moments later, may seem remarkably insignificant, you'll be able to recover your inner balance more quickly and keep moving forward in your life with less anxiety and fewer regrets.[4]

It is our aim to explore some little-known principles that can change the outcome of everyday conflicts—as well as reviewing specific suggestions from experts on ways you might personally apply these principles to potentially violent confrontations.

There are two central and interconnecting dimensions to *safety intelligence:*

Part I is concerned with your *safety in everyday life,* or what we call *sphere of power, peaceful heart.* To establish and sustain this level of safety, you must learn, as we explain in chapter 7, to maintain an enjoyable and vigorous state of energy known as *calm-alertness.* According to researchers, this kind of energy—instead of the much more common state known as tense-tiredness—is an ideal way for most of us to be effective in our daily work and to notice opportunities and problems early on, handling uncertainties and stress with healthy "mental toughness"; similarly, this is an excellent state for noticing, avoiding, or when necessary, effectively managing situations of arguing and potential assault. Another element in *safekeeping in everyday life* is the knowledge and awareness to create and maintain *safer spaces* to live and work, and this involves some sensible steps to be and feel safer. Once taken, these actions can for the most part be put out of mind. The third aspect of *safety intelligence in everyday life* is learning basic skills in *emotional safety* such as valuing, monitoring, and appropriately expressing your emotions rather than attempting to deny or repress them and ending up having them sabotage your life and safety.

Part II of *safety intelligence*—a split-second pause, focused emotional energy, and two+ responses—is designed to be implemented *when you have a sense of danger*. By way of further introduction to these areas, we'd like to share the following insights.

SPHERE OF POWER, PEACEFUL HEART

Unless we each learn to feel safe by mastering fear, we will remain contracted, mistrusting, and disconnected from much of life. We will be victims even when we aren't being victimized. Here are several little-known factors about *inner safety*.

First of all, have you ever walked into a room or hallway or place of business and had some vague "sense" of impending conflict *before* it actually occurred? Have you ever sensed a heaviness or negative atmosphere even though nothing out of the ordinary has occurred—and no angry words have been spoken?

One simple yet profound way to change the way you experience daily interactions—and, at the same time, make it easier to take charge of potential conflicts—is to think of your brain's sensory perception as an invisible energy field surrounding you, as a large sphere. This sphere can expand and contract like a clear balloon. When you are first beginning to sense a conflict or feel fearful, tense, upset, angry, or tired, this energy balloon naturally contracts. On the other hand, when you're in a state of calm energy and relaxed alertness, your confidence and compassion expand and, with them, your energy or *sphere of power*.

Practice using this image. You might think of it as an extension of your spirit or energy field and intuition. It can provide you with an awareness "bridge" between the outer world and your inner safety. It may not only help you sense and prevent or avoid potential conflicts but will also enable you to be more attuned to the needs of others. In truth, all conflicts—and relationships—are affected by this phenomenon of expansion/contraction.

THREE STAGES OF CONFRONTATION

This brings us to an intriguing question: Is there a correlation between verbal and physical attacks and how a person stands, sits, walks, directs the eyes, and holds the body during movement?[5] "Just as the hoodlum planning a mugging is likely to back off and change plans at the discovery that the victim is not helpless," says conflict researcher Suzette Haden Elgin, Ph.D., "so will the verbal mugger look for someone who is not going to be able or willing to fight back."[6]

Scientific evidence suggests that a balanced but *relaxed* upright posture when sitting or standing—which conveys a "tall" position, no matter what your actual height—increases oxygen to your brain by up to 30 percent.[7] In an instant, this sharpens your senses and raises your alertness, whereas slumped posture can magnify feelings of distress, panic, and helplessness. An upright and relaxed posture also projects an unmistakable "signal" of inner confidence and awareness that can deter would-be verbal or physical aggressors. Obviously, when you are alone, it makes sense, as a general goal or rule, never to walk closer than two or three strides from a stranger. If you must pass nearer than this to someone standing in a doorway or leaning against a pole, tree, or car, gracefully change directions and veer around him, providing yourself with a greater chance to sense a threatening movement if a potential attack materializes. Most of us are able to read the signs of potential danger from many different clues: the presence or absence of people on a street, the irritability of people near us, gnawing feelings in the pit of our stomach, hair raising up on the neck, a nagging sense that something is wrong, or the recognition that a circumstance is similar to one in which danger appeared in the past.

Many recent insights on the subject of how human predators choose their prey were sparked by the research of Betty Grayson, Ph.D., a professor of social psychology at Hofstra University in Hempstead, New York. She was teaching a course on nonverbal communication to police officers. Two officers from Manhattan told her they could spot people who looked like potential verbal or physical assault victims. Their candidates were not simply the aged or disabled, the two groups widely assumed to be most vulnerable to attack. Instead, the identified targets were men and women from a broad range of age, ethnic, and social backgrounds. Something about these people seemed to attract attack. When the officers followed these people at a distance, sure enough, they saw them get hassled or mugged. Other police officers told Dr. Grayson of similar experiences.

A series of scientific studies was designed. Dr. Grayson set up a hidden camera in New York City and videotaped hundreds of random pedestrians for about seven seconds each, the time muggers say it takes to size up potential victims. Then she took the tapes to Rahway State Penitentiary in New Jersey where she screened them for a dozen prisoners, whose opinions of each person's "assaultability"—attractiveness as prey—became the basis for a ten-point scale, ranging from "I wouldn't mess with that one" to "an easy target." Next Dr. Grayson showed the tapes to a second group of criminals, all convicted of street assault or rape, and asked them to rate each pedestrian on the assaultability scale. Nearly all of them agreed on the same targets.

"Like most people," Dr. Grayson remembers, "I assumed that the elderly, for example, would be judged the easiest targets. Some were, but many weren't. I was amazed that about a quarter of the younger men and women were also judged as easy prey. The question, of course, was why?"

Dr. Grayson had her tapes reviewed by a movement analysis system called a labonotation. The results were startling. Every one of the "easy prey" shared five movement characteristics: "First, they had exaggerated strides, either too long or too short. Second was the way they moved their feet. Instead of a flowing heel-to-toe walk, they lifted and placed the whole foot at once, as though they were walking on eggshells. Third, they moved 'unilaterally' not 'collaterally,' that is, they swung the left arm and leg together, rather than the left arm with the right leg. Fourth, their upper bodies moved at cross purposes to their lower bodies; their two halves seemed disconnected. Finally, their arm and leg movements appeared to come from outside their bodies, not from within."

According to Dr. Grayson and her research coauthor, Morris Stein, Ph.D., a professor of psychology at New York University: "The prime difference between assault victims and nonvictims . . . revolves around 'wholeness' of movement. Nonvictims have organized movements that come from the body center. In contrast, victims' movements come from the body's periphery and communicate inconsistency."[8] In other words, nonvictims have a natural, confident movement and look "together"; easy prey do not. Studies also indicate that many assault victims get attacked more than once, which further substantiates Dr. Grayson's finding that they broadcast unconscious signals that attract verbal or physical attack. These same nonverbal cues affect many of us in everyday conflicts—such as family arguments and workplace struggles—not just in street assaults.

You can reduce your vulnerability by *balancing your posture* (standing with a comfortably "centered" stance and sitting "taller" with a sense of ease and confidence) and walking with "wholeness of movement." We call this natural, confident movement, and it is an essential part of everyday safety intelligence. Although size, weight, sex, and age are undoubtedly factors in being targeted for conflict or attack, studies suggest they are *considerably less important* than many of us have been led to believe. Muggers and rapists, for example, typically take seven to ten seconds to size up potential prey. To dissuade them, one of the keys is to move with alertness, confidence, and purpose.

Verbal and physical conflicts are almost always characterized by *action chains*—behaviors that take place in a specific sequence and manner.[9] These stages of escalation can be interrupted only if noticed and diverted early on in the confrontation pattern. The purpose of the *action chain* is for the aggressor to (1) select an easy-prey target, (2) demonstrate power over the victim by getting and holding the victim's attention and evoking an emotional response, and (3) carry out the actual attack. Each of the three basic stages of a conflict presents different options for response and escape. As a conflict escalates into all-out attack, the number of possible response or escape choices dramatically diminishes. Your perception and intuition are vital because they alert you *early*, when a potential or actual conflict *first* appears. This is the time when your countermeasures are far more likely to succeed.

These are the times to maintain a high level of *safety intelligence*, including

A. *Calm-Alertness* and *Natural, Confident Movements*
B. *Safekeeping*, including *safer spaces* to live and work
C. *Emotional Safety* to more effectively manage boundaries and the full range of feelings such as fear, hurt, anger, and rage

Stage 1: Unconscious Invitation: The Attacker Seeks Easy Prey

Contrary to popular belief, few people "ask" for a heated argument. And women do not "attract" tauntings or rape by dressing provocatively, for example, or by being in the "wrong" area or neighborhood. Rape education programs have worked hard to debunk this myth. As Michael Castleman, author of *Crime Free*, puts it: "The idea that women who wear alluring clothing invite sexual assault makes as much sense as saying that men who wear expensive suits invite robbery."[10]

What *does* often matter is your *emotional energy*: people who are tense or tired are more likely to find themselves in verbal warfare, and Dr. Grayson's concept of "wholeness of movement" applies to both verbal and physical confrontations.[11] In addition to the five movement characteristics that telegraph vulnerability to aggressors, there are other signals: a fixed gaze up or down, which implies preoccupation; a slow stride relative to other people around you; sifting through a purse or briefcase; listening to music on a portable cassette or CD player; reading a map or book; or anything else that gives the image that you're distracted marks you as easier prey. To find a good victim, panhandlers, muggers, and rapists, for example, will often test out several women, asking for directions, money, or the time. *The attacker will decide his next action based on the reaction he gets from you.*[12] If you are overpolite—to the point of seeming submissive—or nervous, he may take that as an indication that you'd be an easy victim.

To summarize, predators often

- Pay careful attention to the body language of prospective prey
- Are instantly "attracted" to potential victims
- Catch you off guard
- Ask you for money, the time, or directions
- Size you up in seconds, listening to your voice, noticing eye movements, muscle tension, breathing and posture, and how you hold your belongings
- Make up lies and stories to distract you as they prepare to move in

Even in so-called "minor" everyday disagreements, a variety of subtle but powerful conflict/nonconflict signals can exert a pull on your behavior. When you're tense and tired, for example, you may be twice as likely to be selected for verbal or physical attack by a predator, and you may get twice as angry when you lose an argument or may find yourself taking out your frustrations on weaker targets—a younger sibling or one of your children or employees, for example. The old adage "Stuff flows downhill" may, in fact, be far more likely for anyone who does not maintain calm-alertness and, instead, is tense and tired.

Stage 2: Holding Mechanism: Last Chance to Avoid Attack

Stage 2 is likely your last chance to avoid an all-out verbal or physical attack. In his book *The Silent Pulse*, George Leonard, author, social analyst, and aikido martial arts instructor, summarizes the scientific research on an essential but little-noticed factor in a confrontation: the *holding mechanism*. It's the magnetlike psychological tie that operates between people who come in close proximity. The holding mechanism "hooks" the brain's focus field and unconsciously directs our attention toward those who approach us. A verbal abuser, mugger, or rapist needs to capture and hold your attention long enough to lock your brain into knowing that you are captured *prey* and he or she is the *attacker*.

The outcome of a confrontation often hinges, literally, on several seconds, on the initial moments of confrontation—the time when a sense of surprise or uneasiness gives way to the realization that "this *is* trouble!" Attackers and verbal abusers depend heavily on this holding mechanism to freeze you long enough to transform a person into a victim.

Once you recognize the power of this confrontation stage you'll be more alert to it and can use the techniques that follow to bypass the mind's natural tendency to freeze, panic, or lose control. When you break the holding mechanism, you instantly show the attacker that you are not ready to be verbally abused, mugged, or raped. You are, at least for a short string of moments, much freer to respond with confidence and de-escalate the situation, distract the attacker, or escape.

Stage 3: Attack: You're in Trouble!

Many of us who are alert and careful have suddenly found ourselves being yelled at, stolen from, duped, cornered, pinned against a wall, or confronted in some other way. This is the explosion of verbal or physical violence that you want to head off or avoid. Despite the best of precautions, at times you end up in this stage without warning. In this book you'll learn simple, direct, and effective responses to maximize your chances of remaining safe and unharmed in the full spectrum of conflicts—from a heated outburst to an all-out attack.

According to neuroscientists, one of the most effective ways to handle verbal and physical conflicts is to catch the first stimulus or signal of confrontation and trigger an immediate "safety reflex."[13]

The *moment of conflict*, the time danger appears, is the time to call upon the second phase of *safety intelligence*:

A. *Split-second PAUSE*
B. *Focused Emotional Energy*
C. *TWO+ Responses*:
   • Use two or more *de-escalating phrases*
   • Take two or more *unexpected physical actions*

In the next chapter we'll focus on the value of recognizing the *first moment of conflict* and triggering an instant response that we call a *split-second pause*. It's designed to keep your mind alert and open, your senses sharp, and your body in relaxed readiness. In chapter 4, you'll add a second principle—*focused emotional energy*. This is one of the pivotal ways to remain aware and safe while maximizing your ability to resolve conflicts or escape from harm if that becomes necessary.

In chapter 5, you'll add a third principle—a unique, nonaggressive, yet highly effective *outer security* skill that we call *two+ responses*. It's based on brain-science research and will catch many attackers by surprise—suddenly giving you the advantage. In chapter 6, you'll have a chance to put these principles to the test right away using the *split-second pause and two+ responses* together, step by step, in real-life examples. The rest of the book will show you how these two core safety principles can be immediately applied to all levels of conflict—emotional, mental, verbal, or physical.

Beyond this, we're going to build on a foundation of inner safety and consider conflicts from many angles—teaching you a variety of useful new ways to shift your thinking and change your feelings, not just take new actions. The skill sets in each chapter are designed to be easy to learn, remember, and apply. A number of parts of the book incorporate scientific learning methods such as *natural recall* ("learn it and don't think about it again") that promote quicker understanding and application. You'll also gain access to time-saving decisions that make your home, car, office, and travel safer ("take these specific actions and then put them out of your mind").

To take advantage of your natural and very powerful emotional energy, we use a three-step *feel-listen-guide* sequence that quickly enables you to flow away from an attack rather than getting knocked over or absorbing force straight-on. This approach is consistent with certain ancient Taoist philosophies and Tibetan teachings, which indicate that a force—word, thought, or action—that presses against you in attack is experienced along certain patterns of motion known as *dragon lines*. These lines are sensed as "creases" in the atmosphere around you and are often felt or experienced through emotions, not thoughts. If you try to force your way against these lines or across them, you encounter strong resistance. You probably have noticed and reacted to these forces in the past, saying, "I can feel the tension between them" or "The air is so thick over there I could cut it with a knife." Yet if you sense, or read, these lines, you can move safely along invisible paths of least resistance and remain safer and in greater control over an encounter.

Our goal has been to draw on the best of ancient teachings as well as the latest brain-science discoveries to create a direct, uncomplicated set of flexible, fluid responses to moments of conflict that will not only serve you well in everyday life and work but may help enliven your spirit at the same time they reduce your risk of robbery, assault, and rape.

By learning the safety principles in this book, you'll not only begin to more clearly manage moments of conflict—and, by doing so, become healthier and more effective in your life and work—but, as you've already seen, you may also become significantly less attractive to the difficult people who would argue with you and to the human predators who would attack you. *In essence, the safer you feel, the safer you may actually become.*

One of the most essential skills you can learn is to deal in more effective ways with the inevitable moments of conflict that await you. And the best way to encourage our children to feel safe is by example. A study in Israel of children on kibbutzim that had been shelled by mortars and artillery found remarkably little correlation between the level of violent shelling and a child's anxiety level; however, the *parents'* anxiety and children's level of anxiety were closely linked.[14]

According to Richard Weissbourd, Ph.D., the author of *The Vulnerable Child*, who teaches at Harvard's Kennedy School of Government and at its Graduate School of Education, "Whether parents are chronically stressed or depressed often more powerfully influences a child's fate than whether there are two parents in a home or whether a family is poor."[15]

THE BIGGER PICTURE OF SAFETY

We have failed our children. They live in a world where danger
lurks all around them. And the stuff of nightmares when we
were children is the common reality for children today.

Geoffrey Canada

We have seen up close the gauntlet of dangers our children must now run to reach healthy adulthood. As Geoffrey Canada, president of the Rheedlen Centers for Children and Families in New York City, describes it: "What if I were to tell you that we are approaching one of the most dangerous periods in our history since the Civil War? Rising unemployment, shifting economic priorities, hundreds of thousands of people growing up poor and with no chance of employment, never having held a legal job. Growing up under the conditions of war. War as a child, war as an adolescent, war as an adult. War never-ending. Not like Vietnam, where Americans, if they survived, came home. The war today *is* home. You just survive. Day by day, hour by hour. . . . I'm sorry, America, but once you get past the rhetoric what we really learn is that might does make right. Poor people just never had any might. But they want it. Oh, how they want it.

". . . The impact of fear and violence has overrun the boundaries of our ghettos and has both its hands firmly around the neck of our whole country. And while you may not yet have been visited by the specter of death and fear of this new national cancer, just give it time. Sooner or later, unless we act, you will. We all will. . . . If I could get the mayors and the governors and the president to look into the eyes of the five-year-olds of this nation, many dressed in old raggedy clothes, whose zippers are broken but whose dreams are still alive, they would know what I know— that children need people to fight for them. To stand with them on the most dangerous streets, in the dirtiest hallways, in their darkest hours. I want people to understand the crisis our children face and I want people to act."[16]

The key is to start today creating greater safety in your personal and family life, with a plan that makes sense to you. Once that's under way, it is our hope that all of us will join together to right what's wrong in our society, and to make it safe again for children, all our children, to keep themselves and their dreams alive in this dangerous but hopeful world.

Part I

SAFETY INTELLIGENCE:
CORE PRINCIPLES

The foundation of *safety intelligence* includes *calm-alertness* and *natural, confident movements*, along with an awareness of *safekeeping*—of creating and maintaining *safer spaces* at home and work (chapters 10 and 14) and *emotional safety* (chapter 7). Insights and resources in each of these areas are woven throughout this book.

The other dimensions of *safety intelligence* are used in times of verbal conflict, emotional turmoil, or physical danger. The next chapters introduce a trio of simple yet powerful skills: *a split-second PAUSE, focused emotional energy,* and *two+ responses.*

Chapter 3

SAFETY INTELLIGENCE PRINCIPLE #1: A SPLIT-SECOND *PAUSE*

Avert the danger that has not yet come.

THE BHAGAVAD GITA

Depending on your level of awareness and emotional safety, the *first moment of conflict* could register in your heart or mind at any of the three stages of a confrontation discussed in chapter 2. Ideally, you will notice the signs of an emerging conflict at Stage 1 or, at latest, Stage 2, and right then make a *key choice in how you're going to respond* to the potential attack situation. This is the turning point, the single most important place to influence what happens next.

Unless you take control at the opening moment, automatic *alarm reactions*, triggered out of unawareness, can instantly compound the situation, increasing the level of conflict. This can quickly turn simple problems into much worse ones, placing a whole new set of even heavier stress-burdens on your mind and senses. These automatic reactions prevent you from seeing clearly and from resolving conflicts creatively and effectively.

It's essential to understand that safety intelligence *is an ongoing state of calm-alertness and is not* reactive *or* impulsive.

It was a terrible tragedy. It happened because of a deep desire for family safety that went wrong in a single impulsive, erroneous action. Fourteen-year-old Matilda Crabtree was excited about playing a practical joke on her father. After hiding in the hallway closet of their home, she jumped out and yelled "Boo!" as her parents returned home late one night after visiting friends.

However, Bobby Crabtree and his wife thought Matilda was away that evening staying with one of her friends. Hearing noises in the bedroom area when he entered the house, Crabtree had reached for his .357 magnum handgun and went into Matilda's room to investigate. When his daughter jumped from the closet and shouted "Boo!" he shot her in the neck. Matilda Crabtree died in the hospital twelve hours later.[1] Her last words were "I love you, Daddy."

Fear and a concern for safety made Mr. Crabtree grab his gun and search his house for an intruder. Afraid, he reacted impulsively when Matilda leaped out from the closet, pulling the trigger the instant before he recognized who it was or heard his daughter's voice or saw her beaming face while playing what she thought was an innocent practical joke on her father. Automatic, fear-driven reactions such as this may be set deeply into our human nervous systems through evolution. And while at times in the ancient past such instant reflexes may have served us well, they can hurt us in today's complex world—plunging us into needless everyday arguments and unnecessary inner turmoil as well as contributing to tragedies such as the one that occurred in the Crabtree home.

At the first moment of a conflict, maintain your sphere of power, peaceful heart and take a split-second pause before responding.

At the core of *safety intelligence* is the ancient spiritual wisdom to pause, to reach for a higher vantage point before acting or reacting.

Pausing is more than a moment in time—it is a conscious process that can instantly help bring out the best in you, enabling you to rise to the challenge. When this happens in a moment of conflict, you tap into a rare energy that exists beyond aggression, a creative, heartful intelligence that enables you to scan for solutions and de-escalators (and, when needed, protective measures or escape) *instead* of getting bogged down with fear, blame, or justification. By using this *split-second pause*, you bypass the brain's ancient, inherent tendency for *premature cognitive commitment*—the seemingly instant mind-set of judging, assuming, reacting, that escalates everything or blinds you to openings for solving a conflict or escaping from an attack.[2]

Scientific and medical research suggests that with some regular rehearsal, you can *voluntarily* trigger a split-second pause.[3]

> *When in doubt, take a split-second PAUSE and raise your vantage point.*

No matter what pressures you face—an ongoing series of verbal clashes at home or work, a real-life threat of physical attack in your neighborhood, school, or job site, performance challenges in your career, or haunting self-doubts that flare up every time something or someone reminds you of past trauma or attack—to pause for a split second at the moment of conflict is a simple, powerful awareness skill you can begin using right away. With practice, your brain and nervous system can enact the pause in a fraction of a second, using "fluid intelligence" pathways in the nervous system where messages travel at speeds measured in thousandths and ten-thousandths of a second and produce complex interactions in perception, attention, neuromuscular activation, and responsiveness. The power of this phenomenon is exemplified by the fact that the brain can recognize the meaning of more than one hundred thousand words or images in less than one second.[4] It takes only one-hundredth of a second for the eye to blink completely, and at least six hundred individual muscular actions can occur in a single second, "and the number may be much higher," say researchers.[5]

You can elicit the split-second *PAUSE* at the very first moment you feel a flash of anger, surge of fear, or any kind of increased negative stress. Because a split-second *PAUSE* is performed while you are fully alert, with eyes open, the technique may be used unobtrusively in a wide range of circumstances—from everyday confrontations to all-out physical challenges—and can be used successfully whether you're standing, sitting, or moving.

Some scientists believe that skilled actions—such as a split-second pause—may be stored in the nervous system as "chunks of instructions . . . that can be called up and executed by a single command."[6] This may account for the deep relaxation and control—the "flow state"—felt by jet-fighter pilots, artists, and athletes.[7] You've already been using this "chunking" process in your brain for years. Whenever you drive a car, for example, think of how the complex interactions of perception, eye-hand coordination, and responses that involve instantaneous visual shifts (such as keeping your attention to the danger in front as you simultaneously flash a quick glance in the rearview and side-view mirrors) while, at the same instant, you respond with hands on the wheel (and perhaps one on the horn) with feet working the brakes and gas pedal. Literally thousands of independent sensory and motor actions seem to happen all at once, in concert, in this moment of conflict as you sense an icy stretch of road or a dangerous oncoming or tailgating driver.

In large part, what you do with your mind and energy in the initial moment of a conflict may determine the outcome. That's the key to a split-second pause—learning to insert calm-alertness, a gap, at the very start of each stressful or fearful scene. With practice, you can enlarge this gap between stimulus and response and use your creative imagination to seek out new solutions; to focus on what you *can* control rather than what you can't; to divert your mind from knotting you up, again and again, in imaginary fears; to listen for an extra moment with an open mind instead of blindly talking back; to be skilled enough to protect yourself and to do it, wherever possible, without harming others.

In case you're concerned that the split-second pause might sacrifice some flash of protective advantage, there's no need to worry. As you'll learn in the upcoming section on two+ responses, scientific research on reflex-reaction speed shows that when dealing with high-pressure situations in the critical first instant of a confrontation, you're better off *pausing* for a moment and *then* making a quick, appropriate reponse—rather than reacting too quickly with a hurried, less focused one.[8] Unfortunately, few people know this.

Let's take a closer look at some of the advantages of a split-second pause. Just to keep things interesting, we've arranged the following section under letters of the acronym P.A.U.S.E. There is absolutely no need to memorize these steps; however, you may find one or two of the insights helpful in deepening the effectiveness of your pause.

Perceive Deeply

At first glance, perception seems simple enough. It is the act of knowing what your senses have discovered. Light hits your eyes; you see. Sound waves vibrate your eardrums; you hear. But to perceive *deeply*, to gain knowledge of what's between the lines, beneath the surface, and beyond the obvious, is a rare skill. A skill that, beyond safety, enriches your life. A skill you can develop with simple practice. Yet few of us ever do.

To perceive most effectively you must be in a state of relaxed alertness. What that means is you are calm *and* alert, thereby allowing you to pay greater attention to what is unfolding around you. Only then can you be aware of hidden details *and* the full context of the situation you face. This enables you to avoid the unconscious fear-response from a small area of your brain called the *amygdala*, which helps read social signals and give the "fear" alarm to body and mind.[9] You can stay calmer and in far greater control when you perceive more deeply and can quickly examine things more closely to be sure of what you're sensing. According to brain scientists, *logic and reasoning must build on the results of your feelings and perception.*[10]

Your decision-making in a moment of conflict depends on your brain's ability to trust the reality of the identity, meaning, and structure you've discovered through perception. With *deep* perception you are seeking a "snapshot" of the depths and scope of any situation. This transcends the brain's orderly rules of procedure and sequence that invariably bog down or freeze up in moments of high stress.

Deep perception happens instantaneously. It absorbs your senses in the experience of the moment and draws upon superfast creative powers. "In effect," explains Daniel M. Wegner, Ph.D., a professor of psychology at Trinity University in San Antonio and a leading researcher on the psychology of mental control, "when we are absorbed in what we are doing, we are immunized against unwanted thoughts."[11] Because of this, one of the keys to perception is to acknowledge reality.[12] This is essential to what psychologists call the flow state, in which skilled martial artists and elite athletes perform at their absolute best—responding to problems in split seconds—by avoiding the *paralysis of analysis.*[13]

Fortunately, you do *not* need to be a martial artist or athlete to gain the benefits. Here's why this works: When you fail to acknowledge the reality of a difficult or threatening situation— that is, by wishing it weren't happening, regretting you didn't have more time to prepare, wanting to be somewhere else, or anguishing over life's unfairness—you set off a biochemical avalanche of victimizing thoughts and feelings. Without realizing it, you actually help yourself lose control by loading up with anxiety or anger. Your calm, clear thought at the moment of a split-second pause is, *What's happening is real—and I'm going to make the safest, smartest response.*

Surprisingly small shifts in the mind's operations can change us greatly.

ROBERT ORNSTEIN, PH.D., Stanford University,
The Evolution of Consciousness

Assess the Situation

Let's use the possible—but highly unlikely—scenario of a car-jacking to help envision some of the advantages you could gain from a split-second pause. However, keep in mind that there are just as many advantages to be had during a daily argument.

Imagine that you're pulling up to a stoplight on your way home from work or an errand. It's already been a hectic day. It's a lower-middle-class neighborhood where crimes aren't that common, and this is a route you often take home and your mind is mulling over the day as you drive primarily on autopilot. You're humming to the music from the car stereo when you hear a sudden crash of glass and turn to see the passenger window shattering and an arm plunging in, groping for the handle to unlock the door. Now, freeze this image for a moment.

In a split-second pause, you can choose to perceive deeply, to keep breathing and observing whatever is happening. Acknowledge that you're at a stoplight and the window has been broken and someone is trying to enter your car. By doing this instantly you are better able to take the entire situation into your awareness and remain calm, bypassing the tendency to criticize yourself for not paying enough attention, not picking a different route home, or getting paralyzed in any of countless other ways with denial or analysis. The truth is, *what's happening is real—you feel threatened—and what happens next should be up to you.* Perceive deeply—Are the other doors locked? Is there a gun pointed at you? Is your car in gear? Is there cross traffic at the light? Anyone behind you in the rearview mirror? Could you lay on the horn and stomp on the gas—either forward or in reverse? Any policemen or lighted businesses nearby?

Here's a key insight: There is no point in trying to *force* yourself to pay cold, emotionless attention to making the best decision in the heat of conflict. The reason? It won't work. The rationalist approach is to try to obtain the best results in a conflict by keeping emotions *out*. But that's a mistake. According to several leading brain scientists, what you *feel*—when in a state of calm energy and alertness as you enter a conflict—is a vastly important whole-brain/whole-body "marker" signal of what's really happening in this conflict, and instantly—at a level far deeper and a scope far more inclusive than the rational, sequential brain can compute or comprehend—you begin to sense, in a nanosecond, what the best response may be.[14]

Unlock Your Position

Did you know that *a rigid posture or position increases* closemindedness? Or that, similarly, *rigid belief systems may be a root of violence?*[15] With rigidity—in mind or body—anything that encroaches on your inflexible boundaries must be defended against. There is no adapting, no flexibility of thoughts or position, and there's a natural reactive urge to condemn or attack other belief systems and physical forms (such as appearance or race) in a prejudging manner.

Think about it: When we are completely absorbed in our own feelings, views, and objectives, it is virtually impossible to defuse, escape from, or resolve conflicts. And if you happen to be sitting, standing, or walking with slumped posture or in a stiff, tension-loaded manner, no matter what *words* you speak, they can instantly be canceled by your resistive body language.[16] Therefore, in a split-second pause it's vital to make certain your position is unlocked—relaxed, upright, neutral, "tall."

Test this yourself right now by standing up and assuming a tight, slumped posture, perhaps in front of a full-length mirror. Say something. Does it feel natural—or strained, weak, or grouchy? Now choose to unlock your position—both mentally and physically, with a balanced, "neutral" stance and open, peaceful hands. Begin talking again. Do you notice the difference?

Unlocking your position is one of the best and quickest ways to overcome a common, debilitating reaction to fear or danger known as *somatic retraction,* a slight slouching posture characterized by tightening or collapsing the chest, rolling the shoulders forward and down, tensing the abdomen, back, or neck, and feeling beaten down or victimized. Even thinking of a threatening situation can make you automatically tense up.[17] Somatic retraction not only restricts breathing and reduces blood flow and oxygen to the brain and senses, but also adds needless muscle tension, slows reaction time, triggers arguments, and magnifies feelings of panic and helplessness.[18]

One of the ways to head off somatic retraction is based on the fact that certain areas of the body have large corresponding "maps" in the brain that can help you respond more quickly and effectively. Two of these "signal" muscle areas are the face and hands. One of the ways to unlock your position in a split-second pause is to flash a mental "wave of relaxation" beginning with the muscles in your face and around your eyes, then through your whole body, right out through your fingertips and toes—as if you're standing tall, shoulders elevated but loose, under a waterfall that clears away all excess tension.[19]

Let's continue with our carjacking scenario: In the first moment of conflict you've already perceived the situation and acknowledged feeling threatened at the same instant you've triggered a deeper feeling of inner safety and control. This action naturally flows into the third step of a split-second pause—to unlock your position, in this case keeping your posture tall and hands loose on the wheel so you can respond in a variety of ways, such as whirling the wheel and honking the horn as you accelerate through the light, or by opening your driver-side door and running into a well-lighted restaurant or store at curbside, or any of a hundred other unexpectedly effective responses—none of which can be implemented if your body or mind are locked up with tension or panic.

Sense the "Line"

Every conflict has a primary *line*—a core channel of attacking energy, a path of greatest danger (escalation) and others of least danger (escape). Only by sensing this line can you easily and effectively move out of the way of an attacking force instead of confronting it head-on. If you avoid freezing up and follow your automatic reactions to conflict, you may likely dig in your heels, tense up, and get "run over"—or will struggle valiantly to push back the attacker's incoming force, shoving your fists or words against the other person, intensifying the situation and making it more hurtful and dangerous.

The key is to recognize your alternatives to panicking, stiffening up, or getting run over. What it takes is the practiced ability to sense the line of incoming anger or attack. Here's an illustration, adapted from one of our favorite books on safety tactics, *Aikido in Everyday Life* by Terry Dobson and Victor Miller (North Atlantic Books, 1993), that gives an aerial compass view looking down at yourself in the first moment of conflict.

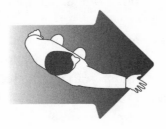

Attacker's *line*

**You are here.
How will you respond?**

Standing still or pushing north will place you in a head-on collision with the attacker. Moving due south may free you for a moment or two, but unless you switch directions, you will be forced to outsprint your assailant. Beyond these two directions, however, *all* the other angles—in particular, the range from NW to SW and between NE and SE—can, with minimum effort, put you off the line of attack. You can therefore choose to *evade the incoming force* (with a small step, for example) or *deflect it* (with a de-escalating word or distracting command). In either case, *you* retain control, and it is this control that can dramati-

Attacker is here.

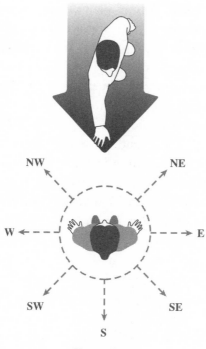

You are here.

cally change the outcome (see the upcoming section on two+ responses).

Once you know the *line,* or angle, of force coming at you, you have a whole range of options to not be *in front* of that attack, but beside it or behind it. In some martial arts this is called *aligning* or *blending,* and it means to tune in to the line of attack so that you can move with it, redirect it, and guide the outcome, neutralizing the attacking force rather than fighting against it, getting knocked over, or giving in. When one person in an adversarial situation does this, the entire relationship changes—even if the other person, the one initiating the attack, is presently unwilling to de-escalate things or change.

Let's continue with our carjacking scenario: You have perceived the threat and gained a deep sensory "snapshot" of your predicament, unlocked your position to free up all available response options, and now, instantly, at virtually the same moment as the other steps in the split-second pause, you sense the primary line of the attacker's force—with his arm through the shattered passenger window, methodically unlocking the door and beginning to jerk it open. The most natural reaction might be for you to scream for help and grip the wheel in a surge of panic, or to turn on the seat and attempt to kick the attacker as he climbs in. Either of these responses could escalate the danger. Think about it: The carjacker wants you *quiet* and he wants you *out* of the car, not glued to the wheel. He's in a rush and you're in the way. He's pumped up with adrenaline and also anxious, probably hostile, and if you kick at him, he may go berserk and shoot or stab you.

Consider just a few other alternatives: Once you've sensed the primary line of attack, you'll "feel" a whole range of *other* directions that may enable you to survive and remain safe. One of the angles of safety is straight ahead—accelerating through the light. Another is in reverse, stomping the gas pedal as you throw the car in reverse. Or, if you're blocked in by traffic, you might ram the car ahead, then the one behind, then throw open the driver's door and run for safety. The main point here is that when you sense the line of attack, you simultaneously sense your lines of possible escape.

Energize for a Swift Turnaround

Here's a simple exercise that symbolizes how the flexibility to change—to get off your position or unlock your mind-set—can dramatically transform the energy of a conflict.[20] Have another person stand behind you, with outstretched arms and hands on the back of your shoulders, and begin slowly and gently but relentlessly pushing you forward so that you must start walking in the direction they dictate. As you walk, have the other person continue to increase the pushing pressure. After six or seven steps, spin to one side, in the same speed or rhythm as the pusher, rolling along your partner's outstretched arms, maintaining contact, so that you end up "rolling" to your partner's back, and placing your hands on his or her shoulders, gently pushing the person who was pushing you. This exercise demonstrates that as soon as you are willing to unlock your position and sense the line of attack in a conflict, you find yourself in a powerful position of choice.

This exercise represents the notion that another person may be pushing you in a direction you don't want to go. Or the force of attack might be coming from within yourself—driving you to do something you really don't want to do, because of money, guilt, anger, or some other reason. As with the push from a partner, with practice you can learn to spin your thoughts out of a rut and move in a new direction.

When you step outside a building on a blustery day and are caught full force by the wind, you don't have to think about turning your body away from the line of attack—you simply go with it, turning on your feet so that you're facing away from the onslaught, as if "riding the edge of the wind." This is the position that gives you the most personal power and control.

Think back to our earlier image of considering conflict as the interaction of two spheres of energy. Your attacker's aggression will contract his energy sphere and push it ahead in a principal line. If you resist and tighten up, you contract your own sphere of energy and become trapped or immobilized. Therefore, the final step in the split-second pause capitalizes on the fact that moments of conflict are, in truth, moments of choice, and you can choose to end the habit of contraction—and, instead, extend your awareness and expand your energy to fill the gap left by the other person's contraction.

This may take many possible forms, such as moving off the line of attack (expanding *away* from the attacking force) or expressing understanding or projecting a sense of calmness and strength in the face of adversity. In many conflicts what this means is that when you take a split-second pause, it can throw an attacker off-balance because you project an immediate sense of nonaggression and confidence. This signals that you're *not* "easy prey" and the other person may instinctively realize that you cannot be readily intimidated or overwhelmed. The aggressor may even relax a bit, brought up short by the mental dissonance or contrast between *his* aggression and *your* self-assured yet nonaggressive position.

This can make other people, even *very* angry people, less hostile, providing even the slightest opening for acknowledging and coming to terms with differences or reaching some kind of peaceful resolution or escape from harm or, as Dr. Edward deBono calls it, *deconflicting* the situation.[21]

With practice, you can expand your energy and attention toward solutions, instead of contracting and getting locked on resisting problems, toward what you *can* control rather than getting bogged down in what you can't. This is the place to clearly choose an *intent to learn* instead of your old reactionary habits; to listen with an open mind instead of blindly talking back; to let go of trying to change other people and, instead, to apply your personal golden rule or spiritual philosophy in place of a rush of anger, impatience, or anxiety; to be skilled enough to protect yourself without harming other people.

Chapter 4

SAFETY INTELLIGENCE PRINCIPLE #2: FOCUSED EMOTIONAL ENERGY

The second principle of *safety intelligence* is one to *actively guide* your emotional energy toward outcomes that are constructive or protective rather than destructive or paralyzing. If you are angry or are faced with an angry person, for example, you will feel a rush of emotion in response to *their* emotion, and if you are not in control of this energy, it can overwhelm you or push you into a reaction that you regret, and perhaps one that escalates—rather than defuses—potential or real violence.

British psychologist and martial artist Khaleghi Quinn, Ph.D., claims in her book *Everyday Self-Defense,* "Ninety-eight percent of aggressive people were once on the receiving end of mental, emotional, or physical abuse, who then went on to use aggressive behavior to compensate for an inner sense of powerlessness."[1]

Learning to distinguish your deeper feelings from the other whirling masses of stimuli and information all around us is certainly one of the most necessary and profound paths to personal growth and fulfillment. As you learn to accept and experience even the most uncomfortable of emotions, rather than suppressing them, a deep inner healing can begin to occur, one that liberates new sources of energy and freedom from the past.

In our busy lives, we assume a lot of things. We make presumptions about what other people think and feel, we criticize as if we actually, even instinctively and automatically, "know" the exact intentions and motives of others, or we pull away, all because we *think* we know. But all too often we are proven wrong when we learn what the other person was really feeling and, at the deepest level, intending and attempting to convey in words. In safety intelligence, when the *heart* listens, it always listens to what is unspoken. When you listen *not* to what is being said but to what is being *conveyed*, whether through facial expressions or hand, eye, and body language, you begin to enter the depths of feeling in another person, the place where the truth is communicated and needs are expressed and responded to. If you are in real danger, chances are you'll *feel* it.

It is not only your mind but also your senses and your heart—which is tied to all of your senses and to the nervous system and brain—that is highly capable of reading the private feelings of an individual by perceiving *beneath* the look on their face, the pattern of their posture and gait, the unspoken messages beneath the sound of another's voice.

Emotions arise quickly—usually in the present moment. This is where safety intelligence must be practiced, because if your emotions are not acknowledged and guided into some form of constructive expression, they do not disappear; instead, they go underground and become a powerfully destructive force. Think about how much time and energy is wasted protecting ourselves from people we do not trust, avoiding problems we cannot talk about, faking acceptance of decisions with which we do not agree, remaining silent about the first signs of danger or risk, putting up with situations that aren't right for us, or turning away when others ask for our help.

"Our culture encourages us to be emotional illiterates, repressing our feelings or living at the mercy of emotional storms," says Daniel Goleman, Ph.D., the author of *Emotional Intelligence*, who reports on the brain and behavior for the *New York Times.* "The price we pay for emotional illiteracy is in failed marriages and troubled families, in stunted social and work lives, in deteriorating physical health and mental anguish. . . . Academic intelligence offers virtually no preparation for the turmoil—or opportunity— life's vicissitudes bring. Yet even though a high IQ is no guarantee of prosperity, prestige, or happiness in life, our schools and culture fixate on academic abilities, ignoring *emotional* intelligence, a set of traits—some might call it *character*—that also matters immensely for our personal destiny. Emotional life is a domain that, as surely as math or reading, can be handled with greater or lesser skill and requires its own unique set of competencies."[2]

Emotions are a vital tool for feeling safe and getting along in the world, says Richard S. Lazarus, Ph.D., professor emeritus of psychology at the University of California at Berkeley. "Emotions evolved as they have in our species because they aid us in making our way successfully through life. In fact, whenever we experience an emotion, it indicates that something personally important has happened to us. . . . Emotions are products of personal meaning, which depends on what is important to us and the things we believe about ourselves and the world. . . . It takes knowledge and understanding to control and express our emotions effectively. . . . On the face of it, emotions appear to be highly fluid, changeable events, unpredictable and irrational. But when we dig deeper, we see how they make sense, and we uncover personal meaning. . . . Emotions are an extremely important source of knowledge about ourselves and of information about how we are faring in our lives."[3]

Another new and important discovery is that emotions are powerful organizers of thought and action and are, in fact, indispensable for reasoning and rationality under difficult circumstances, such as times when you first begin to *feel* unsafe. One of the new realizations is that every time we experience an emotion, especially a strong one, *every dimension of our being* is called upon— our attention and thoughts, our needs and desires, and our bodies. "These are times when the fabric of our society seems to unravel at ever-greater speed, when selfishness, violence, and a meanness of spirit seem to be rotting the goodness of our communal lives," adds Dr. Goleman. "Here the argument for the importance of *emotional intelligence* hinges on the link between sentiment, character, and moral instincts. There is growing evidence that fundamental ethical stances in life stem from underlying emotional capacities. For one, impulse is the medium of emotion; the seed of all impulse is a feeling bursting to express itself in action. Those who are at the mercy of impulse—who lack self-control—suffer a moral deficiency: the ability to control impulse is the base of will and character. By the same token, the root of altruism lies in empathy, the ability to read emotions in others; lacking a sense of another's need or despair, there is no caring. And if there are any two moral stances that our times call for, they are precisely these, self-restraint and compassion."

My bedrock advice is for people to pay attention to their gut feelings, hunches, or premonitions. These are not products of black magic or superstition. They are products of a sophisticated protective system which exists in all of us.

HUGH C. McDONALD, former chief of the Detective Division, Los Angeles County Sheriff's Department, and author of *Survival*[4]

To further your quest to master your emotional energy and to employ useful self-restraint and empathy during times of stress and danger, here, briefly, is a sense & guide sequence for safety intelligence.

1. Sense
"What Strong Feeling *Is Getting My Attention Right Now?*"

Feelings flow inside each of us like a river and pass beneath or through our consciousness in a continuous pattern. Without skills in feeling and responding appropriately to even the darkest of emotions, problems of fear and danger are magnified. "When shame or helplessness become intense," observes Harvard's Weissbourd in *The Vulnerable Child*, "when violence is seen as a legitimate means of resolving conflict, and when children have few day-to-day opportunities to cope emotionally or to gain respect and prestige, the chance of their crossing the border into violence or degrading other children is multiplied many times. . . . They seek to obliterate their helplessness and rage through primitive forms of vengeance."

One of the simple questions to begin with is, Where, in your body, do you feel the *sensations of each emotion?* For many people, one of the most effective ways to deal with feelings is to identify where in the body they are located. Feeling your emotions as *body sensations* can take much of the fear, confusion, or resistance out of getting in touch with them. Each emotion is located somewhere: a heaviness in the chest, a lump in the throat, a tightness in the abdomen, a weight on the shoulders, a knot in your stomach or back. As soon as you locate a feeling in time and space, it becomes less threatening. Best of all, when you describe emotions as body sensations, you free yourself from judgments or criticisms of yourself or others: you are simply reporting what *is*. The emotion *feels* this way in my body. And because you can locate it, you can work with it more directly. Anger that is experienced in the throat, for example, may require a different means of releasing and guidance than anger that stiffens your shoulders and knots up your fists.

Begin by asking yourself these questions:

• When was the last time you felt *angry?* What were you angry about, and where, in your body, did you feel the anger sensations?

• When was the last time you felt *afraid?* What was the fear about, and where, in your body, did you feel the most noticeable fear sensations?

The signals you receive from emotions are coming to you constantly: I feel excited, concerned, cared for, threatened, valued, rejected, enthused, and a thousand other things. Being able to read your feelings and understand the messages behind them is a basic safety skill. This, in effect, connects the heart with the head.

Even a flash of so-called negative emotion sends a message. For example:

Anger and *outrage* arise to tell you that what is happening is unwanted or threatens your beliefs or values or safety. Anger prompts us to take action to protect our safety, and the safety of others, or to express our need to be treated well by those who profess to care about us.

Fear may convey that you are about to lose your safety, or that something you value is at risk.

In many circumstances, to whatever degree we repress a feeling or ignore the truth, the mind begins to chatter with distraction, wasting our time and pulling us away from what we truly want or need, leaving us feeling paralyzed or overreactive and thereby less safe.

The main point is to realize that whatever emotions you feel are appearing for a reason, and they are offering you an opportunity—and a source of natural energy—with which to guide yourself.

If you feel a flash of anger and try to block it, you may end up becoming emotionally exhausted or physically tense, further jeopardizing your safety and triggering an avalanche of other things to go wrong. If, on the other hand, you acknowledge that anger or fear is trying to pull you off-balance, then you may be able to respond more appropriately and constructively.

Of course, in every human interaction and potential confrontation, pitfalls may lead you to *feel under mental or emotional attack from another person even when this feeling is wrong.* Unfortunately, the human brain has been programmed over thousands of years of evolution to capture and then magnify the most negative assumptions. Think about it: When someone ignores you or criticizes you, is your first feeling one of empathy? ("Oh, he or she may be upset about something else or so busy today that they simply didn't notice me.") Not likely. Instead, you may feel or think such things as "Is this a threat to my safety?" "Why is this person angry with me?" "I wonder if I've done something wrong." Or perhaps you even jump to conclusions: "That's no way to treat someone! I'll get back at you for this." Isn't it incredible how often our first reation is "There is something wrong with me" and then this seems to mean "I am not worthy enough"? And these thoughts may trigger needless fear, emotional turmoil, or feelings of loss of safety. What a waste!

Feelings can be a source of truth and power. But only if we read them correctly and honestly. Then we can decide how to *guide* this emotional energy and respond effectively.

2. Guide
"How Can I Best Guide *This Emotional Energy?"*

> *The freedom to choose is not something we have and therefore can lose, it is something we are.*

Emotions should serve us as messengers, not controllers. Unfortunately, many people try to control their feelings through resistance and repression. And, as we've mentioned earlier, this does not eliminate them; in fact, repressing a feeling will eventually make it more powerful. It actually wastes a tremendous amount of energy trying to keep feelings held down. And it becomes more of a struggle to stay in control.

On the other hand, if you accept each strong emotional message as an *inner wake-up call* and are open to listening, you can start flowing with the conflicting force and automatically stop resisting and straining against accepting your deeper feelings. Once you hear an emotional signal, even if it is negative, you can think to yourself, "Thanks for letting me know this," and commit to yourself that you will fulfill this need as soon as possible in the healthiest and most appropriate way.

Now, a key question is, How do you want to consciously focus, or *guide*, this new emotional energy? It is important to recognize that you can feel your feelings without having to act on them, especially in the case of anger and sexual feelings. Sometimes, the most valuable way to guide emotional energy is to do nothing except allow yourself to experience what you are feeling.

To start the guiding process, imagine yourself being handed a surge of emotional energy. Ask yourself, *What's the best way to guide this energy right now?*

There are situations when the smartest response may be *to feel the danger or fear and do nothing.* To let the ire of someone berating you blow over without your saying a word or lashing out at them. In times of danger, you can call upon the inherent emotional energy of almost any feeling such as anger or fear or rage and guide it into an appropriate, constructive *physical response*—such as turning to flee, dodging out of the reach of a mugger, sprinting to escape, or distracting one assailant while jumping away from another, and so on.

On the other hand, as parents one of the wisest things we can teach our children when it comes to facing bullies, for example, may be *to not fight back* under certain circumstances, and instead to walk away or use humor to defuse aggression—"Look, Johnny, please back off. I don't want us to be late for school!"—or to assertively tell the bully, "Get a life! Leave me alone!" and then walk away. This latter approach may be a smart defense for girls in particular. As a recent report in *Psychology Today* observed, there are many times when "fighting back can be the worst defense. In most instances, victimized children really are weaker and smaller than the bully—thus their fears of losing these fights may be quite real. Besides, not all bullying takes the form of physical aggression. Counteraggression to any form of bullying actually increases the likelihood of continued victimization."[5]

In everyday dialogues and arguments or misunderstandings, one of the most useful focuses for emotional energy is to clearly *ask for clarification—or ask for what you want or need.* This is such a simple and profound thing, yet few of us actually do it. Instead, we make assumptions as to the ill will of another person, or we talk in circles, we hint, we hope, we expect, we fume when no one seems to notice. Or we resort to withdrawal, sarcasm, or back-stabbing, instead of asking for clarification, for what we want.

Asking for what you need or want reveals your true humanity. The more you ask, the greater the chances you will stay safe and get more of your needs met. It also makes it easier for your children to talk openly with you about even their darkest feelings. As Dr. Weissbourd has found, "Children are less likely to be scarred by violence when they are able to talk about it to an adult soon after their exposure to it, when they have ongoing opportunities to discuss their fears, and when adults are able to give violence some meaning that is logical."

In some situations, during family or work-related arguments, for example, the best way to guide emotional energy may be to not say anything negative to yourself or another person. Instead, simply refocus your attention so that you now use your emotional energy as a "fuel" for a few minutes of creative thinking, or to take a brief walk or do some other form of exercise, or to find a quiet space for some personal learning, healing, planning, or reflection.

To be able to say to a love partner, friend, or coworker "My feelings are hurt by what you just said to me. Did you really mean . . . ?" or to be able to read another's feeling and clarify what you sense, "Have I offended you in some way? I can tell you pulled away. Are you upset with me?" can create a greater sense of confidence, clarity, and safety in your everyday life.

Have the courage, one question at a time, to be honest with yourself about what you feel, to go deeper, to speak up, to clarify what your senses are telling you, and move toward more authentic communication with others. Sometimes this may mean saying no to requests or speaking up to clarify what you sense is a put-down or put-off but may, in fact, not be. In many circumstances being direct—and appropriately expressing your anger or other feelings—allows you to honor both yourself and the other person, who may have done something, or at least appeared to do something, that offends or distresses you. You stay safer by quickly revealing the limits of what you will tolerate, and you honor the other person by inviting him or her to become more aware of the effects of words and behaviors. Once you release the uncomfortable feelings of confusion or anger inside you, the negative "spin" of this energy is shifted—and a more caring part of yourself is revealed. You will eventually find yourself spending less time on needless emotional "recovery work" and "rework" that results from misperceiving others.

Chapter 5

SAFETY INTELLIGENCE PRINCIPLE #3: TWO+ RESPONSES

The split-second pause and a readiness to guide *emotional energy* both set you up to take effective action using a strategy we call *two+ responses*. When you first learn this skill, it may feel counterintuitive—that is, in some conflicts you may be taking an action that seems at odds with what you might naturally do if you reacted by reflex alone. With two+ responses, you use timing and surprise to go around the point of greatest resistance. Instead of attempting to outshout or outmuscle an aggressor, you outmaneuver him. When someone stonewalls you, do *not* give in to the instinct to react in kind. When an adversary insists on his position, do *not* push back by rejecting it and asserting your own. When he applies pressure, do *not* react with direct counterpressure. The reason? If you react to conflict by trying to push against an adversary's resistance, you usually end up *increasing* it.

RECOGNIZING THE BEST *ANGLES OF RESPONSE*

To better understand the dynamics of conflict, it's helpful to view it through a simple "energy geometry" of attack and response.[1] This accesses another part of your memory for instant recall and application. Symbols can prove useful in instantly perceiving or sensing your situation during a split-second pause and in the actions that follow it. In each illustration, we are looking down on you and your attacker(s), as if viewing the conflicts from a helicopter hovering above. X marks the spot where you are standing.

The principle at work here reminds us of a story by Terry Dobson, aikido martial arts instructor and coauthor of *Aikido in Everyday Life: Giving In to Get Your Way*:

> There was once a man of great strength who, for his own reasons, engaged in a fight with a revolving door, determined to win in this great contest. He walked up to it and pushed with all his might. The door made three full revolutions before it came to rest again. He pushed even harder, and the door swung around four times. In desperation, the strong man got inside the revolving door and pushed and pushed, running as fast as he could to keep from being smacked by the door that followed him around and around. As onlookers gaped, they saw the strong man run faster and faster, until finally the centrifugal force he had created tossed him back out onto the street in a heap. Frustrated and angry, he picked himself up and walked over to a conventional locked door which sported every known security device on its steel casing. In a few seconds he'd knocked down the door and derived some consolation from his victory. Some of the onlookers who'd watched decided that the conventional door needed stronger dead bolts and heavy-duty brass hinges. Others cheered the revolving door but lamented the fact that it still let people in. A few

suggested that the strong man might do well to increase his protein intake. A small boy looked at the whole situation and smiled.

Be the water, not the rock.

The revolving door's appointed task was not to keep people out or bar their way. It was to welcome them. It gave nothing up, nor did it lose its ground or compromise its ideals. The strong man, in his anger, destroyed himself by pushing harder and running harder while the revolving door only accommodated his wish to go faster.

We can, symbolically, choose to be the revolving door and be capable of facing even the strongest, most off-balanced of mankind, or we can put more locks on ourselves, learn boxing, invent strangleholds, carry tear gas, shout more loudly, and stand more resolutely.

Be the water, not the rock.[2]

TWO+ RESPONSES: NEUTRALIZING AN ATTACK BY LINKING TWO OR MORE RESPONSES WITH TIMING AND SPEED

To respond with greatest effectiveness during moments of conflict, it makes sense to have your own simple steps for split-second decision-making. The approach we favor is founded on several key capabilities. Unfortunately, the following insights and explanations are necessarily rather technical. They are included to provide you with a brief glimpse into the scientific basis for *two+ responses.*[3]

• There are several uncommon-yet-basic patterns of *response programming.* Once these are learned, you'll have considerably greater ability to choose, on the spot, from a variety of *simple, preferred means of response*—which include de-escalating words and sudden, unexpected actions. This set of specific, easy-to-remember-and-do response options is, of necessity, free of intricate or complicated movements because such movements are difficult, even impossible, to remember or do when you're in a dangerous, pressure-packed situation.

• At the first moment of conflict, trigger a *split-second pause* before responding. According to neuroscientists, this not only keeps you calmer and more focused, it also prevents you from blindly plunging into action that can unintentionally escalate any conflict and increase your own danger. In a rushed reaction, for example, you may incorrectly anticipate what your aggressor is about to do and end up committing to move but in the wrong direction. Studies indicate that the time required to compensate for moving incorrectly can force you to take ten times longer to find an effective response. By then, it may be too late. In addition, some conflicts quickly dissolve tension and resolve themselves *if you remain calm and do not immediately react or jump in,*[4] and here is where the ability to *acknowledge and guide emotional energy* pays off—because:

• When it's time to respond, you gain a major advantage by using the energy of emotion as a fuel for making two or more responses *within a half second.* If the responses are simple enough, virtually anyone can learn to do this because your brain will link the words or actions in a "chunking" process for instant recall and application. The result is what neuropsychologists call a sensory overload in which an aggressor, no matter how big or strong or angry, must rely on his brain's *psychological refractory period* in which he or she can *only* react to the first sudden, unexpected word or motion you make. If you immediately follow with another sudden, unexpected word or movement, the aggressor's reaction time to the second stimulus (what reflex neurologists call RT2) and third stimulus (RT3) are blocked, making it nearly impossible for him to react effectively—by grabbing, striking you, or "capturing" you—and this empowers *you* to de-escalate the situation or escape.

• Brain scientists have also determined that performing a longer-duration movement (for example, lecturing the aggressor or stepping into a tense, formal martial-arts stance and cocking your arm before striking), *lengthens* your response time and puts you at a disadvantage. Instead, you are usually better off responding later (after a *split-second pause*, for example) with a faster, unexpected set of responses rather than earlier (*without* a pause) but with more complicated, longer-duration responses.

• Another amazing insight is this: If you happen to be caught unaware and an aggressor suddenly grabs you—seizing your arm, for example, the pressure of that grip provides a sensory shortcut for the brain that enables you to naturally, instantly speed your response time. Evidence supports the idea that skilled responses, including those that are cued on pressure or being grabbed, are stored in the nervous system not as a separate series of steps but as complete "motor programs." This can accelerate your response time even more. And the more unexpected you make your movements, the more you may also benefit from what neuroscientists call the *double-stimulation paradigm* whereby your opponent's reaction to your unexpected movement can increase (lengthen) his reaction time in responding to your second and third responses, briefly and essentially freezing him in place.

• On a final note, neutral stances (mentioned several times throughout this book), where you are upright and relaxed with knees slightly bent and palms open, give two added values. First, they convey a universal signal of peaceful intent. This nonaggressive position can, all by itself, help you remain more calm and alert. When an aggressor sees a *neutral stance*, he may hesitate for a moment or two, trying to read if he has misjudged the defense capabilities of his prey. This brief opening may enable you to de-escalate certain confrontations. Second, a *neutral stance* enables you to *open your heart with a feeling of nonviolence and to read the emotional signals of the conflict.* This also enables you to hide what your *two+ responses* might be. And when you avoid telegraphing your initial response, you make it even harder for an aggressor to trap you since he can't begin processing, thus reducing his reaction time.

During times of potential danger, we favor several basic types of responses to moments of conflict:

- *Use two or more de-escalating phrases*
- *Take two or more unexpected actions*

Use Two or More De-escalating Phrases

In some cases, you can readily de-escalate an argument or confrontation by using distractors. Researchers have found, for example, that one key difference in couples who, in conflict, keep their negativity in check and thus prevent things from exploding, is *repair mechanisms*—often a simple comment or caring, peaceful gesture that can lower their bodily arousal and break the cycle of escalation that pushes conflicts toward total chaos and violence. Couples who don't use repair mechanisms don't or can't use these signals to calm each other—and instead, become trapped in a warlike posture that can trigger violence.[5] The unstemmed escalation of hostilities produces a red alert called *flooding*—a state of violent physiological and psychological reactions: the heart feels as if it will burst, blood pressure soars, the stomach constricts, breathing becomes ragged, and stress hormones hurtle through the body. Whenever a conflict reaches this stage (and it can happen within moments), it is virtually impossible to resolve. All attempts at communication tend to be futile or harmful or both. Men are especially susceptible to flooding—hitting a physiological boiling point more rapidly than women—and remain aroused and obsessed with getting even long after the adversary, especially if a woman, may have left the experience behind.

But what about words in a *physical* confrontation? Do they help at all? Can verbal self-defense *really* be effective against physical violence? Sometimes.

The fact is, words can have tremendous power. According to scientists, the human brain has an ancient biological *language instinct* that powerfully shapes what we hear and say.[6] As you are reading these words, a precise series of ideas and feelings are arising inside you. The right word, spoken at the right moment in the right tone of voice, can stop violence in its tracks, if only long enough for a victim to escape or turn the tide. "Yet language is usually deployed without awareness of its underlying power and potentials," observes Steven Pinker, Ph.D., professor and director of the Center for Cognitive Neuroscience at the Massachusetts Institute of Technology.[7]

In general, when you follow a split-second pause and attunement to guiding *emotional energy* with words, whatever words you speak have the most impact when communicated suddenly and unexpectedly, and in a *neutral voice* and from a *neutral position.* As mentioned earlier, most people who are primed to hurt you physically need to see you in fear and hear you act like a victim, pleading for mercy. To some aggressors this matters more than the act of violence itself. Your goal is to keep the level of tension low, to keep your attacker from panicking—a very real danger if you just start screaming and freeze in place within the aggressor's reach. Do not lecture, blame, or plead. Speak clearly. Link at least two sudden words or statements, or combine a sharp command with an unexpected and nonaggressive rotational movement. For example, firmly say, "You seem upset. Please repeat what you just said, only more slowly!" as you simultaneously and smoothly step back *and* turn your stance to begin moving confidently and alertly away from the aggressor at the safest angle. As you leave, you might firmly add, "Thanks for wanting to talk, but I prefer to be alone now." And keep moving to safety—toward a lighted or busy area nearby.

What are some of the important words to use in a moment of conflict? You have many useful choices. Here are a few initial considerations (see chapter 8 for examples on de-escalating hostility):

• *When . . . ?* In a confrontation, the questions *why* ("Why are you doing this to me?") or *what* ("What's the matter with you?") give your attacker an invitation to blast you again, whereas a *when* question ("When did you start feeling so angry?" or "When did you lose your job?") may actually help defuse the confrontation by avoiding the presupposition that your attacker actually has a valid reason for the attack. Furthermore, many assailants love the drama of making certain the prey knows it's captured—and when you suddenly, unexpectedly switch the attacker's attention onto expressing some of his genuine complaints about life or society or social injustice, for example, it may calm him down or buy you a precious few moments of time or provide a brief smoke screen. It's usually difficult for a person confronting you to talk *and* physically attack you at the same time—that gives you a better opportunity to escape.

• *It's not your fault!* or *Yes, I can* understand *why you're upset!* Communication experts call these *leveler phrases,* and they may trigger a flash of surprise in an aggressor's mind, producing a moment's hesitation or disorientation in the attack pattern (few verbal or physical assailants enjoy attacking someone who is truly empathetic or may share their perspectives on injustice, for example). By acknowledging the aggressor, you create what psychologists call *cognitive dissonance,* a momentary inconsistency between perception and reality. The aggressor may think of you as prey, but when you acknowledge him personally with an unexpected leveler phrase, you may instinctively draw him away from the predator-prey mind-set. When a leveler phrase is used with several motions to gain distance—at least a step or two—from an aggressor, it may interrupt verbal escalation and help defuse anger. This is particularly potent against men.

• *Let me understand* . . . *Allow me to help* . . . *Please* tell me more . . . These are variations on the leveler-phrase concept. When spoken in a confident, nonpleading tone, expressions that begin with *let* or *allow* can be anger- or aggression-interrupting words that, at least in some cases, may be unexpectedly calming to an attacker's nervous system, says Keith Sedlacek, M.D., medical director of the Stress Regulation Institute in New York City.[8] When linked with another expression and perhaps an unanticipated change in your physical position, they may permit you to de-escalate the interaction or have greater control of what happens next.

• *Listen!* As an argument escalates, this word can stop some aggressors in their tracks because it taps into memory and language instincts in the brain. When linked with at least one more expression or several unanticipated but nonaggressive physical movements, it can interrupt the pattern and, at least for an instant, give you an opening.

• *Stay back!* or *No!* When shouted in a strong, sudden "command voice"—rather than a terrified or pleading tone—these words may cause an involuntary pullback by an assailant. These commands may be anchored in memory to parental warnings and create a moment of confusion or distraction. These words should instantly be linked to physical movements that put you farther out of harm's way.

• *Fire! Fire!* See the upcoming scenarios to learn why, if your goal is to enlist help from bystanders, "Help!" is sometimes the *wrong* word to scream as you break free and flee from an assailant.

Take Two or More Unexpected Actions

What about conflict situations where words alone are not likely to protect you? What if you're physically grabbed or attacked? Our first piece of uncommon advice is to use your voice as one element in the linked set of responses that set you free. A sharp question, single word, or bloodcurdling yell can, if combined rapid-fire with sudden, unexpected physical movements, turn the tables on an aggressor and enable you to break away. Throughout the book you'll learn the simplest, most effective ways to use physical responses to violence—and to inflict *the least harm to your assailant.* Here are several things to be aware of right away.

When you respond in a physical way, never make just one lunge or rotation or strike. Instead, *make at least two unexpected, contrasting moves.* After a *split-second pause* in a *neutral stance* (paradoxically, power *is* born from a no-power stance), you can respond, for example, using *angular lunges* and *rotational breakaways,* or some appropriate combination of words, movements, and—if needed—defensive strikes. All of these responses can be launched suddenly and unexpectedly with precision and speed. Remember, *speed* is a relative term; no matter what your age or physical size, you can indeed generate plenty of speed. The key is to be certain an aggressor has no idea what's coming. If you're yelling in anger, for example, and suddenly add a shout, it has far less stunning value than standing silently in a relaxed neutral position as you talk in a firm but low voice and then, without any warning, launch a set of *two+ responses,* such as a *sudden, forceful command* combined with a linked set of two or more *physical movements in contrasting directions* that enable you to neutralize the attack and escape.

Note: According to the law and common sense, three criteria must be present to determine the judicious use of force in personal defense:

> *Ability:* The aggressor must have the apparent physical ability to seriously harm you.
>
> *Opportunity:* The aggressor must be close enough to you to actually use his/her force.
>
> *Jeopardy:* The aggressor must be acting in such a manner that a reasonable and careful person would believe the aggressor was about to attack an innocent person (you or someone else). In this case, the attacker is saying, "I'm going to attack you," *and* is big and strong enough to do it *and* is clearly moving forward to do it.

An impending attack may be clear before any physical contact has been made. Ask yourself, "Am I in immediate and apparently unavoidable danger of grave bodily harm?" If the answer is yes, you don't have to wait to be struck first. If this level of danger exists, you can take a variety of uncomplicated, unexpected actions. For example:

If you're being grabbed, rather than resisting it in the usual push-pull manner, you might choose to suddenly tense your arms as you rotate, knees bent, elbows out, whirling your upper body a quarter turn clockwise and then instantly reversing direction and rotating counterclockwise, enabling you to easily slip out of the aggressor's grip and into a lunging charge step at an oblique angle, breaking free and then running on the best route to safety. As another alternative, if you have a purse, briefcase, book, coat, pocket change, bottle of iced tea, cup of coffee, can of soda, umbrella, keys, or any other object in hand, you might power throw it at your attacker (as you'll discover in chapter 11, having a "nonweapon" may turn out to be a great aid to personal protection) as you simultaneously rotate and sprint away in another direction. With minimal practice, any combination of the above two+ responses can provide you with maximal stunning power on your assailant's senses but will cause little or no lasting harm.

If a more forceful response is needed, the most important thing—as we mentioned earlier—is to have a simple, preferred means of response (no intricate or complicated moves). Depending on the size, stance, and number of attackers, you can draw from any two or more of the following sampling of basic protective strikes and use them, always in combination, to stop an assailant in his tracks, giving you an opening to resolve the situation or, if necessary, escape.

1. Eye jab (full hand, angular, natural, sudden)
2. Ear clap (cupped-hand, circular-palm strike)
3. Head butt (top of your head driven into attacker's face)
4. Forearm/elbow (to side of head/jaw, throat)
5. Knee slam (to the groin)
6. Bite (the arm that is choking you or hand clamped over your mouth)
7. Power throw/push/spin away

It is absolutely important to learn sound, basic martial arts techniques—including any of those listed above—from a caring, highly qualified instructor who can personalize the teaching of each skill to fit your size, temperament, and circumstances. (A list of key questions for assessing the quality of instruction is provided in chapter 11.) For women who fear assault and rape, one widely praised program offers a carefully developed combination of awareness, assertiveness, de-escalation, and physical defense skills. It is called Model Mugging (a listing of the classes held nearest you may be obtained from Self-Defense & Empowerment

News, Box 986, San Luis Obispo, CA 93406; 805-995-1224). If you are unable to find reputable, personalized martial arts instruction in your home area, you might wish to consider training via video. Your local law enforcement agency or rape crisis centers may have knowledge of the best martial arts programs and may also provide a lending library of self-defense videos that you can view free of charge.

However, you may be wondering, what about a situation where this doesn't work or if, despite your best plans, you're caught unaware and are trapped or seized and you can't get free? Any of us could suddenly find ourselves in such a perilous situation. If this happens to you:

• Stay calm with another split-second PAUSE to gain a higher vantage point and gather another surge of *emotional energy*.

• Wait for an opening—for a moment when, for example, the aggressor puts down his weapon, turns his head away, or shifts his grip on you.

• When you make your move, use two+ responses that combine surprise (suddenness), distraction (an unexpected battle scream), leverage (rotating and striking with sudden direction changes that force your assailant to break contact and pull away), and flight (escaping the scene of the attack)—triggering all of these responses as close together as possible so they seem nearly simultaneous.

Chapter 6

EIGHT SCENARIOS: HOW WOULD *YOU* RESPOND?

We invite you to consider the following practical examples of moments of conflict, ranging from negative thoughts to everyday arguments to physical attack. Imagine you are there, envision the situation happening to you. Once the scene is set, honestly ask yourself, "What would *I* do if this were happening to me?" Or imagine one of your children or loved ones in this situation. Think through each scenario from beginning to end. Then visualize the possible differences in outcome if you were to apply the opening strategies of this book: A split-second pause and guided *emotional energy*, followed by *two+ responses.*

Brief rehearsals—both imagined and enacted—are one effective method of replacing unconscious reactions with conscious responses. By vividly envisioning the best way for you to use the tactics and tools in this book to deal with a variety of possible conflicts, you create a mental blueprint for effectiveness in the future. The scenarios in the pages ahead—and throughout the rest of this book—can be used to help set these new skills in your memory. With practice, you can program your brain and nervous system to respond more and more effectively under pressure.

Moments of conflict cease to feel like mysteries and become *moments of choice*. If you look around, you'll find lots of everyday conflicts, large and small, in which to practice new ways of responding. If, at the end of the day, you realize you've reverted to old reactions and blown it in an argument, for example, you can sit down in a quiet spot and spend a few minutes reenvisioning the circumstances and rewriting the script in your mind with the outcome you would have preferred. Each real or envisioned success in moments of conflict—a split-second pause and *two+ responses*—reprograms the brain to respond more rapidly and effectively. This work is simple and direct—but it requires rolling up your sleeves and working on yourself. With practice, you'll be able to respond instantly and more effectively to even the most difficult encounters.

Note: The described actions in each of these eight sample scenarios are provided *solely* for the purpose of stimulating your own ideas and choices. To successfully prevent, deter, or defuse a mental, verbal, or physical attack, you must respond in whatever way works best for *you* as an individual.

1. An inner mugging—When the attacker is your own mind.
2. "Now I'm really getting MAD!"—Everyday arguments.
3. "I can't stand criticism!"—Facing the sting of another's words.
4. "What's your hurry?"—Getting grabbed.
5. The echo of footsteps—Being followed.
6. If looks could kill—Predatory stares.
7. Under the club—Facing a hooking attack.
8. "Get in the car or I'll shoot!"—A nightmare at gunpoint.

Scenario #1: An Inner Mugging—When the Attacker Is Your Own Mind

At times the most hostile aggressor isn't "out there"—but "in here." You are the aggressor. And you are the victim.

Every day there are billions of internal muggings—attacks on people's self-esteem and confidence—that go unresolved.[1] In a typical day, most of us seem to attack ourselves at least once or twice an hour: "You fool! Why did you do that?" or "There you go, messing everything up again" or "Hey, when are you ever going to get things right, huh?" At other times our minds turn what we see as ambiguous behaviors in others into negative stabs at ourselves: "He didn't really mean that compliment or kind word. I'll bet he really thinks I'm a _____!" Even worse, the *absence* of a compliment becomes an insult; the absence of a greeting becomes disapproval; the absence of a phone call becomes a rejection.

Under ideal circumstances, in cases such as these the best response is to stay detached from and simply flow with, rather than resist, the negative thoughts—because, as brain scientists have discovered, resisting them simply increases their power.[2] But this is often far from easy. At first, the best you may be able to do is to defuse or deflect one attacking thought at a time. You won't always succeed, but it can happen more often than it does now. In you. In all of us.

Remember, if an attacking force, in this case a thought, comes straight at you, once you've used a split-second pause to gain a higher vantage point and sense the line of the thought attack, you can allow yourself to feel the surge of anger and then guide this emotional energy by, for example, telling yourself *Release!* as you give up the impulse to struggle with the attacking thought—and, instead, become the "energy" shape of the circle, using two+ responses in your mind to imagine yourself flowing, rotating around the negative thought and letting it slip past you, missing its target (remember, the thought can be like an attacker who is off-balance charging straight ahead) as, for the second movement, you turn your attention to something else: *This doesn't matter—something else matters more to me.* If the negative thought returns, once again imagine smoothly, nonaggressively "rotating" your mind and shifting your focus elsewhere, moving on instead of getting angry, rigid, or stuck. In scenario #2 we'll briefly discuss a *mental shielding* technique that can be a direct and powerful tool to protect yourself from negative thoughts.

The American philosopher Henry Ward Beecher wrote, "The world's battlefields are in the heart." To a great extent, scientists today would agree. Throughout this book, we'll be emphasizing emotional safety. Whenever a person begins to *feel* safe, it helps invoke a sense of real-life protective spirit, which in turn helps prevent the gnawing sense that parts of you are off-balance or that you aren't whole, or that others have something you lack. It is the sense of protective spirit that helps you put the pieces back together, reestablishing contact with your own safety intelligence and inner power, making yourself whole again, no matter how unsafe the world actually is or may become. The path to this transformation begins with you—in your heart and mind, and with how you learn to deal with something as basic and pervasive as daily negative thoughts.

Scenario #2: "Now I'm Really Getting MAD!"—Everyday Arguments

While angry confrontations are common and all but inevitable in everyday life, they are also a high-stress nuisance that can throw you off-balance, attacking your inner sense of safety almost like a physical assault.

Simply trying to understand an angry incident is not enough. Even when you manage to say and do the right things, becoming livid with anger can leave you deeply shaken. The goal, instead, is to learn to remain calm and alert with the *mental shielding* skills to disengage from hostile comments and stay in control.

In chapter 7, we'll explore a deeply calm and open state in which it may be simplest to imagine a *mental shield with protective properties.* You can practice using this shield—a technique that has been developed by a neuroscientist[3]—to deflect or defuse many emotional or verbal attacks.

How often have you been in an argument and, in the grip of anger, spent all of your energy trying to be right, trying to deny the other person's views or feelings? Neither of you was really listening or perceiving the needs of the other. All that emerged were differences, right versus wrong. The more right you tried to be, the more separate you became and the more the conflict escalated.

To de-escalate a confrontation and mentally disarm an aggressor, you need to start with a split-second pause, guide the emotional energy of the emerging confrontation, then respond with two+ responses. Be patient with yourself, especially at first. It takes practice to step off the line of attack. "Stepping to the side is probably the last thing you feel like doing with a difficult person," admits William Ury, Ph.D., cofounder and director of the Harvard Negotiation Project at Harvard Law School, and author of *Getting Past No*. "When your opponent closes his ears, you naturally feel like doing the same. When he refuses to recognize your rights or point of view, you certainly don't feel like recognizing his. When he disagrees with everything you say, you may find it difficult to agree with *anything* he says. Although entirely understandable, these responses lead to stalemate or even disaster. To break through an opponent's resistance, you need to reverse this dynamic."[4]

Many everyday conflicts arise from power struggles—when you try to get something from another person and he or she doesn't want to give it to you. Or when others try to get things from you that you don't want to give. Have you ever been in conflicts that keep getting worse the longer you debate or argue? Did it seem that each side got more rigid and closeminded, and everything ended in hurt or frustration? Sometimes, the harder you and the other person try, the more resistance and anger appear. They may be centered around just about anything. You may even forget what started the argument; all that matters is the power struggle.

The real issue in most of these conflicts is control, with one person indicating, "I'm *not* going to be controlled by you." A rapid escalation kicks in, and if it happens often, you may throw up your hands and say, "The issue here seems so simple. Why can't the *other person* understand things. What's the problem?" The problem is that the other person feels or acts as if their identity or integrity is at stake.

To break the cycle, you might begin by acknowledging that a willingness to accept another's sense of the truth does not invalidate your own, no matter how conflicting your feelings or viewpoints may seem. If your intention is to creatively resolve everyday clashes that occur at home, on the street, or in the workplace, a willingness to understand the other side is essential. Remember, your goal in many situations is not to win arguments, not to prove your point; your goal is to be and feel *safe*. Don't get suckered into a verbal fight. And try to refrain from antagonizing others.

Relax for a few moments. Take a deep, long breath and recall a recent "minor" conflict that turned into an angry exchange or an argument, one that didn't end up as well as you would have hoped. For example, suppose someone lit up a cigarette in a no-smoking area or cut in front of you in line at the supermarket, and when you spoke up, they launched into an angry war of words. The situation could be any kind of verbal assault, but one where, at least at first, there was no physical violence.

Relive the experience in your imagination. Exactly what did it look like, sound like, feel like? Did you pause and remain calm? Or did you react right away? What were the facial expressions and voice tones like? The posture you each had? What specific words, gestures, gazes, or sounds seemed to make things better— or worse? Did any word or action *almost* turn things around and resolve the conflict? Were you or the other person, or both, trying to listen or to be "right"?

Now rewrite the script. Review the conflict in your mind as if it were happening right now. At the first moment you feel the clash beginning, trigger a split-second pause. Perceive more deeply this time, heightening your sensitivity to whatever the other person may be struggling with. In a friendly but assertive manner, say something like, "My intention is not to hassle you. I thought perhaps you had missed seeing the no-smoking sign." The point here is to try to give the other person the benefit of the doubt *and* a face-saving, argument-deterring opportunity. If the other person still lashes out in anger, rather than lashing back, pause once more and commit yourself to working toward the best possible solution or outcome. "Acknowledging your opponent's point of view does *not* mean that you agree with it," says Dr. Ury. "It means that you accept it as one point of view among others."[5] Here is where you can channel or guide the emerging emotional energy.

"I can tell you feel strongly about this," you might say, "and perhaps there's another place nearby where smoking is permitted." Rather than criticizing the other person, unlock your position—first in your posture, letting any sudden tightness go from your muscles, and then in attitude, remaining open to the other person's needs or view of truth or anger. Sense the line of conflict—the emotional energy that is present—and move off this line and focus all the available energy of your own feelings to de-escalate things as you begin a two+ response. Perhaps using a *mental shield* (explained in the paragraphs that follow) as you speak a calm, neutral-toned *leveler phrase* backed by a nonaggressive opening of your hands and a half step to the left or right, smoothly guiding your body off-line to give the other person a little extra "space" to calm down. You may even be surprised that your calmness prompts other bystanders to speak up and urge the smoker to find another area in which to smoke.

As discussed further in chapter 7, one scientifically based "mental shielding" technique is based on imagining a point of light in front of you, then stretching that point of light into a window of light.[6] You use the light to mentally construct an instant titanium-like shield, a curtain of light or screen or wall. You may want to wrap the shield or light all around you in a circle or protective sphere. Use whatever image is most comfortable for you. With practice, you can focus your thoughts to give the shield protective qualities so that nothing angry, critical, or manipulative can pass through it. You can still *see* through this shield as an observer, and the protective barrier allows positive thoughts and feelings through. You are reminded, according to psychologist

Richard Driscoll, Ph.D., "that you should be protected and that it is right and good for you to feel safe. If you believe in God or a higher being, you might see the protective shield as the love and protection of God."[7]

With mental rehearsal, you remain relaxed and alert as you imagine a troublesome person in front of you making an accusation or threatening comment. You envision yourself observing the comment being hurled toward you and see it strike the shield, disintegrating or being deflected, then passing harmlessly by. You realize that the anger attached to the words does not have to affect you, and thus you experience being protected. This mental shielding technique is particularly invaluable in light of evidence that, when facing criticism and rudeness from others, to remain *safe* it is often best to remain as *alert, detached,* and *uninvolved* as possible.

The truth is, by brushing off insults and degrading words you are not merely pretending. *What you take as important or unimportant can literally help construct the reality of what follows.* Perceiving an ugly comment as small and distant helps you keep the attack itself small and distant. You subsequently gain considerable power in controlling the meaning of your experiences. Likewise, no slight is so small, no rude word so minor or petty, that it cannot be made huge and destructive by getting upset about it.

Even when you are unsure of precisely how to respond, take the safest route and PAUSE again. It helps prevent thoughtless and automatic reactions. At the least, when you let a barbed word go unanswered, you do no harm. By mentally shielding yourself against hostile comments, you dissolve some or even all of the other person's power to force you into feeling victimized.

By remaining in a relaxed, alert neutral stance—and, in some circumstances, even keeping a small yet disarming smile, something courteous yet assertive, on your face—you help de-escalate the situation and we find it easier to *feel* and then *guide* the emotional energy the situation elicits. When necessary, you can follow up with a second pause and set of two+ responses. The next time a stressed-out person crosses your path, use a split-second pause, determine the direction they're heading, and then, if possible, step clear of the path and yield the right of way, avoiding a verbal collision.

Here's an example, which we have adapted from a story by Tom Crum, aikido instructor and author of *The Magic of Conflict*.[8] You're in line at the supermarket as the person ahead of you takes her receipt and heads for the door. No one is behind you in line. You've had a really rough week at work and are in a hurry to get home. But all of a sudden, before you can step forward to the cashier, a large man with a Cat-n-Fiddle Tavern jacket cuts ahead of you with a twenty-four-pack of beer under his arm.

"I'm in a hurry" is all he mutters, placing the beer on the scanner.

"Excuse me," you say in a rigid tone, "but *I* was here in line!"

He turns with an icy stare as his unshaven face stiffens. "Well, *I'm* in a big hurry!" he snaps impatiently.

"So am I!" you reply, going red.

"Not the kind of hurry *I'm* in," he says, turning back to the checkout counter.

Let's stop the scene right there. Do you think that right now in *your* mind you perceive this line encroacher as someone's loving and helpful husband in a hurry to bring home beer for a twentieth-anniversary party that he's late in attending because of an ice storm that delayed his truck on its return route home from Omaha and he's been driving all night? No way. Instead, what you likely perceive, with a flash of indignation and tightened jaw, is a lazy, good-for-nothing, chauvinistic slob who probably leaves the toilet seat up, underwear on the floor, and does virtually nothing around the house to help. Sound familiar? It takes only a split second (clock this the next time something similar happens to you) for you to jump to such a conclusion and react.

And what about the man in the Cat-n-Fiddle Tavern jacket? He hears you criticize him for cutting in line. Now, do you think *his* response is "Aha! A *moment of conflict*—what a splendid opportunity!" Not a chance. Instead, in his mind the I-work-my-butt-off-all-week-for-my-family-and-now-I'm-missing-my-wife's-party scoreboard lights up. As linguistics researchers have discovered, if he's like most men, deep in the *language instinct center* of the male brain he intuitively knows he "wins" if he can dominate things.[9] Besides, he's tense and tired and would find it extremely difficult to take a calm, well-reasoned approach.

"I think you should get behind me in line," you say as the scene continues to unfold.

"Oh, *yeah?*" he snarls, eyes beet red, striking his fist against his palm. "I work my butt off all week while you're probably sitting at home gossiping and watching soap operas. I *deserve* to be at the front of the line right now! I *earn* my money and pay taxes!" Now we're into money and taxes.

Your turn: "How *dare* you say that, you rude . . ."

Now, within a matter of seconds, the conflict is spiraling out of control. Winning at any cost has become the goal. Any sense of fear you may have is getting lost in the heat of anger. It's winner take all—and you can imagine the lingering, destructive effect in the hours and even days ahead.

Let's stop the scene and ask ourselves, How could the two of you break out of this pattern and use conflict as a positive signal? Here's one possibility:

What if you had taken a split-second pause? What if you had chosen a different vantage point and perceived that this man was stressed-out and rushed, feeling as if he actually *deserved* or at least *needed* the shortest path to the door and home after a hard week's work. What if you saw yourself making an altruistic gesture, actually *welcoming* him—a random act of kindness?—just as you began to acknowledge your surge of emotional energy at the start of the interaction and chose to unlock your position by shrugging your tense shoulders and breathing deeply? What if you had sensed his lost-in-the-rush state of mind and realized it probably *wasn't* a deliberate act on his part to insult you—and what if this realization enabled you to remain less judgmental about him during the first moments, as a kind neighbor might? Now you are in a position of far greater control to influence the outcome of whatever comes next.

Following with two+ responses, you might kindly have stepped aside and, if still irritated, moved to another checkout aisle if one was open. That could have ended the potential conflict in a relatively positive way.

Here's another possible rewrite of the scene: What if the man, at hearing your angry voice, "Excuse me, but *I* was here in line!" had delayed his reply for a moment by using a split-second pause? What if after perceiving the tension in your voice and noticing that *you* looked as if you were in a rush, too, he had *postponed* feeling angry or defensive (knowing he could always get upset later if he wanted to). What if he had remained calm and unlocked his own position by looking for another open checkout lane, sensing your tiredness and stress as he responded with greater empathy *(I'll bet we both had a helluva week!)*.

And then what if the man had taken a deep breath and replied with two+ responses, perhaps with something like "Sorry, I've been so wrapped up in trying to get home for an anniversary party and my truck got delayed in that ice storm west of Omaha"—and he began moving toward another line.

Wouldn't you be more likely to say, "No, you go ahead. It's fine"?

Of course, these alternate responses are not easy, especially if the air is already charged with tension or hostility. Yet only by pausing and acknowledging do we show others that we value them. Whatever the exact words, it's the quality of your calm sincerity and kind intention that convey the real, deeper message.

But what if *you* wouldn't give in that easily? How about saying something like "I can see you're in a rush, too," as you scan the lanes for an open checkout counter—and, if you spot one, say, "There's another open line over there. Would you mind taking that one?" Chances are, even with some grumbling, the answer may be yes.

One of the main points in this scenario is that even if you stay angry or the other person turns into a royal grouch, you'll have a greater chance of realizing that *all it takes is for one person to change.* Even if the other person is verbally putting you down, when you remain calm and use a mental shield and let go of the need to fight back and "win" and, instead, move to understand the stress this other person feels, your actions offer a sign of strength—not weakness or "giving in"—and that dramatically reduces the chance that things will escalate into violence and helps the other person calm down.

In their book *Getting to Yes*, Roger Fisher and William Ury, of the Harvard Negotiation Project, explain, "It is not enough to know that they [your "opponents"] see things differently. If you want to influence them, you also need to understand empathetically their point of view and to feel the emotional force with which they believe in it."[10] Being willing to understand another person is a chance to perceive all aspects of a conflict, not just the anger of the moment.

Physical self-protection skills are your last line of defense. While it is true that some conflicts cannot be de-escalated, it is also true that a large majority of attacks can be avoided or de-escalated before they reach a physical level of violence. Throughout this book we emphasize inner safety and avoidance or de-escalation skills. The following scenarios offer you a brief snapshot of times when nonaggressive physical actions can be a valuable option.

Scenario #3: "I Can't Stand Criticism!"—Facing the Sting of Another's Words

Let's face it—no one likes to be criticized. Whether it's by a total stranger or a loved one, even constructive criticism can trigger arguments. Both giving and receiving criticisms, or honest—and often unpleasant—words from other people, is a necessary and difficult part of life, frequently leading to misunderstandings and hurt feelings. Ask yourself, when during the past several weeks did criticism get under your skin or throw you off-balance? Did your spouse or a friend confront you with an old habit that you were not ready to change? Did a parent say something that made you feel guilty, ashamed, or defensive? Did someone at work imply you weren't doing a good job? Did a stranger on the street try to panhandle you for money and then criticize or insult you when you said no and walked away?

What was it about each of these criticisms that made you feel most angry, guilty, defensive, victimized, or enraged? Did the situation get resolved safely or did you continue to feel off-balance or hurt? In many cases, we're either accused of being too sensitive or else we're criticized for how we criticize. At the heart of the matter is that constructively intended comments—the original meaning of *criticism*—are vital to honest and fulfilling relationships at home and work. If we discourage others from criticizing us, then irritations and resentments pile up and will eventually destroy friendships anyway.

Let's assume that when you sense the good intentions of another person's criticism, you can hear the message without anger or defensiveness and respond appropriately. But what about those times when the critical remarks are really barbed? In every conflict, it's the small choices that often make the biggest difference in the outcome. In these cases, the approach we suggest is to be aware that you're actually under *verbal attack* but *don't take the bait.* Here are several examples:

"If you really . . ."

"If you *really* cared about this family, you wouldn't *do* that!"

"If you *really* noticed how hard we all work around here, you wouldn't *make* decisions like that!"

"If you *really* loved me, you'd stop ignoring me!"

This verbal attack pattern begins with the presupposed attack—"If you *really* . . ."—followed by the *bait,* the openly insulting or hurtful part of the sentence intended to grab your attention and lock you into a victimizing argument. Classic stabs here include "you wouldn't be the _____ you are!" or "you wouldn't do something so stupid!"

To neutralize this kind of verbal attack, first remain silent for an extra moment with a split-second pause. Be certain to unlock your position by delaying judgments and loosening both your shoulders and your perceptions. You might perceive things this way: The other person isn't actually yelling *at* you, he's yelling *for* himself. Imagine that this expression of feelings may actually be good for him. Don't take this emotional energy as a direct strike *against* you; instead see it being sent *past* you, then dissolving in the air.

When you begin your two+ responses, make it a point to keep your voice and body language neutral. Don't let yourself sound insolent or become sarcastic. Avoid the mistake of taking the verbal bait and letting the presupposition escape your attention. If you do, you will play right into your attacker's plans and inadvertently admit, by default, that there's truth in what the attacker is saying. Instead of beginning your reply with "What makes you think that X . . ." or "Why do you think that X . . . ," the best reply usually is "When did you start thinking X?" *Why* and *what* questions generally give the attacker an invitation to blast you again, whereas *when* questions help defuse the confrontation by avoiding the presupposition—the verbal *bait*—that your attacker actually has a valid reason for the attack and instead presupposes that "at some time you began thinking X." The safer, more effective response is usually one that zeroes in on the presupposition that immediately follows the setup "If you *really* . . ." For example:

ATTACKER: "If you *really* cared about this family, you wouldn't *do* that!"
YOU: "*When* did you start thinking that I don't care about this family? And"—now, for the second part of your two+ responses, you're quickly shifting the focus of the dialogue—"besides, just this afternoon I was working on _____ for [name of relative]."

ATTACKER: "If you *really* noticed how hard we all work around here, you wouldn't *make* decisions like that!"
YOU: "*When* did you start thinking that I don't notice how hard everyone works around here? And"—instantly switching focus again—"one of the things I really appreciated last week about the efforts being made on the _____ project was . . ."

ATTACKER: "If you *really* loved me, you'd stop ignoring me!"

YOU: *"When* did you start thinking that I don't love you? And"—a rapid change in direction now—"just this morning I was trying to think of a way we could begin spending more time together, perhaps this evening or weekend . . ."

Researchers have found that your attacker will often be surprised that you didn't take the bait and will drop the line of criticism or will answer you with a specific incident or deeper personal feelings—and *then* you'll have a far greater chance of understanding what the attack was *really* about and can deal with it in perspective and appropriately.[11] As an alternative, if you're especially pressed for time and don't want to enter into a discussion, you might use two+ responses to first say something like *"Of course* I care about this family" (or whatever the presupposed attack is), then *immediately* break eye contact and change the subject to another area of interest, letting the attacker know you're late for a _____.

Example: *"Of course* I care about this family, and, in fact, yesterday I called about the weekend getaway we've been looking forward to, and I'll probably know more about it tomorrow. Now, I've got to go—" By doing this, you are demonstrating that you refuse to be a victim for the verbal attacker.

Here's one more example of a typical verbal attack pattern:

"Even a . . ."

"Even a *woman* could handle *that* assignment!"

"Even an *elderly* person could figure out how to use *that* computer!"

Again, the key here is to take a split-second pause and skip the bait, focusing your own emotional energy and then responding to the presupposed attack.

ATTACKER: *"Even* a *woman* could handle *that* assignment!"

YOU: "The thought that women are somehow inferior or second-rate is still common, and"—here you want to quickly shift focus for the second of your two+ responses—"I'm surprised to hear it from you" or "I'm sorry to hear that you feel that way."

ATTACKER: *"Even* an *elderly* person could figure out how to use *that* computer!"

YOU: "The idea that older people are somehow incapable of mastering new things is common but inaccurate, and"—change the direction of the discussion—"I'm surprised to hear it from you" or "I'm sorry to hear that you feel that way."

Scenario #4: "What's Your Hurry?"—Getting Grabbed

It's late in the day and the sun is setting. There's a chill in the air as you hurry down the street for your car or commuter train. Out of the corner of your eye you notice a man, tall, barrel-like, and unshaven in a jean jacket. He's standing next to the door of an old, beat-up blue pickup truck at the curb, and his eyes seem to be boring right through you. You look away and begin to walk faster, trying to ignore him, intent on getting home. All at once, he steps out from the truck and grabs you roughly by the elbow as you pass by.

"What's your hurry, anyway?" he growls in your ear as you stop short, his grip viselike, pulling you off-balance. "Don't I know you?" he hisses with a sinister lisp and the rank smell of liquor on his breath.

You gasp, stunned at what is happening, arm aching, heart pounding, breath stopped, throat clamped shut. No, you *don't* know him, and no sooner than that thought crosses your mind, he moves closer and you notice he's towering over you and his eyes are wild. If you're a woman, he may try to extend his other hand to clamp on your breast or squeeze one of your buttocks or start rubbing against your groin. If you're a man, he might shove his free hand into your pockets searching for money or keys or your wallet.

"Let go of me!" you manage to cry, instinctively jerking back from his grip, trying to pull away. But he clamps down harder on your elbow and you feel a sharp jolt of pain as he pushes you toward a nearby doorway or alley. The harder you resist, the more he seems to overpower you. One more time you try to pull your arm free.

"Where do you think you're gonna go?" he snaps, and without warning punches you, a full-fisted hammer blow to the side of your head. Everything starts to go black . . .

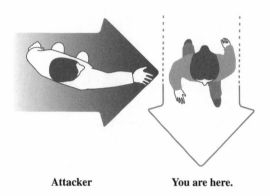

Attacker   **You are here.**

Let's stop the scenario right there and rewrite the script, assuming you were so intent on getting home that you failed to notice the attack until the man was already holding your arm. These things happen. Even the best-trained security experts and martial artists can sometimes be caught by surprise. Next time, with greater alertness, you may be able to choose in advance to cross the street or take some other evasive action. Unfortunately this time you didn't, and now here you are.

The first moment you realize what's happening, take a split-second pause. Remember, in almost every confrontation, even physical ones, a momentary pause can be your ally. Extend your sensory awareness and acknowledge that you've been grabbed. Notice any nearby escape routes to light, safety, or people. Unlock your resistance to the assailant's grip—by relaxing your arm, bending your knees, and *not* pulling against his grip, and for the moment, by blending or flowing with the direction of the attack. If he's already pushing you toward the alley, go *with* his push for the first step or two as you sense the danger and exact line of his force and keep your own balance to flow with the situation. By the end of the second step, gather your emotional energy—fear, anger, and whatever other deep feelings are churning inside you—and direct it into *two+ responses*, a *linked chain* of sudden, unexpected actions to turn things around. One example:

As you stop resisting his grip on your arm, you suddenly move closer to him. This will surprise him but seems to signal his brain that he's absolutely in control of his "captured" and submissive prey. You're his now; he's won and he knows it, and just for a second, he grins and loosens his grip on your arm.

At precisely that instant everything changes.

With a sharp command, "Stay back!" you make two swift, contrasting rotations, for example, with knees bent and body relaxed, with your entire upper body all at once going from loose to tense as you sharply pivot and rotate clockwise, arms braced against the sides of your chest, then suddenly rotating counterclockwise, which in virtually every case, no matter how big the aggressor, will free your arm. The moment your arm comes loose you can break away to safety.

If you feel the danger is life-threatening, an alternative set of *two+ responses* might include—depending, as we mentioned previously, on your martial arts training and abilities—striking in rapid succession before running to freedom. For example, first, an open-hand eye jab that drives all five of your extended fingers on an upward angle into your assailant's eyes (yes, this may cause some scratching of the cornea and howling but, contrary to popular belief, usually causes no permanent damage), followed by an elbow or forearm strike to the side of his face, followed by bending your knees and then thrusting your entire upper body upward, delivering a smashing head butt by ramming the *top* of your head into the *front* of his face. Just as soon as you've finished the head butt and jumped out of reach, his hands may be held to his face as he screams in stunned surprise, as much from the sud-

Attacker   **You are here.**

den reversal of his fortunes as from the pain, as you run to safety, perhaps yelling something—"Fire!"—as you go, hoping to attract the attention of a policeman or bystander.

This is just one example of a *linked sequence* of two+ responses—direct, uncomplicated actions that are *simple to learn* and easy to *remember and execute under pressure*. Skip the complex martial arts moves or trying to reach in your purse to fish out that Mace or pepper spray that needs to be held correctly, aimed perfectly, and sprayed downwind (one study showed that in forty-eight street-assault simulations not *once* did a woman with Mace stop the attacker).[12] In contrast, when linked together, simple strikes such as these tend to be considerably more effective.

Let's talk for a minute about yelling or screaming. You may be astonished at how powerful your voice can be, yet many people, particularly women, are convinced they could not scream if they wanted to. The important part of this statement is the phrase *wanted to*. In a society that extolls politeness, a battle yell can certainly feel outright aggressive. Yet, as part of a sequence of responses, your voice can be a powerful distractor, perhaps even a lifesaving one. *Your voice can be a safety tool in arguments and can play a significant role in breaking a physical-freeze response.* If you're about to be attacked or are under attack, many people think that yelling "Help!" will summon others to your aid. Perhaps, but it's unlikely. For a yell to have the greatest possible "defense value," it depends on knowing:

• *When* to yell: The best time may be at the confrontation stage. When used as part of a set of two+ responses, a yell can help break the dangerous psychological "holding mechanism" attackers use to trap you before striking.

• *How* to yell: Suddenly and forcefully—a medium- or low-pitched, bloodcurdling battle scream, really—has the greatest chance to unnerve your adversary and let you escape to safety. Remember, in a sequence of two+ responses, you *always* want to precede or follow your yell with an immediate set of unexpected, sudden actions.

• *What* to yell: Some experts suggest using a wordless, full-blown war cry—perhaps something like "RAAAHH!" or "KEY-AIEE!"—since words can impose the rationality of language on the listeners' minds and reduce emotional impact. But if you choose to scream a word, make it "Fire!" *not* "Help!" because evidence suggests that during rapes and physical assaults, more bystanders within earshot will turn away from "Help!" than from "Fire!" It pays to remember the Kitty Genovese case in 1964 when, walking to her house in a low-crime, middle-class neighborhood of Long Island, New York, she was raped and murdered. Thirty-eight people heard her cries for help and not one person responded (or even called the police, until thirty minutes later). Hundreds of law enforcement cases confirm this typical bystander reaction. For children, "Help! Fire! He's *not* my father!" may be one of the better tactics.

Here's another variation of the grabber scenario: What if you'd been more alert and had sensed the line of attack *before* he reached your arm? Then you might have followed the split-second pause with focused emotional energy expressed through a set of two+ responses such as shouting "No!" at the same time you launched a power throw (see chapter 11 for a description) of your shopping bag or pen or book or, perhaps best of all, a heavy plastic container of ice tea or juice, as you instantly spin away from his line of attack and reverse directions with a run to freedom.

Here's one more variation on the scenario of being grabbed:

What if we altered the situation into a so-called *silent groping* on a subway or commuter train packed with people? Imagine that some stranger is suddenly getting "too close" or is actually leaning or rubbing against you. Use a split-second pause to remain calm yet maximally alert, taking an instant to gather up your emotional anger and then, *very suddenly,* begin a two+ responses pattern, such as breathing in as you smoothly uplift your posture and "invisibly" tense your upper body muscles, elbows braced against your sides, and suddenly rotate your upper body forcefully to the left and, without any pause, reverse directions suddenly and forcefully—a quick quarter-turn clockwise then, instantly reversing direction, a half-turn counterclockwise. You might also shout a low, firm "No!" as you stand up or step to the side and quickly move away, out of reach. The rotating motion makes the groper's hands slip off your body and neutralizes the aggressor's anticipated cat-and-mouse game of push-pull resistance.

Throughout this book we promote nonaggression, yet we also realize that there are times to fight back.

Being self-righteously nonviolent when we see no other option is practicing passivism, more than pacifism. Increasing your options for self-protection does not contribute to the violence; permitting yourself to be violated allows the violence to exist.

FREDERIQUE DELACOSTE AND FELLICE NEWMAN,
Fighting Back: Feminist Resistance to Violence

Scenario #5: The Echo of Footsteps—Being Followed

Imagine yourself walking home around midnight. It's a nice night and the streets are well lighted, except for a few areas of trees and shrubs. You know the route by heart. All at once you realize that someone is following you in the shadows not far behind. According to conventional wisdom, what happens next is simple: Your brain detects the threat, fires off an instinctive reaction, and elim-inates or reduces the risks. Unfortunately, conventional wisdom is wrong.[13]

The neural and chemical aspects of your brain's response to this detection of possible danger, this first *moment of conflict*, causes a profound set of simultaneous and complicated changes in the way the tissues and whole organ systems of your body operate: altering energy and metabolic rate, readying the immune system, contracting movement-geared muscles in your neck, back, and shoulders, and priming your physiology with a surge of stress hormones. By now, your brain and body are switching into an alarm-reaction mode, probably making you walk faster, then run in a panic incited by a "cascade" of emotions, conscious thoughts vanishing, muscles propelling you, fueled by stress hormones and a burst of pure terror (remember the raw edge of emotion when running from "ghosts" or the "bogeyman" in your childhood play?), with everything narrowing into a desperate-feeling, tunnel-like race toward lights or friendly people or the safety of your own home.

Sound familiar? One problem, of course, is that you may have made a mistake in perception. The other person *isn't* following you, after all. Or it may be Aunt Emma or a friend simply trying to catch up with you. Or, if it *is* a mugger or rapist, will the panic save you? Perhaps not. One of your potential advantages in this scenario is that you know your own neighborhood, the shortcuts, the people to call to, the places to hide, the yards with dogs that might help raise the alarm. If you allow a wave of sudden, primi-tive fear to drive you into a beeline sprint, you've sacrificed these advantages in a single moment.

What if, instead, you took a split-second pause as you kept walking at a brisk yet relaxed pace while breathing calm, steady-ing breaths, extending your perception to notice the *weight* and *rhythm* of the footsteps behind you. Is it a man or woman? Mov-ing fast or slow? How close? Before your chest feels a deep squeeze of anxiety, or instead of stiffening up your strides and rushing them—which may signal "easy victim" to predators—you

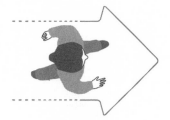

Follower/attacker   **You are here.**

unlock your leg muscles and move even looser, more catlike, with greater ease as you sense the follower's line of motion: Is he on the center of the sidewalk or at the edge of the street? While sensing this line, you expand your energy, imagining it filling the air and drawing strength from the surrounding lights in this, *your* neighborhood.

Now, only a second or more after hearing the footsteps, it's decision time. If you still *feel* a sense of threat or danger, you can channel this emotional energy into constructive action using an appropriate set of two+ responses. There are many options. For example, if the stranger is still far behind and you're close to your door, you might smoothly reach into your purse or pocket for your keys, place the door key outward, and all at once, break into a sprint for your door. If the follower begins to run, too, you may elect to suddenly change directions and head for a neighbor's lighted porch, especially if your own lock is hard to open in a rush in the dark or if in your own doorway, neighbors might not hear your calls for help.

Whenever you're being followed or chased, it's vital to do your best to avoid getting captured from behind. If the stranger is less than ten steps away, for example, you might alter your response pattern by reaching into your purse or pocket for a handful of loose change or bending over in a single motion to scoop up a handful of small rocks from a nearby garden bed or driveway. If necessary, you might then walk under the yard lights of a nearby house and calmly turn to make eye contact with

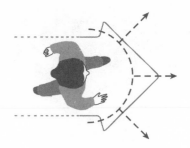

Follower/attacker   **You are here.**

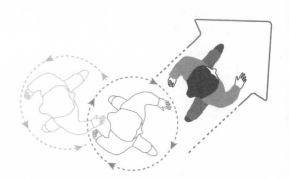

Follower/attacker   **You are here.**

whoever is behind you, yelling, "Stay back!" in a sharp, com-
manding tone.

These two actions give a signal of confidence that deter, or at
least momentarily confuse, a mugger or rapist intent on easy prey.
If the person keeps coming, you can stand in a relaxed, upright
neutral stance and ask a sharp, de-escalating question with another command to stop. If he keeps coming at you, you can gain an
extra few seconds by suddenly power throwing the coins or rocks
or other common object (discussed in chapter 11) and simultaneously giving a bloodcurdling battle scream or two (if you want to
draw the attention of others, yelling "Fire!" may be a good choice)
as you suddenly change direction and head for the nearest area of
likely safety. If you're next to the street, in some cases researchers

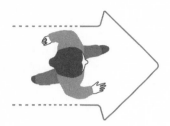

Follower/attacker

You are here.

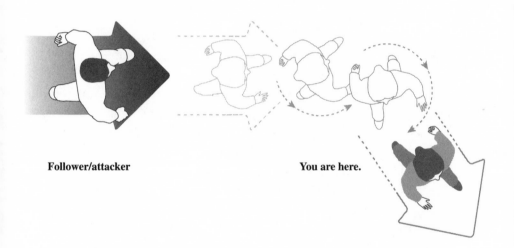

Follower/attacker

You are here.

suggest that the best place to run may be on the side *facing* oncoming traffic rather than on the sidewalk.

Note: If you live in a moderate- to high-crime area, you may want to take advance preventive measures by joining, or starting, a Neighborhood Watch program, which has been shown in some communities to reduce crimes by up to 75 percent.

Scenario #6: If Looks Could Kill—Predatory Stares

You probably know the feeling: Someone is staring at you with terrifying intensity, sizing you up or, perhaps, if you're a woman,

"PREDATORY STARE"

Predator   You are here.

undressing or even visually raping you with his eyes. Or perhaps you're on an airplane, a bus, or a train, or in line at the supermarket, and you look up to find someone glaring at you.

These situations happen to people every day, and the visual violence is far from harmless: the pain inflicted by *predatory stares* is real and potentially dangerous. But how, exactly, would *you* react or respond? By confronting him? Turning away? Cursing under your breath? By telling yourself it doesn't really matter, that sticks and stones may break your bones but words—or looks— can never hurt you? By staring back?

In many cases none of these responses is adequate or effective, because brain scientists know that throughout life, we human beings read our meaning for others and establish our value in the world by the *looks in other people's eyes.* "The looks are far beyond words: eyes speak more profoundly than language," explains Ruthellen Josselson, Ph.D., professor of psychology at Towson State University in Baltimore, and author of *The Space Between Us.* "They express, surely and absolutely, what is real. Words may lie; eyes cannot."[14]

Predatory or hateful looks trigger instant inherent reactions deep in the human brain—along with feelings of pain and victimization—just as surely as other forms of conflict and attack. More and more young people/teens are highly sensitive about people staring at them and may even see it as a form of disrespect, of being "dissed." If you make eye contact with young male strangers, make it brief and nonthreatening. Be alert. And keep moving.

Let's approach this scenario differently. The moment you *first* become aware of a predatory stare, take a split-second pause to gain a measure of inner calm and perspective as you project a feeling of quiet confidence and alertness. You might feel more confident by imagining yourself surrounded by a protective shield or sphere of light.

If the emotional energy is building—fear, anger, outrage—you might direct it into two+ responses. In this case it might make sense to first *nonaggressively* slip out of the visual "trap" that has apparently been set for you. Remember, on the one hand there's a chance you may be misreading the stare altogether; on the other hand, the person staring at you may have physical violence in mind and be sizing you up with his gaze. In either case, when you move, it needs to be suddenly and forcefully but with smooth, deliberate motions that are free from any sign of fear or panic. You might break the psychological "holding mechanism" that predators use to capture their prey by making neutral eye contact—perhaps imagining a protective stream of energy forming a barrier between you and the one staring at you—as you suddenly, smoothly turn, get up, and change positions or walk away, breaking eye contact but without losing your relaxed peripheral awareness of the predator's next actions. Immediately switch the focus of attention by beginning to talk in a steady, low, confident tone to someone else nearby. Ask the time or strike up a casual conversation.

Whatever you do, it's *not* a good idea to fire back a look of hatred or contempt because you may inadvertently goad the predator over the edge into physical violence. *Do* take a smooth, steadying breath as you move away, and—if you're sitting or standing on crowded public transportation, for example—position yourself in a posture of confidence.

If you feel the predator moving toward you, sense the line of his movement and, if you have a makeshift or preplanned protec-

tion weapon (an umbrella, cane, Mace or pepper spray, or loose
change to power throw), clear your access to it, moving in a
smooth, relaxed manner. If the predator tries to sit down beside
you in a cramped commuter train or bus, look at your watch,
gather up your emotional energy, and begin another set of two+
responses—such as suddenly get back up, keeping your knees
slightly bent for faster response time as you move away. Ask
someone else the time ("Excuse me, sir, my watch seems to have
stopped. What time do you have?"), and while this other person
with the watch is looking at you and telling you the time, simultaneously rotate your upper body in a quarter-turn clockwise and
then counterclockwise, which disengages any hand contact as
you deliberately choose another seat or position yourself near the
conductor, driver, doorway, or beside a friendlier-appearing
group of adults, until you reach your stop.

"PREDATORY STARE"

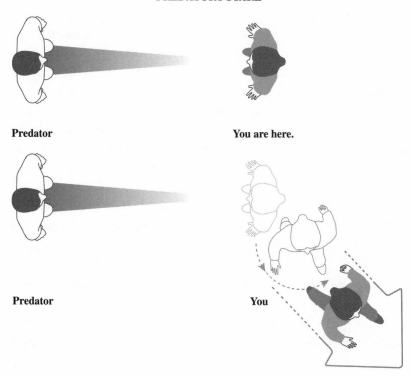

Predator   You are here.

Predator   You

If you are experiencing predatory stares or leers from someone in your workplace, you might at first try to ignore that person and set a firm psychological boundary. Hopefully, he'll soon get the message to stay away. However, if he continues to leer at you or make sexual remarks, speak up assertively and tell him to leave you alone. If he does not, seek the moral and protective support of friendly coworkers and, at the same time, initiate sexual harassment procedures under the laws of your community and policies of your workplace. For further details, see chapters 8 and 14.

Scenario #7: Under the Club—Facing a Hooking Attack

What if you looked up and suddenly someone was yelling at you and lunging toward you in a circular attack, swinging a stick or throwing a hook punch or circular kick toward your head? Most people would instinctively put up their arms in a rapid, rigid motion to protect themselves by blocking the strike, standing stiffly as they are struck. But, if you do this, you are absorbing the brunt of the strike at its most powerful point or impact.

Against a circular attack—in words as well as by physical force—two places are generally free from impact—*inside* the whirling strike or *outside* the range of the attack. With a split-second pause, you can immediately sense the exact line of aggres-

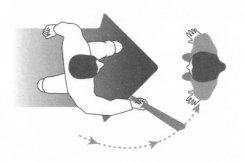

Attacker's *line*   **You are here.**

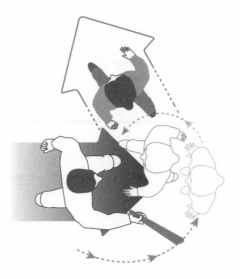

Attacker's *line*   **Your two+ responses**

sion coming at you. Your two+ responses might be initiated by focusing your emotional energy into a sudden, unexpected move *inside* the arc—inside the strongest circular line produced by the words, stick, fist, or club. Admittedly, this response takes some real daring and practice under a qualified instructor, but it's relatively simple to learn and apply no matter what your size and strength, and it's likely a move that will be among the *least* anticipated by an aggressor. Even if contact is made (a bump from the inside of his arm or the edge of hateful words, for example), it will be minimal, and in your second move, break free of the arc and lunge or run to safety.

An alternative set of two+ responses could move you *outside* the circular attack, beginning with a sudden step back so the strike swings past you, then immediately turning in another direction and running to safety. If you're trapped at the end of a hallway or alley or in an elevator, you can lunge in *behind* the strike as it misses you and position yourself at the back of your attacker as his momentum turns him around. What happens next is up to you. You can push him off-balance and run to freedom, or if you feel your life is still in serious danger, you might launch a swift

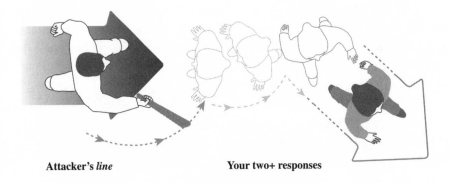

Attacker's *line*   **Your two+ responses**

series of strikes (one example was given in scenario #4) to neutralize his ability to harm you and *then* escape to safety.

Scenario #8: "Get in the Car or I'll Shoot!"— A Nightmare at Gunpoint

You approach your car in a hurry to head for home, and all of a
sudden you realize that there's someone inside with a gun—
pointed at you at close range—who says, "Shut up and get in,
we're going for a ride. I just wanna talk. I'm not gonna hurt you.
Get in, *now!*" Many people believe it would be best to do what the
armed man says. But that may be exactly the wrong choice—and
might give you little or no chance to live to tell about it.

Detective J. J. Bittenbinder of the Chicago Police Department,
puts it this way, "If you get in, you're as good as dead."[15] Victims
rarely survive attacks after being forced into a car, says Jean
O'Neil of the National Crime Prevention Council. Your decision
in a situation like this matters more than ever since carjackers are
exhibiting a disturbing new set of values. "Hatred is hip. Killing
is cool," says Jack Levin, a professor of sociology and criminology at Northeastern University in Boston. "We're seeing a callous
disregard for human life that we've never seen before."

So what's an alternative? First trigger a split-second pause,
which, to the gunman, may look as if—just as he expected—
you're captured and about to comply with his commands. Imme-

diately notice if he's the only person in the car as you sense different escape routes and, with sustained breathing so you remain alert and relaxed, unlock your knees, which may already be trembling, and sense the precise direction of the barrel of the gun. It may also be helpful to expand your energy by imagining a foglike shield around you, throwing off the aim of the gunman. If you feel your life is in grave danger, then you alone must decide if action is warranted. If so, gather up your fear and anger, your emotional energy, and then instantly, *with absolutely no warning*, begin a set of two+ responses. Warning: When facing a firearm, do not yell—since a sudden loud voice may panic the gunman into firing. Among your options: Suddenly whirl to one side, *away* from the barrel of the gun as you power throw anything— even a shopping bag, cup of coffee, book, purse, or briefcase you may have been carrying—and run like hell. But here's where a key difference comes in: run unpredictably. Run shifting your steps obliquely left and right, in a random, changing zigzag style like a football back trying to evade tacklers. (Don't laugh, it works— and, as long as they're not wearing flip-flop sandals or high-heeled shoes, men and women of nearly all ages and conditions can simulate this running pattern.) According to Hugh C. McDonald, former chief of the Detective Division of the Los Angeles County Sheriff's Department, "To shoot a running person in poor light using a handgun takes a real expert, and even then the probability of hitting him is low. I would particularly recommend running with a weaving or some other sort of evasive action. . . . Don't run in a straight line but zigzag, making an evasive turn with every other step."[16] Head for the nearest exit or security guard or public restaurant or store, or a nearby home with a light on.

What few people realize is that, in truth, even handgun experts can have *incredible* difficulty felling a fast-moving, direction-changing target at five paces or more in dim light, or seven paces or more in bright light, and—day *or* night—you're effectively out of range from twenty-five or thirty feet on. But keep running! It doesn't take much practice to zigzag run, and you might even add a few short "practice stretches" of it to your weekly walking or jogging program. In the real-life armed-confrontation scenario described above, even if you're not in great shape, you can dramatically improve the chances you'll be able to foil the aim of the gunman and escape to safety.

LOOKING AHEAD

As these brief opening examples demonstrate, safety is about learning to observe—rather than automatically condemn or resist—our emotions and conflicts, and to respond in specific and appropriate ways that may best protect your personal safety while giving you the greatest chance to escape or resolve confrontations without resorting to hostility or aggression. We encourage you to devote special attention to the upcoming chapter on emotional safety.

As we have stated, one of the rules that governs the subconscious mind is that the *strongest habit usually wins.* Your brain will follow, in split seconds, the pathways that are easiest, most facilitated, most developed *by choice* and *rehearsal.* In the absence of such learned pathways, under conflict the brain will tend to revert to ancient, fear-driven reactions that incapacitate you or plunge you into the wrong, counterproductive, and potentially harmful outcomes.

You can learn to be and feel safer in an unsafe world in many specific ways. You *can* change. You *can* raise your awareness and manage your thoughts and feelings in ways that help you establish and maintain a greater sense of safety. In the chapters ahead we'll review simple, practical ideas and resources for promoting a *strengthened inner sense of personal safety and calm-alertness that, according to research, can empower you—without raising your hand or voice—to avoid, deter, or defuse many, even most, attacks.* In this light, we strongly encourage you to review the upcoming chapters and make a conscious commitment to using your verbal, mental, and emotional skills *first* to minimize the chance any physical skills will be called upon during times of conflict or danger. With regular practice, instead of reacting in fear, anger, or panic and ending up feeling victimized or being victimized, you can respond in split seconds with greater safety—and in ways that honor your own character, heart, and spirit, as well as the heart and spirit of those around you.

Part II

SAFETY INTELLIGENCE:
INSIGHTS, APPLICATIONS, AND RESOURCES

Chapter 7

EMOTIONAL SAFETY: WHY IT'S ESSENTIAL

The world's battlefields are in the heart.

HENRY WARD BEECHER

There is perhaps no other area where each of us can make more of a difference in being and feeling safe than in *emotional safety.* As we mentioned in chapters 2 and 3, when you cultivate greater emotional safety, you begin to live with relaxed alertness and with a heightened awareness of your environment. In this way, you not only feel less stressed but are also better prepared to avoid, prevent, de-escalate, or, if necessary, escape from unsafe situations.

Many people who experience a sense of lost emotional safety assume that they will *always* feel this way and there's just nothing they can do about it. However—based on reviews of more than fifty different research studies on nearly thirty thousand individuals—we disagree.[1] Virtually all of us *can* make small, key changes in how we respond to pressure-filled situations.

James E. Loehr, Ed.D., a well-known sports psychologist who has trained thousands of athletes and professionals who had experienced debilitating fear or choking under pressure, believes that nearly everyone can become healthier and mentally tough by learning ways to be emotionally flexible, responsive, strong, and resilient, tapping into what he calls an ideal performance state (IPS).[2]

"Fear is a feeling we all have in certain situations," observes Joseph Wople, M.D., professor of psychiatry and director of the Behavior Unit at Temple University in Philadelphia, and author of *Life Without Fear.* "We know it when someone pulls a gun on us, when we're told our plane is going to make a crash landing, when a loud noise surprises us on a dark street at night, when the driver of our car does eighty miles an hour on a country lane. The feeling in each of these situations is always, at the bottom, fear. These fears are appropriate and may promote helpful action. . . . However, when a fear gets in the way and impairs our ability to function, then it is a useless fear and, with proper training, must and can be removed."[3]

As psychologist Susan Jeffers observes in *Feel the Fear and Do It Anyway,* "You may be surprised and encouraged to learn that while inability to deal with fear may look and feel like a psychological problem, in most cases it isn't. I believe it's primarily an educational problem, and that you can reeducate the mind to conquer it."[4]

Keep in mind that feelings and emotions should be messengers, not controllers. They are the body's internal eyes and ears. . . . Think of feelings and emotions as flight data from Mission Control, faithfully guiding your journey. They will do that if you control them instead of being controlled by them.

DR. JAMES E. LOEHR, *Toughness Training for Life*

To understand *emotional safety,* it may be helpful to know that it speaks to each of us in simple, direct messages. You must cultivate your ability to feel it. This may seem paradoxical, but think of it this way: Walking is natural, but must be learned; speech is natural, but must be learned. In this chapter and those that follow, we will review a variety of options for monitoring, guiding, and renewing your emotional safety.

EMOTIONAL SAFETY DEPENDS ON CALM-ALERTNESS: THE BRAIN AND HEART MUST WORK TOGETHER

What you see and feel and experience in a situation depends largely on your presence, on what you bring to the situation.

ALBERT EINSTEIN

Einstein was absolutely right. Scientific studies show, for example, that disagreements, arguments, and confrontations of all kinds can escalate or seem overwhelming if you are trapped in a state of either *tense-energy* or *tense-tiredness.*[5] Yet, the same conflicts and problems appear much more manageable when you are feeling strong and vigorous, in a state known as *calm-energy.*[6] According to Robert E. Thayer, Ph.D., professor of biological psychology at California State University, Long Beach, "Low levels of energy appear to increase vulnerability to tension, anxiety, and fearfulness. . . . When you feel highly energetic, and at the same time relatively calm, your perception of both yourself and the world are distinctly different from when you are tired and at the same time tense. Not only are memories of past successes and failures during conflict likely to be different, but perceived likelihoods of future successes and failures are also different."[7]

CALM-ENERGY AND RELAXED ALERTNESS

The word *power* comes from the French and Latin roots meaning "to be able." Few of us recognize that power is closely allied with relaxation. Just as a tense muscle loses in strength, so a rigid, tense attitude will fail to protect you during a conflict.

Think about it: Whenever you are tense or tired, your field of vision narrows, sometimes radically, and your sense of touch and range of hearing are sharply diminished. You become increasingly vulnerable to being caught unaware and suddenly finding yourself blindsided by, or in the middle of, a verbal or physical conflict. On the other hand, with calm-energy, your field of perception—your ability to detect and avoid danger and to be sensitive to creative opportunities and the needs of others—expands dramatically.

At first glance, it may seem surprising that *calmness and relaxation do* not *mean depleted energy or dulled senses.* Instead, they are the foundation for one of the ultimate creative performance states that scientists call *flow,* the sustainable, calm-alert zone of thought and performance in which world-record-setting athletes and artists and leaders in every field are at their personal best for extended periods.[8]

"Energy, tiredness, tension, and calmness are excellent indicators of your *personal resources,*" says Dr. Thayer. "When you think about a confrontation or criticism, you view it—so rapidly you may scarcely be aware of it—through the framework of these personal resources. Thousands of times a day we are confronted with conflicts or tasks that require resources to accomplish them, and in each case there is a momentary—often unconscious—evaluation of the conflict or task in relation to one's resources to meet it, summed up in the basic question, 'Do I have the energy to face this or to complete this?' "[9]

The state of energy and alertness you bring to your daily interactions has a significant influence on how many conflicts you experience and how you react to them.

If calm-energy is so important, you may be wondering, how, exactly, can you increase and sustain it hour after hour? Here are four qualities of calm-energy that you can begin developing right away:

1. Turn on your brain's alertness "switches"
2. Sustain your breathing
3. Be present and aware
   Consider meditating twice a day

High
Intensity

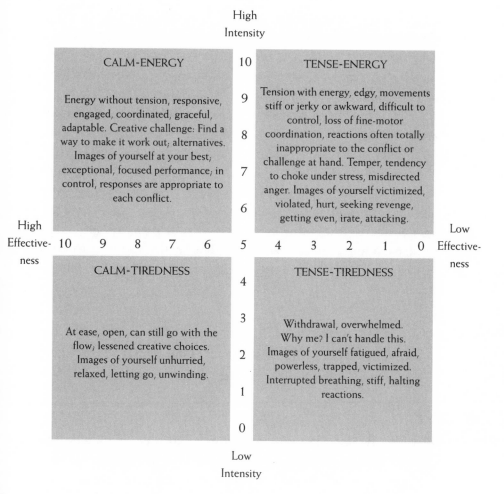

CALM-ENERGY 10 TENSE-ENERGY

Energy without tension, responsive, 9
engaged, coordinated, graceful,
adaptable. Creative challenge: Find a 8
way to make it work out; alternatives.
Images of yourself at your best;
exceptional, focused performance; in 7
control, responses are appropriate to
each conflict.
6

Tension with energy, edgy, movements
stiff or jerky or awkward, difficult to
control, loss of fine-motor
coordination, reactions often totally
inappropriate to the conflict or
challenge at hand. Temper, tendency
to choke under stress, misdirected
anger. Images of yourself victimized,
violated, hurt, seeking revenge,
getting even, irate, attacking.

High Low
Effective- 10 9 8 7 6 5 4 3 2 1 0 Effectiveness ness

CALM-TIREDNESS 4 TENSE-TIREDNESS

3

At ease, open, can still go with the
flow; lessened creative choices. 2
Images of yourself unhurried,
relaxed, letting go, unwinding.
1

Withdrawal, overwhelmed.
Why me? I can't handle this.
Images of yourself fatigued, afraid,
powerless, trapped, victimized.
Interrupted breathing, stiff, halting
reactions.

0

Low
Intensity

4. Learn to instantly "anchor" *inner safety* and maintain a "safe space" within yourself

I. Turn on Your Brain's Alertness "Switches"

According to William C. Dement, M.D., Ph.D., professor of psychiatry and behavioral sciences at Stanford University School of Medicine, "Impaired alertness is one of the greatest potential dangers of contemporary life."[10] This is something that, unfortunately, most victims of everyday conflicts know little about. One of the simplest ways to increase your *calm-energy* any time of the day or evening is to turn on your brain's alertness "switches." These on-the-spot activators bolster your brain's ability to sustain a high level of awareness and energy throughout the day.

"Without alertness, there can be no attentiveness, and without attentiveness you are blocked from effective performance in times of conflict or crisis," says Martin Moore-Ede, M.D., Ph.D., associate professor of physiology at Harvard Medical School, and director of the Institute for Circadian Physiology. "A person's alertness is triggered by . . . internal and external factors that can be considered the switches on the control panel of the mind. Understanding how to manipulate them is the secret of gaining power over one of the most important attributes of the human brain."[11]

Alertness is the optimal, activated tension-free state of the brain. It enables you to make ongoing, conscious decisions about what to pay attention to and how to respond most effectively.

Here are two of the simplest alertness-boosting techniques that promote sustained calm-energy and help set you up to be at your best no matter what conflicts may arise in the hours ahead:

ALERTNESS SWITCH #1: *Increase Your Calm-Energy by Pulling Back for Brief Midmorning and Midafternoon Work Breaks.* Scientists have discovered that when you work nonstop for long periods, the brain becomes less alert and, perhaps scarcely noticing it, you push yourself into a tense, overtired state.[12] Beneath the surface, problems are brewing as your mounting fatigue becomes masked by stress-hormone opiates, such as beta-endorphin, that give you a transient sense of feeling good even when you're increasingly worn down.[13] Throughout your brain and body, the microscopic cellular storage compartments for messenger molecules are becoming depleted; signal hormones—powerful neurochemicals that coordinate memory, perception, and performance during conflict—may be all but gone.

Before long, the increased tension and tiredness (which may seem normal since most everyone around you is probably getting tense and tired, too) not only makes you less aware of your surroundings but also less attentive to other people. In this state, you are more vulnerable to conflicts—giving off unconscious signals that attract attack that may draw you, almost magnetically, into late-day disagreements and stalemates. Later, when you walk out the door to head for home or go pick up the children or run some errands, this mental daze and physical tightness or near-exhaustion serves as a beacon to panhandlers and muggers.[14] It may also prime you for "negative spillover"—making you impatient or irritable with family members.[15]

One of the most effective ways to start turning things around, *today*, is to take a two- to five-minute *midmorning and midafternoon break*. Get up and move around, look out a window or step into an area of natural daylight, shift your train of thought to something besides work, sip some mineral water, ice tea, juice, or a cup of coffee, then eat a few bites of a low-fat snack that has a few ounces of protein. Here's why: During the day when you go for four or five hours without taking a break and eating, your blood-sugar levels drop and your energy wanes, forcing you to fight off needless tension and tiredness. "For every meal we eat, we have actually missed one small meal that our body wants," explains Ernest Lawrence Rossi, Ph.D., a psychologist who has extensively studied brain-body energy cycles. "We incur significant energy deficits and become much hungrier than we should be. Eating six times a day helps spare us from the wide swings of alertness and fatigue that can occur by eating too many calories in a single large meal. Eating smaller, nutritious meals and snacks helps to stabilize blood-sugar levels, which in turn optimizes memory, learning, and performance."[16]

In recent years, one of the surprise findings in nutritional research has been the discovery that, in many cases, eating low-fat, between-meal snacks can actually help reduce feelings of impatience or distress and boost your overall alertness, energy, and effectiveness.[17] Research published in the *New England Journal of Medicine*[18] and the *American Journal of Clinical Nutrition*[19] supports this.

ALERTNESS SWITCH #2: *Stay Physically Active: Get a Few Minutes of Muscular Movement Every Hour or So during the Day.* Nearly any type of physical movement, such as walking up a flight of stairs or down a nearby hallway, can immediately increase your energy and alertness. According to Dr. Moore-Ede, "You do not have to be running a mile or lifting weights—taking a walk, stretching, or even chewing gum can stimulate your level of alertness."[20]

2. Sustain Your Breathing

Surprisingly, most of us halt our breathing for several seconds or more when stress rises at the start of a conflict—large or small, real or imagined. This reduces oxygen to the brain and pushes you toward feelings of anxiety, anger, frustration, panic, faulty reactions, and a general loss of control.[21] "It is the inner breathing of the one hundred trillion cells in your body that enables you to produce biological energy," says Sheldon Saul Hendler, M.D., Ph.D., a researcher and internist who is a faculty member at the School of Medicine of the University of California, San Diego. "Out of this comes what I call the basic currency of life, the energy produced in all of our cells. It is called adenosine triphosphate or ATP. . . . It is ATP that we utilize to act, feel, think. . . . The body and brain are extremely sensitive to even very small reductions in ATP production. This sensitivity is expressed in terms of fearfulness, anxiety, aches and pains, confusion, and intermittent fatigue."[22]

"When we alter our breathing, we alter our consciousness and our life momentarily," explains Charles F. Stroebel, M.D., Ph.D., professor of psychiatry at the University of Connecticut School of Medicine and lecturer in psychiatry at the Yale University

School of Medicine. "Alterations in normal breathing rhythm changes the amount of oxygen available to the brain. The mixture of oxygen and other gases is in delicate balance, and even subtle changes in it change our consciousness. When we experience the emergency (stress) response, our breathing is one of the very first functions to change, and it often does so entirely without our awareness. . . . When you change the way you breathe, you change the way you feel."[23]

What this also means is that, in many instances, your *breath helps sustain self-confidence during moments of conflict* and can be *a pace-maker for your waning attention.* "A quarter of the oxygen in every breath goes to fuel the central nervous system," observes Dr. Loehr. "Breathing is the most direct and most intimate connection from the external world, the world that human beings must perform in, to the inside of the body and the power of the human brain. Under stress, shallow, irregular thoracic breaths are tied to poor performance. This breathing pattern also contributes to feelings of worry, panic, and feeling threatened during a disagreement or conflict. This change in emotional state can arrive solely because of changes in breathing patterns."[24] An active lifestyle and some regular exercise will prove very beneficial, not only for health reasons, but also in expanding your respiratory capacity. Continued, steady breathing during stressful situations promotes calm-energy and a greater sense of mental and emotional control.

3. Be Present in Each Experience: What You Resist Not Only Persists, It Grows

It's a classic paradox: in moments of conflict, whenever you attempt to resist or deny unpleasant thoughts or block strong feelings (in the belief, for example, that if you allow yourself to feel emotions, you'll sabotage rational thinking), you inadvertently *help* yourself lose control by shutting down reasoning and decision-making, thereby magnifying the power of the opposing emotional force.[25,26]

"There is a collection of systems in the human brain consistently dedicated to the goal-oriented thinking process we call *reasoning*, and to the response selection we call *decision-making*," explains Antonio R. Damasio, M.D., Ph.D., head of the Department of Neurology at the University of Iowa College of Medicine. "This same collection of brain systems is also involved in emotion and *feeling* and is dedicated to processing body signals. What you *feel* is vital to providing the brain with an instantaneous, intuitive 'marker' of reality."[27] In part, what this means is that *emotions* are vital to *reasoning*, especially during arguments and confrontations. In a preventive sense, if a situation *feels* wrong, assume that it *is* wrong, advises personal safety expert and former police chief Tim Powers, coauthor of *The Seven Steps to Personal Safety*.

Here's a second paradox: Although *being present* with what you *feel* at moments of conflict is absolutely vital to peak brain functioning, if you're tense and tired, then your emotions can loom up and overwhelm you. It doesn't take much of a confrontation or imagined affront to trigger "flooding"—the mental state when your attention narrows or shuts down altogether and you want to fight or flee, *anything* except what works best—which is to flow with the emotion-charged situation. This is why your "entering state" plays such a pivotal role in moments of conflict. Once you've learned to keep turning on your brain's alertness switches and gained increased control over your breathing patterns, you can more effectively practice *being present* with difficult people and unpleasant emotions. At first, it's a tough job, but it progressively gets easier.

Here's one brief exercise that may help you expand your ability to acknowledge a potential danger or conflict and *flow* with it, to avoid or prevent violence, or, if necessary, effectively deal with it.[28] Take a moment to tune into something you are feeling in your body. This is the easiest place to begin—with a body sensation or feeling. It could be tension, hunger, nervousness, happiness, your breathing pattern, or the feeling of the chair you're sitting in, or the floor surface beneath your feet.

Gently, completely, place your attention on the sensation without trying to fix it or change it. Just be with it. There is a distinction between relaxed alertness and *trying* to pay attention—where you wrinkle your forehead and work at it with effort and judgment. That's the wrong direction to go. Instead, it's mindfulness, pure and simple, that you're after: *being present.* Notice what happens when your attention gets fully connected with the sensation. Other feelings may pop up. Allow them to simply appear and blend with other sensations. There are no right or wrong answers. Just feel whatever you feel and notice whatever you notice.

This ability to flow with circumstances and *be present* with whatever you're feeling frees your mind to identify and respond to whatever hidden opportunities are at hand instead of getting derailed or bogged down by attempting to block emotions. This capability is all the more vital when you realize that feelings often come in packs, in scrambled groups of emotions. For example, if your teenage daughter is arriving home late, you may feel anger ("She better have a damn good reason for this"), regret ("Did I remember to ask her to call home before leaving the concert?"), and fear ("My God! What if she's been in an accident?").

The good news is that with some regular minutes of practice, there is scientific evidence that the ability to *be present* has the power to make unpleasant feelings—such as the first flash of frustration or anger or anxiety—fade or disappear *simply by experiencing them.*[29]

Consider learning to *meditate daily.*

Harold has found that the Transcendental Meditation program is a simple mental technique that cultivates relaxed alertness and inner safety throughout the day. It is easily learned, practiced for twenty minutes twice daily, and requires no change in lifestyle or beliefs. Since the early 1970s, when the first empirical studies documenting the distinctive psychophysiological correlates of TM were published in *Science*[30] and *Scientific American,*[31] four million people have learned the technique. Over 500 studies on TM conducted in over 200 research institutions worldwide make it the most widely researched approach for cultivating inner safety.

Several meta-analyses suggest that TM has a significantly larger effect than other forms of meditation and relaxation in producing relaxed alertness.[32,33]

4. Instantly *Anchor* Inner Safety *and Maintain a* Safe Space *within Yourself*

An *anchor* is a single nervous-system cue that can elicit from memory a full set of sensations of *feeling confident and being at your best*. With a bit of practice, you can create a personal *anchor* that enables you to instantly shift the mind and elicit a surge of confidence and calmness under pressure.[34]

In truth, countless anchors or "triggers" are affecting your behavior every day. For example, think of the immediate wave of emotions and memories when you hear an old favorite song. Or the forceful feelings you get from recalling one of your great moments or worst moments in relationships, parenting, sports, hobbies, or work. These anchors can be good or bad, strengthening or weakening, empowering or victimizing. The important fact is that they're everywhere. You can either choose to take greater charge of your life by forming anchors of inner safety and strength, of tapping into a deep "safe space" within yourself, or make no effort at all and let your environment and the people around you dictate your emotional reactions.

Here's one way to create a powerful personal anchor of inner safety. First, sit in a comfortable, quiet place and gently close your eyes. Direct your attention to your breathing, focusing on the air as it gently passes into and out of your nostrils and chest. Begin to feel the sensations of your body—the air or clothing on your skin, the weight of your shoulders and arms, the texture and support of the surface you're sitting on, and so on. Now draw your awareness to the center of your chest, to your heart beating. Whenever you notice your attention wandering, gently return it to the center of your chest.

Now vividly imagine yourself thinking, feeling, looking, sounding, and performing at your *relaxed best* in a specific past place and circumstance—a peak experience—when you felt safe and calm and confident. Picture the safest moments of your life, as a child, as an adult, in the past year, or in the past month. "Summon an image of yourself at your best, a time when you were able to respond effortlessly no matter how demanding or intricate the challenge," advises one scientific report in *Omni* magazine. "Recall your finest moment in every detail, using every sense . . . etch it into your consciousness so that you can summon it in an instant whenever you need it."[35] Develop every aspect of this mental image of confidence and strength and calmness: How deeply are you relaxed? Do you feel a sense of ease, compassion, or discovery? What does it feel like to have this sense of inner strength and balance? Are you indoors or out? In sunlight or shade, clear air, rain, or snow? What is the temperature? Do you notice air currents? What are you wearing and how does it feel on your skin? What can you see in all directions? How do the muscles in your body feel? What is the rhythm of your breathing? What are the sounds around you and off in the distance? Where was your mind focused? In what specific ways did you feel connected to nature and the universe around you?

Real-life experiences usually form some of the best anchors, but researchers report that you can create anchors by vividly imagining a "safe space" or new sense of inner personal strength and then forming a multisensory anchor to access it.

At the peak moment of your image, make a *unique sensory signal.* For example, choose a *touch* (such as your thumb against the second knuckle of your index finger with a specific amount of pressure) and a *mental picture* (of yourself in a fluid state of safety, confidence, and alertness). This combined sensory signal becomes your personal anchor.

Wait half an hour or so and repeat the process. Later on, test your cue. Re-create the quiet, relaxed scene. Then, in slow motion, imagine the first sign of a moment of conflict or the imaginary appearance of an aggressor or angry or hostile person. But be certain to maintain the feeling that you are in a safe space while viewing the scene. Research shows that with practice many fears can be successfully overcome this way.[36] If you feel yourself becoming tense or anxious, make the antagonist less hostile or move him farther away from you in your mind, until the sense of being safe and strong returns to you. Perceive the vivid scene and then trigger your anchor—in this example we used touch and a mental picture. When your anchor is programmed into memory and activated, you will feel a quick surge of energy, inner calm, heightened alertness, or confidence. With practice, you can make the effect even stronger. If the anchor is programmed well into memory, just by instantly pressing your thumb and forefinger together, for example, you gain an extra few crucial moments of calm-energy and control and are less likely to freeze up or panic and therefore have a significantly improved chance of maintaining *emotional and physical safety.*

If your anchor doesn't seem to be effective at first, you probably haven't used a vivid enough mental image or sharp enough sensory cues. Rehearse it several more times. Go back and again form the signal, increasing the richness and brilliance of the scene. How *exactly* does your best moment look, feel, sound, taste, smell? Sense the lighting, colors, shapes, temperatures, textures, movements, tastes, physical sensations, and feelings. Be certain your sensory cues are unique—try modifying your touch or gesture to see how that works. We think you'll be surprised at how helpful such a simple, practical tool can be in boosting your inner-safety resourcefulness during times of conflict.

RECOGNIZE AND MANAGE EMOTIONAL AND PHYSICAL BOUNDARIES

Good fences make good neighbors.

ROBERT FROST

Our skin marks the limit of our physical selves, yet each of us must be aware of the vital *emotional boundaries* and *physical "space" limits* in our interactions with others. These are invisible, fluid circles or spheres whose outer edge defines you as distinct and separate from others. It is where you end and another person begins. It is how close you can be to another person and still feel comfortable and *emotionally safe*. In his book *Language of the Heart*, James J. Lynch, Ph.D., refers to this as a "social membrane."

Chances are, you become quickly aware when someone stands too close to you. A warm, caring lover or young child can stand much closer than most friends, who in turn can stand closer than strangers. If you sense someone is angry, hostile, dangerous, or threatening, you may only feel safe across the street from them. In the worst cases of being stalked, you may only feel emotionally safe when away visiting friends in another city or state. Without an awareness of healthy and appropriate boundaries, it can be difficult to sense—until it is too late—whom it's unsafe for you to be around. As Anne Katherine points out in her book *Boundaries: Where You End and I Begin*, "A boundary violation is a serious matter. The survivor of the violation bears the brunt of the emotional shock wave created by it. . . . A boundary violation is committed when someone knowingly or unknowingly crosses the emotional, physical, spiritual, or sexual limits of another. Whether a violation is intended or not, it still harms."[37]

We set our boundaries and make others aware of them in several ways: by eye contact, our voice, and our body (posture, gestures, and movements to create distance).

During rush hour in crowded cities, for example, the discomfort you see on many people's faces, and probably feel yourself, is in large part due to the forced closeness of so many strangers. Here, too, traditional safety rules to protect yourself against purse snatchers, pickpockets, and muggers make sense—such as to remain alert, move quickly and confidently, and for women to wear their purse across the shoulder and held securely against the front hip, and for men to consider keeping their wallet in an inner coat pocket or front trouser pocket.

In a hallway or room, do you clearly recognize the signals other people give as they attempt to establish personal boundaries? Do you keep others at a comfortable, emotionally safe distance? Are you able to readily protect yourself against people whose closeness stresses you out or, in cases of abuse or harassment, individuals who advance with an apparent intention of inappropriately touching you?

Each of us is responsible for establishing and managing *emotionally safe boundaries.* If someone moves too close, you can back up or stand so that an object (desk, coffee table, countertop) is between you and the other person. Or you can extend your arm and firmly say, "No closer please," or if you sense danger, you might assertively say something forceful as noted in chapters 3 through 5, such as "Stop! Stay back!" If a lighter touch seems to be called for, Anne Katherine suggests, "You may want to back up. If I breathe on you, you'll be sick for a month."

The best "talking distance" varies according to personal habits and cultural traditions. Usually, you can learn to tune in to the most comfortable and effective distance by using three guidelines:

1. *Choose* a location from which to talk, and begin.
2. If your partner moves toward you—or backs away from you— *remain* where you are until he or she stops.
3. Once the other person has chosen a location and is talking comfortably, you know that this is his or her *preferred personal distance.* Respect it.

SAFELY MANAGE ANGER

We boil at different degrees.

RALPH WALDO EMERSON

While angry confrontations are common to nearly all human relationships, they can deeply shake your emotions and confidence and may even harm your health.[38] When you chronically lose your cool, you lose your perspective, your health, and eventually maybe even your life. We aren't even referring to the anger that provokes some people to beat, stab, or shoot others. Instead, we're talking about the everyday kind of anger, annoyance, irritation, and surges of hostile thoughts and feelings that lurk beneath the surface of the average person. If you're quick to blame or feel anger when faced with everyday delays and frustrations—waiting in line, rude drivers, lethargic elevators, obnoxious teenagers— and if this blaming flashes into heated irritation and the urge (controlled or not) to take aggressive action, then getting angry can be like taking a small dose of *slow-acting poison,* and chances are, it will eventually destroy your relationships and harm your health.[39]

Anger may be defined as *the thoughts, feelings, physical reactions, and actions that result from a blameworthy or attack-worthy physical, emotional, or mental provocation—"a demeaning offense against me and mine."*[40] In many cases, anger is a straight track to *hostility,* the expression of aggression or even attack. It's essential to point out that anger is certainly an instinctive and normal emotion, *and sometimes anger is highly adaptive and reflective of a healthy sense of indignation.* Assertively speaking out against attacks or transgressions against your personal beliefs and values can be warranted and healthy. Feeling anger and rage when defending yourself against a violent physical assault can be both necessary and justified.

However, the problem arises when anger occurs frequently, and at very minor hassles or perceived slights, and is *chronically mismanaged*—leading to feelings or reactions of hostility. For years, researchers have known that mismanaged anger and hostility can contribute to high blood pressure and the risk of *sudden cardiac death* (an unexpected fatal heart attack).[41] Marital discord is strongly correlated with depression.[42] And there may be a link between anger or helplessness and certain forms of cancer.[43] Perhaps worst of all, anger is the emotion that tends to fuel violence.

Recent studies report that suppressing anger *and* explosively venting it may both be linked to a death rate (from all causes) that is over two times greater than that related to "reflective coping." Three standard responses to anger are (1) "anger in"—suppressing your angry feelings altogether; (2) "anger out"—explosively venting your anger immediately; and (3) "reflective coping"—waiting until tempers have cooled to rationally discuss the conflict with the other person or sort things out on your own. Reflective coping is often the best choice because, as researchers have discovered, it restores a sense of control over the situation and helps resolve it. Those people who kept their cool—who acknowledged their anger but were not openly hostile, physically or verbally—felt better faster and had superior health. While venting anger does relieve tension, it can also contribute to feelings of guilt, which become an added source of stress.

Your brain uses neurochemicals, electrical impulses, and trillions of special receptors to spread the influence of your thoughts to every cell in your body. These chemicals change in response to the way we each perceive ourselves and interact with the people and events in our lives. Every pressure triggers a host of questions: Can I handle this? What happens if I can't? What are my options?

Researchers have discovered a number of ways that thinking can distort or magnify the stressful effects of experiences in your life. When you blame yourself for bad events but feel powerless to change them, feelings of distress rise sharply. A pessimistic view of life events makes them more stressful and thus more likely to produce illness.[44] Some researchers call this phenomenon *cognitive distortion*—the automatic negative thoughts that lead to distress and conflict.[45] Each one encourages and amplifies others. It's easy to end up trapped in a labyrinth of pessimism, and it takes dedication to break out.

"Much of our stress is due to conversations we have with ourselves," explains Robert S. Eliot, M.D., professor of cardiology at the University of Nebraska Medical Center, and author of *Is It Worth Dying For?* "Unfortunately, we often talk ourselves into the ground. Our mental tapes are always running, and if they are programmed with negative messages, they become a prime cause of stress. . . .

"The result: feelings become heated up and exaggerated; energy that could be used elsewhere gets tied up in self-talks that make life seem hopelessly out of control; and behavior becomes counterproductive and self-defeating as stress carries the day. . . . Replacing certain negative and irrational self-talks with more constructive, helpful ones lets you cultivate a 'thick-skinned' reaction to stress. People who respond in thick-skinned ways pay the minimum psychological and physical price for stress."[46]

In a study published in *Psychosomatic Medicine,* researchers noted that in married couples, angry or hostile behaviors—including criticizing, blaming, denying responsibility, making excuses, and frequent interruptions during dialogue—were linked to increased blood pressure and heart rate and a falloff in immune response.[47] Women were even more likely to show negative immunological changes than men. According to this study, dealing *effectively* with anger and conflict is a key to a healthy relationship and your physical and mental health. Tragically, over a lifetime, many of us wreck dozens, perhaps hundreds, of relationships in the heat of runaway anger.[48] As a group, hostile people are unhappy people, with more hassles and negative life events, and less social support.[49]

Another impact of anger, far subtler but nearly as destructive, is that a climate of unmanaged anger—and violent arguments—between parents is the most disturbing and depressing event that children witness. Studies suggest that when parents chronically or frequently fight—not when they *disagree,* but when they *argue* and *verbally fight* each other in anger—their children "become unbridled pessimists." In general, these children see bad events in life as permanent and pervasive, and they see themselves as responsible. Years later, research indicates that, on average, this pessimism persists, even after the parents are no longer fighting.[50] It's time for a change.

"Our research has shown that intimate partners must learn how to manage their anger and control the exchange of negative behavior by finding a way to express their feelings in a constructive manner," say Howard Markman, Ph.D., professor of psychology at the University of Denver and director of the Center for Marriage and Family Studies, and Clifford Notarius, Ph.D., professor of psychology at Catholic University in Washington, D.C. "Constructive expression of gripes, criticisms, and annoyances is a matter of knowing how to express oneself and choosing the appropriate time and place for the conversation."[51]

Anger has three core components. First, there is a *thought* that you are being trespassed against. Your angry reaction may be launched so rapidly that you fail to notice this mental turning point, but it's always there.[52] "I'm never appreciated." "*Another* delay!" "He never helps; he just complains." "That idiot changed lanes without signaling!" "Why does this *always* happen to me . . ." "Here we go again . . ."

The second component of anger is your *bodily reaction*. Your blood pressure soars; your heart rate accelerates. Your muscles tense up for physical assault. Brain centers go into a warfare mode. And you're swamped with a subjective feeling of anger or hostility.

The third element of anger is the *attack*, which is what the thought and bodily reaction have readied you to make. You lash out, to blame or accuse, in words or body language, or with some form of physical aggression. Or, on the other extreme, you struggle to suppress your angry feelings. Some say that telling off other people "gets things off your chest," but studies indicate that, rather than relieving aggression, such *anger-out* reactions amplify it, creating more hostility, not less.[53]

Identify Anger "Hot Spots"

Ask yourself, in the course of a typical day and week, what *specific* kinds of incidents trigger your anger? Injustices? Frustrations or annoyances? Interruptions? Threats to your income? Rush-hour traffic? Rudeness? Discourteous drivers? Waiting in lines? Slow-moving coworkers or employees? Unsolicited romantic advances? Snubbed romantic advances? A partner's anger? Family disagreements? A nagging financial or legal issue? The perception that your spouse or parent or mother-in-law or neighbor is nagging or criticizing you? Does ranting and raving make you feel better or worse? How *long* did the feelings of anger or hostility last? After the incident, do you feel guilty, ashamed, or remorseful? Did you accomplish what you wanted? Do others seem to like you more, or less?

In short, *what are your patterns of anger?*

All of us experience anger, and at times, it's completely appropriate to act on those feelings with safe, assertive behavior. The challenge, however, is to take "reasonable" action, without lashing out, becoming violent, or sabotaging your relationships. And only when you're clearly *aware* of your own anger and hostility patterns, and "hot spots" or "triggers," can you effectively choose the tactics to dampen or dissolve your hostile reactions, turning negative emotional energy into something more healthful and constructive.

Value the "Voice" of Emotions

In many cases, anger is fueled by judgments about others. Therefore, if you can learn to communicate in more caring, trusting, less-judgmental ways, you may be able to prevent arguments and even extend your life.[54] Researchers have found, for example, that the frequency with which a person refers to himself or herself— that is, how often you use the words *I, me, my,* and *mine* in ordinary conversations—may actually predict the recurrence of a heart attack.[55] "In short, anything that promotes a sense of isolation leads to chronic stress and, often, to illnesses like heart disease," says Dean Ornish, M.D., assistant clinical professor at the School of Medicine, University of California, San Francisco. "Conversely, anything that leads to real intimacy and feelings of connection can be healing."[56]

"How we approach other people each day can determine whether we experience isolation, chronic stress, suffering, and illness, or intimacy, relaxation, joy, and health," adds Dr. Ornish. "Of course, touching, hugging, and massage are ways of increasing intimacy. . . . Another powerful technique is that we can learn to talk to each other in ways that allow the other person to hear us better."[57]

Dr. Ornish and other researchers recommend communicating our feelings in ways that are likely to be heard without causing the other person to feel attacked. The basic principle is this: Our *feelings* tend to help connect us to others; whereas our *thoughts*—

especially judgments—tend to isolate us and increase distress. Thoughts connect our heads, feelings join our hearts.

That's because thoughts are more likely to be heard as criticisms than are feelings. "I think you're stupid" or "I think you're wrong" puts the other person in the position of feeling verbally attacked—making the walls go up . . . and stress levels with them. As soon as we feel criticized by someone else, it's extremely hard to hear anything else the attacker has to say. If you communicate feelings, such as "I feel hurt by what happened" or "I feel upset by what you just said," you are less likely to be perceived as an attacker, and it's easier for both people to be better understood. It's important to note that although expressing feeling makes many of us feel somewhat vulnerable, it actually makes us safer.

In contrast, some typical judgment-centered *thoughts* include "I'm right"; "You're wrong"; "You're always _____"; "You're never _____"; "You're not listening"; "You're a jerk"; "You should have _____"; and so on. Sometimes thoughts disguise themselves as feelings, such as "I feel that you're wrong"; "I feel that I'm right"; "I feel you're being stupid and shortsighted"; "I feel you ought to _____." The words *that, like,* or *as if* following *I feel* are a signal that what follows is probably a judgment thought instead of a feeling. Words like *you should, you ought to, you never,* and *you always* are thoughts that are often heard as criticisms.

Here are several ways to get closer—and reduce stress—by talking:

• *Be willing to express what you're feeling.* It can be a healthy, healing experience to let a loved one or friend know what you're truly feeling—in the spirit of informing this person rather than judging or criticizing. Just as, similarly, it helps when you know what others are really feeling. To ask another person, "How are you *feeling* about _____?" can provide you with a very different insight than you may receive by asking the more common question "What do you *think* about _____?" When two people share a greater willingness to express not only what they think but also what they feel, it helps them in many ways, including spending less time arguing and more time dealing with real issues in life, work, and relationships.

• *Listen with openness and empathy.* Stress often eases when we listen to each other with empathy—trying to understand what the other person is feeling, and acknowledging what we are sensing and hearing.

Steer Clear of Stressed-Out People

It's amazing how many conflicts begin as simple collisions between a stressed-out person and an "innocent" person who just happened to get in the way. The next time an angry, fuming person crosses your path, breathe deeply and remain relaxed, noticing where the person is headed. Then, step out of his way. This is a matter of awareness and common sense. First of all, it generally pays to avoid saying no to stressed-out people.[58] Realize that their present outlook and abilities are severely restricted by their anger. You are yielding—saying nothing, or at least nothing that will trigger an escalating argument, and moving out of the way— to keep yourself safe.

Become an Anger A.C.E.

Notice how anger is so often incredibly fast and furious. We're primed to accuse or deny, blame or feel victimized. Anger, unchecked, is volatile and potentially harmful. More often than ever, in our modern society people say and do things they later regret. Yet the effect of these words and hurtful actions cannot be undone or erased simply by saying, "I'm sorry." When you're provoked to anger, the time between the trigger and your reaction is often extremely brief.

Chances are, when you're upset, you tell yourself, "I'm angry *because* that person made a critical remark" or "I'm angry *because* my wife doesn't understand me" or "I'm angry *because* that person cut in front of me in line." The problem is that automatic comments such as these set the blame for feeling angry on something *outside* ourselves. This perception forces you to wait to feel better until some outside event happens, or someone else changes—and these things are often beyond your control.

When you blame some*one*, or some*thing*, else for how you're feeling, you give this person or thing the power to cause *your* emotional state. In contrast, if at the first moment you feel yourself getting upset or angry, you *pause for five seconds* (you may literally count from one to five if you like)—without saying a word, to recognize this and take full responsibility for how you feel and respond—it's easier to see how many choices you have, and to realize that you can choose *not* to feel like a victim of outside circumstances. Transforming your anger requires expressing yourself while preserving and nurturing your relationship rather than arguing and attacking each other.

For some people, acronyms are helpful devices to remember specific skills under pressure. Here's a useful acronym for recalling constructive anger-management skills whenever you feel the first rush of anger:

   A: *Assess Accurately*
   C: *Choose Constructively*
   E: *Express Effectively*

A: *Assess Accurately*. Especially with a loved one, it's easy to assume inaccurately that he or she is angry. Instead, the loved one may be rushed and tense due to the pressures of school or work, or accumulated daily hassles. He or she may not actually be anxious or short-tempered. Ask clarifying questions, such as "I'm sensing that things are tense for you right now, is that right?" "Are you upset with *me* about something? Or is it work . . . or school . . . or . . . ?" It's important to be able to quickly and readily distinguish between everyday stress-related "baggage" and genuine interpersonal anger, and to avoid assuming that your loved one *intends* to ignore you or snap at you because of anger at something *you've* done or haven't done. Unfortunately, if you fail to assess things accurately and jump to the conclusion that there's a fight already under way or keep pressing this person for what he or she simply cannot give right then, your pressure itself can be hurtful and trigger an angry reaction. Many anger-generated arguments have little to do with the issues or concerns being discussed. For instance, you and a loved one or friend may quarrel over finances, the children, politics, housecleaning, errands, or even your reactions to a recent movie or book. Yet the anger and heated words are often less about the issue being discussed and more about the frustration that comes from a failure to listen and acknowledge each other's needs, feelings, and points of view.

C: Choose Constructively. Don't say, "Why are you *always* . . . ?" or "There you go, getting *angry* again!" Rather say, "Did something at work make you late for . . . ?" Don't say, "That's an ugly, cheap-looking outfit." Rather say, "You are a handsome man (or great-looking woman), and *I* don't happen to like this outfit on you." Don't say, "Get off my back—I hate your guts!" Rather say, "Right now I'm really feeling (upset, stressed, worried) and I'm getting (or I'm not) angry at *you*."

E: Express Effectively. Stop for a moment whenever you feel a surge of anger and ask yourself, "Why am I starting to feel angry, and what, specifically, do I want to change?" Rather than being "right" (and the other person "wrong"), you must be committed to being *effective*. Ask yourself, "How can I best express my anger to get the results I/we want?" Remember, it's essential to *be specific*. For example: "You keep promising to come home for dinner at seven, but it's been seven-thirty or eight almost every day the past week. Not once did you call to let me know you'd be late. It makes me feel like you don't care, and that hurts; I'm angry." It would have done no good to say, "You make me furious because you're *always* late. You don't love me and you're a selfish, inconsiderate slob!" Effective anger management asks for an acknowledgment of your hurt *and* moves on to a commitment to avoid the same frustrations or mistakes in the future.

Becoming an *anger A.C.E.* is not a competition. Instead, the goal is to make stress and anger opportunities for you and your lover, for example, or friend or child, to learn more about each other, to meet each other's needs, and to affirm your bond by working out conflicts *together*—in ways so that both of you feel good about the outcomes of interactions about anger. This requires skill in expressing your own anger and also acceptance of the other person's anger as well. Acknowledge and reaffirm each other's efforts to clarify irritations and manage anger effectively.

Practice the three A.C.E. skills. Rehearse imaginary dialogues geared toward specific frustrating situations at work, school, or home. Write things down, if that feels helpful to you.

Use the Fishhook Technique

In your first response to anger, you may be inclined to call upon the old saw "Count to ten." It's good advice—to a point. But pausing, by itself, may do little to dampen the anger you feel. Go ahead and count to ten—better yet, when possible, sleep on it (see "reflective coping" in chapter 9 on safe relationships). During your pause, challenge and review the thoughts of trespass or affront that have made you angry. Envision yourself as a fish swimming along a stream.[59] Hundreds of fishhooks, symbolizing insults and criticisms, dangle in the water. Each offers you the choice of whether or not to bite.

Take an "Anger Release" Walk

For years, scientists have known that exercise can be one of the best stress relievers around. In fact, research suggests that, in many cases, it's a highly effective way to defuse anger, lift moderate depression, raise self-esteem, and spark creative thinking.[60] And it's a pleasure to realize that the psychological benefits of physical activity can often be felt quickly—in only five minutes or so—of brisk walking.[61]

The central idea is to combine the brief bout of exercise with a shift of mind, by choosing something else—a natural outdoor scene, humming a pleasant song, taking a "mental vacation"—to capture your attention.[62] One of the reasons this can work so well is that the conscious mind has difficulty focusing on two things at once. It's hard work to hold on to the heat of anger when something else draws your focus away.

Write an Emotional Safety "Feelings Letter"

This exercise is recommended by John Gray, Ph.D., and has proven successful in his work with emotional healing and emotional safety. It can be a good, sensible place to begin safely expressing personal hurts and "negative" or "unsafe" emotions.

Instructions:

Don't edit your feelings. The purpose of the feelings letter is to let all of your emotions out. A part of your mind might disagree with your feelings, and some statements you write down might not make any sense, but don't edit what you write. Your feelings will never make sense unless you clear out all of the bottled-up, incoherent, "negative" emotions you've been holding on to.

Don't try to be rational! Allow the wounded, frightened, angry feelings inside to come out on paper. You can sound like a child throwing a temper tantrum. You can be a bitch or a jerk. You can bring out all the parts of yourself you are afraid to show. This is not the time to be nice, understanding, or reasonable, especially in the first few sections of this letter; wait until you naturally get down to the section on love and forgiveness. Even if only 1 percent of you feels angry, express it openly as if all of you feels that way.

When you begin the letter with anger and blame, indulge that part of you that feels you are right and the other person is wrong. "You are so mean, you selfish jerk!" Let all that anger out. Don't intellectualize it.

Don't expect yourself to be aware of the love when you start the letter. When you begin your feelings letter, you may just feel anger and resentment, maybe a little hurt, and not much else. Once you begin expressing the anger and blame, you will likely see how, quite naturally, your emotions will progress into the next and then subsequent levels of feeling.

With these guidelines in mind, take out several pieces of paper and answer the following:

1. **Anger and blame**
   I don't like it when . . .
   I resent . . .
   I hate it when . . .
   I'm fed up with . . .
   I'm tired of . . .
   I want . . .
2. **Hurt and sadness**
   I feel sad when . . .
   I feel hurt because . . .
   I feel awful because . . .
   I feel disappointed because . . .
   I want . . .
3. **Fear and insecurity**
   I feel afraid . . .
   I'm sorry for . . .
   Please forgive me for . . .
   I didn't mean to . . .
   I wish . . .
4. **Guilt and responsibility**
   I'm sorry that . . .
   I'm sorry for . . .
   Please forgive me for . . .
   I didn't mean to . . .
   I wish . . .
5. **Love, forgiveness, understanding, and desire**
   I love you because . . .
   I love you when . . .
   Thank you for . . .
   I understand that . . .
   I forgive you for . . .
   I want . . .

Head Off Negative, Distorted Thoughts That Fuel Anger and Conflicts

"But what can I do about it?" many of us ask when anger keeps throwing us off-balance and threatens our relationships. One thing you can do is to change the way you *think* about the events of your life. Nearly all of us tend to make some specific mistakes in thinking—mistakes that make us angry or hostile, that create problems or block us from finding solutions.[63] These mistakes in thinking cause us to misinterpret what we're experiencing, misjudge others, and misjudge ourselves.[64]

These mistakes in thinking often involve *distorted thought patterns*—rigid, unrealistic ways of perceiving what's happening to us. In an instant, distorted thought patterns can make you jump to conclusions—or provoke you to anger or worry or doubt or resentment. Or they may impart a nagging sense of frustration, impatience, or helplessness. No matter how irrational they are, distorted, automatic thoughts are almost always believed, and they often appear in incomplete sentences—several key words or a visual image flash. Emerging research also suggests that, in many cases, the amount of *emotional arousal* you feel when negative thoughts arise may be influenced by a variety of additional factors, including excessive muscle tension, tiredness, or even low blood sugar from going more than two or three hours without eating.[65]

Fortunately, there are some rapid, well-proven ways to identify—and correct—distorted, unproductive thoughts. Let's begin with a review of some of the most common distorted thought patterns (listed alphabetically):

- *Argumentum populum.* "If everyone else thinks this way, it must be right."
- *Availability.* When you accept and advocate an explanation or solution that comes quickly to mind without considering other, less obvious, or less readily available solutions.

• *Being right.* You believe confessing ignorance or confusion makes you look ineffective, so you pretend to know things you really don't. You need to always prove that your statements and actions are right. You are quick to launch into defensive rationalizations whenever your "rightness" seems in question.

• *Blaming.* Your problems are either *never* your fault (other people and situations cause whatever goes wrong) or *always* your fault.

• *Change illusion.* Your happiness and success depend on other people changing their bad habits—"bad" from your perspective—and you believe they will make these changes if you keep pressuring them enough.

• *Composition illusion.* With this fallacy, you reason that what is true of parts of a whole is necessarily true of the whole itself.

• *Control illusion.* You feel either externally controlled—and therefore victimized—by other people and circumstances or internally controlled, which leaves you feeling that you cause everyone else's unhappiness.

• *Disqualifying the positive.* You reject positive experiences on the grounds that they somehow "don't count" when compared with the endless list of problems at your job and in your life.

• *Division illusion.* You assume that what is true of the whole is necessarily true of each individual part of that whole.

• *Either/or thinking.* There is no middle ground—things are either good or they're bad. Either you perform perfectly or you're a total failure.

• *Emotional reasoning.* You automatically assume that your feelings are facts and therefore must reflect the way things really are. If you *feel* incompetent or indecisive, then you must *be* incompetent or indecisive.

• *Failure to make distinctions.* Distinctions are subtle differences among things.

• *Fairness illusion.* You think you know exactly what's fair in all situations but feel victimized when other people often don't agree with you.

• *Filtering.* You find negative details in any situation and dwell on them so exclusively—ignoring the positive—that no matter how bright an experience may initially be, it soon looks bleak.

• *Invalid disjunction.* Here you only examine one or several possible solutions to a question or problem and assume that these are the only solutions that could possibly be relevant.

• *Jumping to conclusions.* You quickly leap to negative interpretations of statements and situations even though you usually lack the facts to support your conclusion. This includes *mind reading*—without checking to find out the truth, you assume that you know precisely why other people are thinking, feeling, and acting the way they are—and *fortune-telling*—you anticipate that a future event will turn out badly and act as if this is a predetermined fact.

• *Justification of effort.* This is a powerful force in human thought and action. Once you've invested a substantial amount of time or other resources in a given course of action, you seek reasons to justify that investment and become overly defensive if anyone questions it.

• *Labeling and mislabeling.* This is an extreme version of overgeneralization. When you make an error or become irritated with others, you emotionally assign a label to yourself ("I'm a loser"; "I'm an idiot"), another person ("He's a quitter"; "She's a liar"), or situation ("It's a lost cause").

• *Magnification* (catastrophizing) and *minimization*. You exaggerate risks, anticipating disaster; you overplay your mistakes or the importance of someone else's achievements; or you erroneously shrink your positive attributes or another person's imperfections until they appear insignificant.

• *Overgeneralization.* You make a sweeping assumption based on only a shred of evidence—a single negative event becomes a never-ending pattern of defeat.

• *Oversimplification.* Simplification can be valuable and enlightening. However, in oversimplification, you omit certain essential information or ignore complexity. Oversimplification distorts reality and confuses discussion.

• *Personalization.* You see yourself as the cause of some negative work occurrence for which you were not primarily responsible. You think that everything other people say or do is a reaction to you. You keep comparing yourself to others, wondering who's smarter, more successful, better looking, and so on.

• *Resistance to change.* Old beliefs provide a sense of comfort and security. New ideas are resisted simply because they are new.

• *Shoulds.* You try to motivate yourself and others with guilt, using statements filled with *should* and *shouldn't, must* and *ought.* When you or others break your rules, you feel anger, resentment, and frustration.

• *Ultimate reward illusion.* You talk and act as if monumental daily sacrifices and self-denial are what will ultimately bring you great rewards. You feel resentful when the rewards don't seem to come.[66]

Distorted thinking is contagious—the habit spreads. "If you consistently respond to events pessimistically," says Martin E. P. Seligman, Ph.D., professor of psychology at the University of Pennsylvania, "that negative style can actually *amplify* your feelings of helplessness and spread to other areas of your life."[67]

Therefore, resist the natural tendency to accept distorted thoughts as true simply because they seem reasonable or "feel right." Begin paying closer attention to the way you explain unpleasant situations and outcomes to yourself and others. Catch negative, stressful thoughts and examine them clearly and carefully, looking for supporting evidence, contradictory evidence, alternative explanations, and more logical inferences. Derail the temptation to resort to habitual, self-defeating reactions, such as defensiveness, retaliation, or withdrawal. The next time you feel yourself losing control, stop. Keep breathing and release physical tension. Reflect: Ask yourself questions, such as "What's going on here?" "Why am I so distressed?" "What's the worst thing that will happen if I'm late?" "Will worrying about it help?"

For some of the large indignities of life, the best remedy is direct action. For the small indignities, the best remedy is a Charlie Chaplin movie. The hard part is knowing the difference.

CAROL TAVRIS, *Anger: The Misunderstood Emotion*

SUPPORT EMOTIONAL SAFETY IN OTHERS

In upcoming chapters we'll look more closely at teaching safety to our children and creating safer relationships. But what can you do when you witness neighbors or complete strangers who are apparently being emotionally or physically assaulted? More than 4 million U.S. women are battered every year. This means that nearly all of us know someone involved in an abusive relationship. It's natural to want to help, but what do you do? Let's consider several examples.[68]

What if you hear a couple next door screaming and shouting through argument after argument? If you sense the situation may be on the verge of getting out of control and nearing violence, you might call the couple and say something like "I thought I heard something break, was it a window? I just wanted to make sure everything was okay there." This brief interruption may provide a valuable distraction and temporarily de-escalate runaway anger, says Esta Soler, executive director of the San Francisco–based Family Violence Prevention Fund.[69] If you are female, you might also consider approaching the woman involved, when her male partner is away, and offer to let her use your phone, look after her children, or give her a ride to the hospital if necessary. If she lives in the apartment next to you or above you, you might consider creating an SOS system when, after three hard knocks on the wall or floor, you will call 911.

What if, through an open window, you see a neighbor being struck by a male or hear a loud thump followed by screams for help? The answer is straightforward: call 911. Do not try to rush in and intercede yourself. There are too many dangers. It is only safe for trained police personnel to intervene, and the appearance of law enforcement officers may have an immediate calming effect on the abuser, whereas the appearance of a nosy neighbor may escalate things even further.

What if one of your friends or a coworker appears bruised and battered? First, none of us should assume that everyone with an occasional bruise is being battered. According to Mary Ann Dutton, Ph.D., a George Washington University clinical psychologist specializing in domestic violence, it may make sense to say something nonthreatening, such as "Wow, you seem to bruise easily." Even if the woman is not ready to talk about what happened, you have opened the door for further conversations. Once a dialogue on abuse is opened, acknowledge that it must be hard to ask for assistance and offer to help by looking in the yellow pages under "Social Services" and providing a list of telephone numbers for local shelters, hot lines, or counseling services (see the resources section in this chapter and chapter 8). In short, be supportive. Most battered women feel ashamed and alone. Volunteer to accompany this friend or coworker if she chooses to see an attorney or counselor.

Donna Edwards, president of the Washington, D.C.–based Coalition Against Domestic Violence, suggests offering to keep a safety box for an abused friend. It should contain extra house and car keys, money, a change of clothing, and photocopies of her birth certificate, driver's license, passport, social security card, divorce papers or protection orders, and bank and credit card information. You might also suggest that she secretly open her own savings account and develop options for where to go and whom to call if she decides to leave.

It's important to note that it's often *not* a safe idea to offer your own home as a protective haven unless you can be absolutely certain it will not be dangerous for both of you. As an alternative, you might share the name and number of a supportive friend in another area or state. It's also vital never to tell an abused or battered woman that she is doing something wrong by staying in the relationship with her husband or boyfriend. Then she may feel even more ashamed and view you as another person trying to control her life.

Beyond the above options, here are several other ways we can each contribute to increased *domestic emotional safety* and help put an end to domestic violence:

• *Advocate establishing more shelters.* The United States currently has three times as many animal shelters as it has shelters for battered women. In Oregon, four out of every five women and children are turned away due to limited space. In Massachusetts, shelters in 1994 closed their doors on seven thousand women and children because of lack of room.

• *Stop insurance companies from discriminating against battered women.* A number of women are denied coverage or are charged higher premiums for health, life, and disability insurance when their medical records reflect a history of abuse.

• *Put domestic hot line numbers in the front of telephone books, next to other emergency numbers.* When violence appears, phone numbers for help must be readily accessible.

• *Help victims escape and stay safe.* Local governments should provide women who don't own a car with coupons for taxicabs for getting to shelters, just as they provide taxi coupons to make it easier for senior citizens to go to doctors' offices. The federal government should support a national protection program for battered women and children, especially in the most severe cases. Perhaps this initiative could be modeled after the federal witness-protection program.

• *Zap movie and television violence—especially against women and children.* It seems imperative that movies that show women or children being beaten or killed be considered for rating as NC-17.

• *Ensure that specially trained domestic-violence units are in every prosecutor's office.* It takes specially qualified prosecutors and victim advocates to effectively and fairly deal with the rights of victims of domestic violence.

• *Recognize and acknowledge* emotional *abuse.* Physical wounds leave visible scars, but emotional abuse and terrorism leave even deeper scars on many women and children. Everyone from relatives, neighbors, police officers, physicians, journalists, and attorneys needs to recognize the brutalities of emotional and mental abuse as well as physical abuse.

• *Parents: School your children in fairness and nonviolence.* It is essential for parents to teach young children to defuse anger and deal with conflicts in nonviolent ways. Studies indicate that many batterers simply don't know how to negotiate for what they want and end up resorting to violence. That's why, as odd as it may seem, many treatment programs provide male batterers with assertiveness training.

For insights on dealing with more violent emotions such as rage and hostility, see the next chapter.

SAFETY RESOURCES

• *Anger Kills* by Redford Williams, M.D., and Virginia Williams, Ph.D. (Times Books, 1993). Seventeen scientifically based strategies for controlling the hostility that can harm your—and your loved ones'—health.

• *From Stress to Strength: How to Lighten Your Load and Save Your Life* by Robert S. Eliot, M.D. (Bantam, 1994). Timely, well-founded advice by a pioneering cardiologist investigating the sudden cardiac deaths—unexpected fatal heart attacks—caused by mismanaged stress.

• *When Anger Hurts: Quieting the Storm Within* by Matthew McKay, Ph.D., Peter D. Rogers, Ph.D., and Judith McKay, R.N. (New

Harbinger Publications, 1989). A practical program of anger management based on cognitive-behavioral therapy.

Calm-Alertness

• *Toughness Training for Life* by James E. Loehr, Ed.D. (Plume, 1993). An excellent, practical guide to "mental toughness" and emotional resilience under pressure.

• *The Twenty-Four Hour Society* by Martin Moore-Ede, M.D., Ph.D. (Addison-Wesley, 1993). Intriguing insights on the brain's alertness "switches" and body clocks.

Boundaries

• *Boundaries: Where You End and I Begin* by Anne Katherine, M.A. (Park Ridge, Ill.: Parkside Publishing, 1991). A practical guide filled with exercises.

• *Options for Avoiding Assault: A Guide to Assertiveness, Boundaries, and De-Escalation for Violent Confrontations* by Mary Tesoro, 1994 (an international publication of the nonprofit organization Personal Safety Options, P.O. Box 986, San Luis Obispo, CA 93406; 805-995-1224). This is an outstanding book, written primarily for women but of considerable value for men, too.

Domestic Safety

• The National Domestic Violence Hotline (800-799-7233). The first twenty-four-hour, toll-free national hot line that anyone suffering from physical abuse can call for help. Established in 1996 by the U.S. Department of Health & Human Services and staffed by trained, multilingual counselors. Battered individuals, their families, and friends can call for counseling. They can also be hooked up immediately with local law enforcement agencies and emergency shelters. The hot line provides referrals to more than two thousand local shelters, legal-aid offices, and health-care centers specializing in abuse victims.

Meditation

• For more information on the Transcendental Meditation program contact: TM Science & Research, 1000 North 4th Street, DB 1137, Fairfield, IA 52557, (515) 472-1200, (515) 472-1165 (FAX).

Chapter 8

DE-ESCALATING HOSTILITY

All cruelty springs from weakness.

SENECA

A verbal assault can distress, intimidate, shame, or aggravate you and create emotional shock waves that last for days or even years after the incident. It is one thing to tell yourself you shouldn't get upset by antagonism from others, but it's not easy to stop being strongly affected by it. Complicating things is that there is no one kind of "right" advice—you must match your response, as best you can, to each specific circumstance. That is one reason why, throughout this book, we discuss various *options* for responding.

First, it's essential to assess the situation you are facing. Do you feel that your boundaries are being invaded? If so, then does it seem intentional or unintentional? Does this feel like an impending attack, or is this person merely rude or upset? Do you sense this person's anger can be de-escalated? What is the environment around you (is it light, dark, quiet, noisy, wet, or dry)? Are there other people near who could come to help? Are there avenues to flee or escape? As you speak or move, how does the hostile person seem to respond to your words and voice and movements?

Each moment, you must keep assessing your situation, checking the aggressor, the surroundings, and your own capabilities. What is the other person doing now? Am I breathing steadily? Am I in a good, balanced protective stance with flexed knees and relaxed shoulders? What am I feeling? Where is safety? Are there other people anywhere nearby?

According to Mary Tesoro, author of *Options for Avoiding Assault* and a black belt martial artist and expert on helping women avoid and neutralize attacks: "If you have assessed that the aggressor is highly agitated, will 'lose face' if he doesn't perceive himself in charge of the situation, and has responded to your strong words by becoming more agitated, then it is probably not in your best interest to yell, 'Get out of my space!' Instead, you might give him a reason to discontinue the assault that allows him to keep his sense of being in control: 'Look, why don't I give you my money and you can leave before anyone else enters the park.'

"On the other hand," adds Tesoro, "if your aggressor is obviously hesitant about whether or not to attack and reacts to strong words by backing off, it might be more appropriate to say something like 'I want you to leave now!' In any event, assessment of each present moment gives you the ability to determine your most appropriate strategy for setting verbal and physical boundaries."[1]

In a research study on destructive conflict, M. Deutsch noted that "both rage and fear are rooted in the sense of helplessness and powerlessness," and both rage and fear make it impossible to effectively communicate a message from one person to another.[2] In a related study, the escalation of violence, particularly the violence that results in homicide, seemed tied to the quick flare-up of rage and perceived humiliation.[3] In fact, the topics of argument or conflict (money, power, sex, roles, responsibilities, jealousy) had little to do with escalation; *anything* could become an issue. The key, then, is how *you* respond—what can you do that might be protective while defusing hostility and heading off possible violence?

Extend Empathy and Avoid Ridicule, Threats, Blame, or Denigration

This may seem obvious, yet few of us remember it when tempers flare and we inadvertently toss fuel on the flames. This can be especially dangerous when confronted by a person prone to violence, whether due to mental, emotional, or physical causes. Anger and rage can arise whenever a person merely *feels* disparaged, ignored, deceived, threatened, or blamed—whether it is true or not or even if you intended it this way. Shame can be even more powerful, since it concerns the *whole self*, a deficiency in your eyes as well as the eyes of others, triggering a sense of helplessness and alienation, of being cut off from others, followed by a desire to lash out or hide. If intense shame is evoked by not being acknowledged, then rage may quickly follow. No matter which of these triggers produces an escalation of conflict, researchers have found that it is essential that the hostile person *save face* if there is to be a peaceful resolution or de-escalation.[4]

Always and everywhere men seek honor and dread ridicule.

C. H. COOLEY, *Social Organization* (1909)

In *Coping with the Stressed-Out People in Your Life,* psychology professors Ronald G. Nathan, Ph.D., and Marian R. Stuart, Ph.D., suggest that one of the most effective ways to disarm some verbal attackers is by "agreeing with them. In this way we flow with them and redirect their energy rather than wasting ours in fight-flight-or-freeze. In addition it honors the fact that most attackers are really feeling scared, incompetent, and alone. This is why agreeing can be so powerful. Do we honestly agree with everything they say? No, just some small part." According to Drs. Nathan and Stuart, an example phrase is

"'You seem upset.'

"This phrase demonstrates that the other person has your full attention and you are acknowledging that the antagonist feels very strongly about an issue. . . . The qualifier *seem* clarifies that it is his opinion and not a fact. There is agreement in 'You seem upset,' but it is not expected to disarm, just to temporarily defuse. Then to lower the volume of the attack. When someone goes off tilt, gets angry, and ventilates through criticism, he or she often does it in front of others in a loud voice.

"Could you run that by me more slowly?

"When you make this request in a calm, warm voice, you force him to lower his volume. Have you ever tried to yell slowly?"[5]

Remain Calm and More Effective with Protective Images

To develop this capability, find a quiet place to sit down and relax, taking some long, deep breaths. Plan to devote at least ten minutes to this exercise.

Picture an antagonist. Begin by imagining someone at a safe distance away coming toward you. Imagine that this person is someone who irritates you and who, today, appears hostile, critical, or manipulative toward you. This person can be a partner, friend, boss, coworker, or a complete stranger. With this image in your mind . . .

Relax more deeply, visualizing yourself calm and alert, protected by your inner safety and the physical distance between you and the antagonist, who continues to come forward. Breathe smoothly and deeply, keeping your muscles loose and free from excess tension, feeling a sense of inner peacefulness, your inner calm.

Extend an imaginary protective shield. Imagine a point of light out in front of your chest, perhaps three arm's lengths away, and expand it from a point into a thin wall of bright, warm light, then into a glowing *sphere of power* that surrounds and protects you. Find whatever image is most comfortable to you and give this protective shield the power to deflect critical or hostile remarks, yet you can still see through it and accept friendly words and kind gestures. While you are imagining this shield, keep your hands open and relaxed, or neutral. Do not assume gestures or stances of fighting or aggression, since these can inadvertently make you more tense and antagonize the antagonist.

Imagine that the antagonist is now nearing the edges of your protective sphere of power. As the person says hurtful things, imagine them being deflected or striking the shield and disintegrating to dust, falling harmlessly to the ground. Feel the experience of being alert and protected. If you notice yourself becoming anxious by the nearness of the imagined antagonist, then move him farther away and take some of the sting off his hurtful words.

When you begin to use this protective-shield image in your everyday interactions, it pays to remember that some angry individuals are not open to genuine, honest dialogue, and no matter what advice you try to give or rational questions you raise, they take offense and things heat up even more. In these cases, the most appropriate response may be no response at all—simply listening with a neutral expression on your face and in a relaxed stance. Sometimes, the aggressor will calm down on his own if you don't take the bait. You are carefully choosing where and when you invest your precious time, attention, and energy.

If someone insults you, you have two basic choices: first, to magnify the insult by getting upset about it; second, to perceive the hurtful comment as small or irrelevant and of no real importance to anyone. By making this latter choice—and it *is* a choice—you preserve your emotional safety and inner sense of calm-alertness. Furthermore, you control the impact and meaning of your experiences around negative, antagonistic people. By shielding yourself, you take away their power to upset you or force themselves upon you.

Certain feelings are part of our nature: we need to "look good."
Nothing makes us more angry than being made to "look bad."
  LYALL WATSON, PH.D., *Dark Nature: A Natural History of Evil*

Wherever Possible, Extend Respect and Acknowledgment to Others

According to researchers, the main ingredients in spontaneous de-escalation of hostility and conflict are respect, acknowledgment of feelings, and a brief sense of validation or connectedness.[6] The truth is, social bonds and status are at risk in all encounters; if they are not being built, maintained, or repaired, then they are being damaged or destroyed. *Loss of face* is one of the many metaphors for damaged bonds, loss of self-identity, and deeply felt shame. Saving face—which enables an angry or agitated person to still look good and present himself in a favorable light to others—is an important concern.

Studies show that alienation and shame often precede each episode of angry escalation of conflict.[7] Therefore, when you refrain from verbally attacking another person (and, by attacking, demonstrate disrespect and antagonism) and, instead, *remain neutral* or, when possible, show respect in some brief way for the deeper value of this human being—"I can understand how difficult it is to be laid off"—or provide some other acknowledgment of connection or empathy, you allow the antagonist to save face and may have a realistic chance of heading off an escalated conflict.

DE-ESCALATING A VERBAL ATTACK

Verbal de-escalation of conflict is not an easy thing to accomplish, but it is possible in more situations than most of us would guess, times when it makes sense to try to get an antagonist to back off by using the right angle of communication. Caution: If the verbal de-escalation doesn't work, you will need immediate access to other options—such as breaking free and fleeing or defending yourself if cornered. *Always remember that your voice power is a safety tool!* In de-escalating hostility, *what* you say is often not nearly as powerful as *how* you say it. According to recent findings reported in *Self-Defense & Empowerment News*, pitch, intonation, and volume are the keys:

Pitch refers to the frequency and range of your voice. In stressful circumstances, the voice tends to rise to a higher pitch, sometimes becoming shrill. Speakers using a low pitch are more likely to be perceived as telling the truth and being able to stand behind their words. In light of this, for an assertive de-escalating message keep your voice as steady as possible and at its lowest natural pitch. For women and some men, this takes practice. You might start by practicing with a friend or in front of a mirror.

Intonation refers to variations in the voice's pitch while speaking. For assertive power, it's best to keep a level intonation. Many people sabotage their own communication power by ending statements on a *rising* intonation, which causes strong statements to sound weak, as if questions. Consider, "I want you to leave now!" Say this with all the words at the same pitch. Then try it with the last word in a high pitch. When the *now* sounds like a question, even a polite listener may be confused about what you really want.

Volume is the loudness of your voice. In de-escalation, you do not necessarily want to yell or shout. Many successful verbal de-escalations have occurred with the speaker using a calm, firm voice. It depends on the specific situation. Some antagonists may turn and run if you shout the command, "Get away from here now!" Another assailant, upon hearing the same message, could pull out a weapon and attack you. In many circumstances, the best approach may be to speak in a firm, clearly understandable voice with a level tone and a strong sense of conviction behind your words. This may get your point across without triggering the aggressor into a more agitated or violent state. If you choose to raise the volume, be certain to maintain a steady, level pitch. Closely observe the response you get. If the other person's agitation is increasing when you raise the volume, then lower it and keep adjusting, as needed, to remain in control and give yourself the best chance to safely end the confrontation.[8]

Be careful about *mixed messages*. When attempting to de-escalate a dangerous situation, smiling unintentionally (which is often a nervous, unconscious reaction to stress) or cowering are two examples of self-sabotage, negating your words and making you seem weak or easy prey to the aggressor.

As discussed in chapter 5, *leveler phrases* may immediately help you defuse hostility:

• When . . . ? In a confrontation, a *when* question ("When did you start feeling so angry?" or "When did you lose your job?") may help defuse the confrontation by avoiding the presupposition that your attacker actually has a valid reason for the attack. When you suddenly switch the attacker's attention onto expressing some of his genuine complaints about life or society or social injustice, it may calm him down or buy you a precious few moments of time (it's usually difficult for a person confronting you to talk *and* physically attack you at the same time) and a better opportunity to escape.

• It's not your fault! or Yes, I can understand why you're upset! Few verbal or physical assailants enjoy attacking someone who is truly empathetic. By acknowledging the aggressor, you create what psychologists call *cognitive dissonance*, a momentary inconsistency between perception and reality. When a *leveler phrase* is used with several motions to gain distance—at least a step or two—from an aggressor, it may interrupt verbal escalation and help defuse anger, for men in particular.

• Let me understand . . . Allow me to help . . . Please tell me more . . . These are variations on the leveler phrase concept. When spoken in a confident, nonpleading tone, expressions that begin with *let* or *allow* can be anger- or aggression-interrupting words that may be unexpectedly calming to an attacker's nervous system.[9] When linked with another expression and perhaps an unanticipated change in your physical position, it may permit you to de-escalate the interaction or have greater control of what happens next.

• Listen! As an argument escalates, this word can stop some aggressors in their tracks because it taps into memory and language instincts in the brain. It can be most effective when linked with at least one more expression or several unanticipated-but-nonaggressive physical movements, interrupting the pattern and, at least for an instant, giving you an opening.

Here are several other examples for practice:

1. *For situations of no apparent personal danger.* Assume for the purpose of this exercise that the person to whom you are speaking will get the message the *first* time you give it. Put yourself into a relaxed and balanced stance and a "neutral" face—not smiling, not forcing a dark frown. Use the statements below to practice pitch, intonation, and volume, all backed with enough firmness or assertiveness to be taken seriously.
   "It's time for you to leave!"
   "I'm sorry, but I'm not interested."
   "I'm uncomfortable being touched, so please don't."
   "Thanks for being friendly, but I prefer to be alone now."

2. *The situation has not changed from (1) above—the person did not respond to your first message.* Assume that the lack of response had nothing to do with your assertiveness or verbal skills. Use the same statements as in (1) above but preface them with "Excuse me, I said . . ." and follow them up with "Do you understand what I mean by that?" Keep your nonverbal communication—stance, face, and gestures—neutral and refrain from sarcasm, aggressiveness, taunts, threats, or put-downs.

   It's essential to choose words that fit the situation. If you are a woman on a date with a man who doesn't seem to understand the word *no*, if you use the statement "I said no—and I mean it—if you continue, this will be a sexual assault," you might shock the aggressor into realizing the possible consequences of his actions and cause him to stop. However, what if this assailant had jumped out at you from the bushes in a park or near your front door? That same statement might escalate, rather than defuse, the confrontation.

3. *Situations where someone is acting inappropriately toward you.* Assume that you don't know enough about the person to determine whether this is a potentially dangerous situation. In addition, assume that help is nearby, if you need it. Practice the following statements:

> "I want you to leave now."
> "Don't come any closer."
> "Stop touching me *now*."

Example: Assume you are in a large park and a stranger comes up to you and asks for directions to a local coffee shop. Alert signals should be flashing in your head as you assess the situation. Use body language and movement to establish your boundaries and further assess the other person's motives. Take a step away, in a balanced, neutral stance, with shoulders relaxed and knees slightly flexed, and say something like "I'm uncomfortable being so close to someone I don't know. Now, what was your question?" Observe the response you get, then plan your next move. Always remember that it never pays to get drawn into a verbal argument, since this takes your attention away from staying safe, throws you off guard, and can escalate the conflict.

A multitude of case histories attest that many would-be assailants are talked down, and you may be able to convince an aggressor to leave. As Mary Tesoro reminds us in *Options for Avoiding Assault*, "This comes as a surprise to many women—it's okay to *lie* to an assailant: 'Nothing has happened yet. If you just leave now, I promise not to tell anyone or call the police.' A word of caution about pleading or begging: recent studies indicate that pleading and begging often result in a greater severity of sexual abuse. Understand the difference between pleading/begging and negotiation."[10]

4. *The situation has not changed after you communicated in (3) above.* Add the words below and alter your pitch, tone, volume, and non-verbal behavior (stance and face) to strengthen your message without becoming aggressive or denigrating.

   "Listen, I *said* I want you to leave now. If you don't leave, I'll call for help."

   "Look, I *said* don't come any closer. If you continue to move forward, I'm going to call for help."

   "I *said* I want you to stop touching me now. If you touch me like that again, it will be an assault and I will call for help."

5. *For more dangerous situations.* As the risks increase, you may elect to use a more assertive command:

   • "Stay back!" or "No!" These commands may be anchored in memory to parental warnings and create a moment of confusion or distraction for your assailant, giving you a chance to escape or summon help.

   • "Fire! Fire!" If your goal is to enlist help from bystanders, "Help!" is sometimes the *wrong* word to shout as you break free and flee from an assailant.

If a situation calls for lying, you'll have a variety of deceitful statements to call upon. If, however, an aggressor orders you to "Shut up," it may not be a good time to keep talking. Instead, switch to another tactic. You might feign sickness or craziness or even give the appearance of going along with things, if that might give you an edge to escape.

SAFETY RESOURCES

• *Coping with the Stressed-Out People in Your Life* by Ronald G. Nathan, Ph.D., and Marian R. Stuart, Ph.D. (Ballantine, 1994). A sound, practical guide to defusing arguments in personal relationships.

• *Options for Avoiding Assault: A Guide to Assertiveness, Boundaries, and De-Escalation for Violent Confrontations* by Mary Tesoro, 1994 (an international publication of Personal Safety Options, P.O. Box 986, San Luis Obispo, CA 93406; 805-995-1224). This is an outstanding book, written primarily for women but of considerable value for men, too.

• *Mental Shielding to Brush Off Hostility* by Richard Driscoll, Ph.D. (booklet and training cassette; Frontiers Press, 301 Gallaher View Road, Suite 302, Knoxville, TN 37919; 615-690-0962). A simple, practical program for troubled relationships with irritable coworkers, an angry boss, an upset love partner, or other hostile people.

• *The Gentle Art of Verbal Self-Defense* and *More on the Gentle Art of Verbal Self-Defense*, both by Suzette Haden Elgin, Ph.D. (Prentice Hall, 1983). Classic works on protecting yourself against critical, hostile people.

• *Verbal Judo: The Gentle Art of Persuasion* by George J. Thompson, Ph.D., and Jerry B. Jenkins (Quill, 1993). A method of verbal protection and de-escalation devised and tested by Thompson, who is a former police officer, martial artist, and English teacher.

• *Self-Defense & Empowerment News* (an international publication of Personal Safety Options, P.O. Box 986, San Luis Obispo, CA 93406; 805-995-1224). An inspiring newsletter for women, filled with real-life stories of successful de-escalations and thwarted attacks, plus resources, instructional insights, and a listing of endorsed schools across the United States and abroad.

• *Violent Emotions: Shame and Rage in Marital Quarrels* by Suzanne M. Retzinger, Ph.D. (Sage Publications, 1991). A scholarly text on some enlightening research about the escalation and de-escalation of conflict.

Chapter 9

MAKING YOUR RELATIONSHIPS SAFER

Surround yourself with people who respect you and treat
you well.

CLAUDIA BLACK

*To establish and sustain a state of emotional and physical safety is the central
requirement for loving relationships to flourish.* At the core of each interaction it's the thoughts and words—spoken and unspoken—that
draw us together or drive us apart. And even when two people
care deeply for each other, communication is often mishandled or
gets mixed up—igniting arguments, fueling fears, and soundless-
ly shattering our bond. We ask for help but no one answers. We
talk, not understanding what needs to be understood. We listen,
not able to hear what's in the other person's mind or heart.

One of the most consistent predictors of marital unhappiness is
destructive conflict.[1]

SUSAN E. CROHAN, PH.D., of the University of Wisconsin,
Madison

Perhaps more than any other single factor, the way you handle
misunderstanding and conflicts determines whether your relationships are safe and thrive or even survive.[2] One of the most difficult tasks in a loving relationship is managing differences and

disagreements without escalating anger and hostility. Too often we fail: suddenly you stop talking in a caring manner and start hurting each other—blaming, complaining, accusing, resenting, demanding, threatening, and doubting. "We live together under one roof, but cope with problems like total strangers," you think to yourself. And it's true. "We're married, but speak different languages," you complain to your close friends. And you're right.

To appreciate and respect the unique "languages" of others, including loved ones, is one of the keys to increasing emotional safety. One of the principal ways to keep relationships safe, healthy, and growing, and to head off bitter arguments, is this: No matter what problems we face together, we each naturally have different points of view—and those differences must at all times be respected rather than ignored or invalidated. In fact, some researchers are convinced that men and women use language so differently that they actually speak to each other with cross-cultural perspectives.

According to some researchers, the single most important strategy to head off defensive communication is to consciously choose to hold a positive image of your partner and keep reintroducing praise and admiration in your relationship.[3] If you arrive home to a grouchy partner or find clothing unwashed or on the floor, instead of ranting and raving about it—and then wasting time and energy feeling uptight or arguing—you can choose to remember that your spouse was tired last night and busy all day. "We've been handling a hectic schedule recently," you might think to yourself or say aloud. "It's remarkable to me how many thing *are* getting accomplished!"

Another powerful, on-the-spot way to get closer and stay closer is to *recognize—and adapt to—the other person's "conversational style."* For women, the key is intimacy and connection, explains Deborah Tannen, Ph.D., professor of linguistics at Georgetown University and author of the well-researched book *You Just Don't Understand: Women and Men in Conversation.* "For men, it's about preserving independence and negotiating status." To men, simply spending time together—eating at the same table, running errands, or watching television—is part of being intimate, while having a conversation isn't. Whereas women often want to talk about what's happening in—or to—the relationship, men usually just prefer to "be" in the relationship.

"To a woman, talking often means relaxing," says Dr. Tannen. "That's what she does with her friends. But a man sees talking as a kind of display—it involves competition, getting the edge, showing what you know." For example, a man says, "I'm tired—it's been a long day." In reply, the woman says, "I had a hectic day, and I'm really worn-out, too." Because conversation is usually perceived as a contest to men, he thinks she is trying to belittle him. But from her perspective, she's trying to make him feel better, showing empathy, deepening the connection. According to Tannen, when a woman asks, "What do you want to do tonight?" she's initiating "a free-flow give-and-take, but the man thinks she wants him to decide." Or sometimes, even more irritating, he simply responds, "I don't care, what do *you* want to do?"

Social intelligence is given far too little value in societies which measure worth by standards of technical prowess.

LYALL WATSON, PH.D., *Dark Nature: A Natural History of Evil*

Adapt to the Other's Inherent Communication Needs

In truth, it's unrealistic to revamp your own conversational style or expect others to change theirs—especially since there's evidence that, to a significant extent, personal conversational style is a biologically centered instinct of the brain.[4] Therefore, what's called for may simply be greater flexibility—in seeking out what, precisely, other people *really* mean, and in being more responsive to the other's needs when trying to get your own meaning across. A good three-point guideline is this:

1. Listen attentively—and respect each individual's preferred "conversational style."
2. Get to the point early on.
3. Give enough details so that what you *mean* to communicate comes through.

Three of the most damaging reactions to conflict are defensiveness, stubbornness, and withdrawal from interaction. How *flexibly* a couple handles points of disagreement may be the key to the health and longevity of their relationship, says John M. Gottman, Ph.D., professor of psychology at the University of Washington in Seattle, who has spent more than a decade researching how men and women react to stress in relationships.[5] Some of the elements once thought to be vital to relationship success—love, similar backgrounds, coming from well-adjusted families—are secondary to how well a couple communicates and even argues, says Howard J. Markman, Ph.D., director of the Center for Marriage and Family Studies in Denver, who along with his colleagues has spent nearly two decades studying what makes successful marriages work.[6]

One of the worst consequences of escalating arguments is that they can quickly lead to what some researchers call *flooding*—feeling so overwhelmed by your partner's negativity and your own reactions that you experience "systems overload" and feel swamped by upset or distress, feeling unfairly attacked, misunderstood, or wronged.[7] Within moments you may become defensive, hostile, or withdrawn. Once you're feeling this far out of control—and some of us feel this far out of control often—constructive discussion is all but impossible.

"In any intense exchange with a spouse," explains Dr. Gottman, "it's normal for some negative thoughts and feelings to arise. As long as they don't get too extreme, most people are able to handle them. We each have a sort of built-in meter that measures how much negativity accumulates during such interactions. When the level gets too high for you, the needle starts going haywire and flooding begins."[8] A few of us have high thresholds for negativity. Others feel flooded at the mere hint of a complaint. Flooding is also influenced by how much pressure an individual is facing outside the relationship; the more stress, the more quickly flooding occurs. You may be surprised to learn that research indicates men become flooded far more easily than women. And the most common reaction is withdrawal—which represents a last-ditch effort to protect oneself from feeling trapped and overwhelmed.

To a large extent, the way you see yourself depends on the way you *assume* other people see you. As Aaron T. Beck, M.D., professor of psychiatry at the University of Pennsylvania, explains it, such perceptions are shaped, in turn, by our interpretation of "signals" we get from others. But these interpretations can be biased by old, reactionary habits and by our current state of mind. For example, as noted in chapter 7, when you're feeling tense or tired, feelings of anxiety and doubt tend to be magnified.[9]

"When a partner doesn't live up to imagined expectations, the other becomes as upset as if a legal contract had been violated," explains Norman Epstein, Ph.D., associate professor at the University of Maryland. "It's as if a basic trust has been broken."[10] And once that trust is lost, *a catastrophic shift occurs in how you think about your partner and your relationship.* Even your *memory* gets altered—you come to recast your earlier, happier times together in a negative light. You start to react with dread to almost everything your partner says or does: "What *now?*" You feel continually on guard against attack. Your spouse says, "We have to talk," and you instantly think, "Here comes another fight," even if all he or she wanted was to invite some friends over this weekend.

You begin hesitating to say what you really mean and begin misreading each other's mind, imputing the worst possible motives to each other, and overgeneralizing complaints: "You *always* ignore me." "You *never* help out around here." If this pattern isn't headed off, eventually hostility colors everything. Based on long-term research,[11] here are two important pieces of day-in, day-out advice for men and women:

MEN: *Try Not to Avoid Emotional Dialogues.* Sidestepping a problem or complaint won't make it disappear, it will probably just upset your partner more. Uncomfortable as it may be, by venting feelings she's able to help keep your relationship healthy and secure. To the best of your ability, stay detached and flexible—rarely is it her goal to attack you personally, even if frustrations prompt her to employ sarcasm or contempt. If you listen attentively to her complaints or criticisms without putting her down, she will feel validated and will likely calm down. If you refuse to listen, she'll be increasingly upset and may escalate the conflict, pushing you toward flooding.

WOMEN: *Confront Him Clearly but Gently.* Due to a host of genetic and cultural reasons, in most relationships it's up to the woman to raise the majority of important issues. But it's essential to be flexible enough to do so *in a calm, clear, and gentle way.* If you don't, your partner will likely resist or withdraw. Be pleasantly persistent if he seems driven to keep changing the subject. Let him know you are *not* attacking him, and that you need him to join with you in facing issues and conflicts in your relationship. You might say something like, "This may not seem so important to you right now, but it really *is* important for me—and we need to talk, *together*, about what's bothering me so we can keep the love alive in our relationship."

If He Stonewalls, Give Him a Little Extra Space

At times, someone—usually a man—will suddenly stop communicating and become silent. Dr. Gottman, in *Why Marriages Succeed or Fail*, calls this emotional reaction *stonewalling.*[12] Apparently based in part on genetics and in part on learned behavior patterns, stonewalling occurs, for example, when a man hears—or just anticipates—criticism, or senses that his partner is bringing up a difficult issue. He feels threatened—and withdraws. He avoids eye contact, barely moves his face, keeps his neck rigid, and even neglects to say such simple acknowledgments as "Yes, I see" or "Uh-huh." Many women think out loud, sharing their struggles with an interested listener, and to some extent discover what they want to say through the process of talking.[13] But many men process information differently, and tend to first silently "mull over" or think about what they've just heard or experienced.

Even though it's not fair, when a man stonewalls it often seems to be up to the wife to take control of what happens next. Dr. Gottman and other researchers have discovered that, in happy marriages, the wife usually interrupts the argument cycle.[14] She ignores a negative comment or says something positive in the face of stonewalling behavior. *It may surprise you to learn that it's less important to solve marital "problems" than to be able to deal with the emotions they bring up.* Distressed marriages are characterized by one, and often both, spouses getting flooded and escalating arguments into fights.

The man is likely to be too "rational" and downplay his partner's emotions. Experiencing his reaction, the woman is then more likely to complain and criticize her partner, feeling she must raise the intensity of the interaction to keep him responsive. Then, as she demands more emotional confrontation, he withdraws even more, which escalates her demands. Often perceiving her partner's withdrawal as a lack of caring—which it usually isn't—she may become irate and further escalate the conflict, and trigger what Dr. Gottman calls "kitchen-sinking"—"bring up all kinds of past and present complaints and mixing them with sarcasm and contempt."[15] This tactic, of course, immediately overloads most men and causes further withdrawal.

"The biggest challenge for women is to correctly interpret and support a man when he *isn't* talking . . . ," says John Gray, author of *Men Are from Mars, Women Are from Venus.* "Women need to understand that often when a man is silent, he is saying, 'I don't know what to say yet, but I am thinking about it.' Instead, what women hear is 'I am not responding to you because I don't care about you and I'm going to ignore you. What you have said to me is not important and therefore I am not responding.'"[16]

Pause and Say, "It's Not Your Fault"

According to some researchers, men "hear" far better when they don't feel they're receiving unsolicited advice or being attacked. Often, when a man feels challenged, his attention zeroes in on being right and he forgets to be loving or to listen. And he is unaware of how uncaring he sounds or how hurtful this may be to his partner. Requests turn into commands; frustrations fireball into attacks. He has no idea that by his response *he* is starting an argument; on the contrary, he thinks *she* is arguing with him. He defends his point of view while she defends *herself* from his barbed comments—which hurt her feelings.

To end this down spiral of misperceptions, pay careful attention whenever you're complaining about a problem to be sure that the listener knows that you're not blaming him or her for causing it. Whenever appropriate, say, "It's not your fault." And if you feel as if the other person's complaining is really blaming, ask, "It seems to me that you're saying this is my fault. Is that true?" Chances are, it isn't. By getting clear about it, you can avoid blowing things out of proportion in your mind and be a far better listener.

"In a sea of conflict," explains Dr. Gottman, "men sink while women can swim."[17] While neither men nor women enjoy conflict, women generally seem able to handle it better, whereas men are more likely to crumble under the stress.[18] "Men are less able to cope with negative expressions of emotion," says Dr. Markham. "As a result, men withdraw further and further and feed the vicious cycle."[19]

"A man commonly feels attacked and blamed by a woman's feelings, especially when she is upset and talks about problems," says Gray. "Many men don't understand the female need to share upset feelings with the people they love. With practice and awareness of our differences, women can learn how to express their feelings without having them sound like blaming."[20] She could make a comment such as "It sure feels good to talk about this" or "I'm feeling so relieved that I can talk about this. Thank you." That kind of simple change can make a world of difference and can help men remember that complaining about problems does not mean blaming and that when a woman complains, she is generally just letting go of her frustrations by talking about them. "The four magic words to support a man are 'It's not your fault,' " says Gray.[21] Or the man can take matters into hand by saying, "It feels like you're saying it is all my fault that _____. Is that true?" In most cases, it isn't.

Here's another example: "What's your problem?" This phrase triggers many a you-versus-me battle. The typical reaction is one of defensiveness. "It's not *my* problem—*you're* the real problem!" A better question to ask when you notice a friend or partner feeling angry or upset is "What happened? And how may I help?" And, if someone asks you the barbed question "What's your problem?" one constructive response recommended by George J. Thompson, Ph.D., in *Verbal Judo* is "It's not a problem, it's something I need to discuss. Can we talk?"

Be Safety Conscious about Your Mood When You Arrive Home

At the end of a difficult day, when you may be exceptionally tense or tired or hungry, and your partner asks, "How was your day?" your answer may sound more negative than you intended, as a result of your mood and fatigue. Similarly, your partner may *hear* your question "What's for dinner?" as an attack (it may sound more like "Why isn't dinner ready yet?") and respond angrily and argue. To avoid this common problem, take a different approach. Whenever you—or your partner—greet each other at the end of the day, make it warm and brief, then give each other a "buffer zone" lasting at least five or ten minutes to wind down and relax. *Then* talk.

Keep Things Feeling Safe—and Fair!

Even the most destructive relationship conflicts begin with good intentions. The most important focus is how to tap into these good intentions and the reservoir of safety and hope beneath them. Evidence continues to mount that it's not *what* you fight about, it's the *way* you fight that's a key to either marital happiness or disaster.[22] "The more a couple is able to fight constructively, the higher their level of marital happiness," says Susan E. Crohan, Ph.D., of the University of Wisconsin, Madison. She bases this observation on her research with colleagues at the University of Michigan.[23] Many of us have never learned how to express disappointments and frustrations and hurt feelings without a battle. It takes two to argue, but only one to stop an argument. So get in the habit of asking yourself, "Is this really worth arguing about?" If the answer is yes, ask again.

One way to disengage from the start-up of an argument is with *no-fault communication phrases,* such as "We seem to be caught in a cycle" or "We seem out of sync" or "There seems to be a push-pull pattern going on right now in our relationship" or "We seem to have fallen into a pattern where you have this understandable reaction, which causes me to have an understandable reaction, which then causes you . . ."[24]

When you and your partner can pinpoint whatever pattern you're locked in, you can recognize its power. Then it also becomes easier to see why blaming each other is a waste of time and energy. Even though every negative feeling occurs for some important reason, you can frame negative emotions as symptoms of problem patterns: "Lately I've been feeling (jealous, guilty, depressed, anxious, angry, critical) . . ." and then immediately add, "and I think it's because we're starting to fall into a pattern of . . . What do you think?" Healthy, emotional intimacy requires knowing your own feelings and letting them be known—in a safe, caring "space" in your relationship.

Some other recommendations for easing relationship anger include avoiding using words and phrases that make your partner livid. But don't turn away from conflict at all costs, either, since there's evidence that "avoidance means couples never get to the issues, which blow up later," Dr. Crohan says. When conflict is handled constructively, it can be "positive," she explains. "You learn more about yourself and your spouse. You build a trust that you can weather the storms." According to Dr. Crohan, constructive fighting means "calmly discussing issues; really listening; saying nice things and making your spouse laugh to defuse anger." And some hurtful tactics need to be truly off-limits—such as mudslinging, playing psychologist, dumping loads of grievances on each other, acting like an ostrich and refusing to acknowledge that a problem exists, storming out of the room, or maneuvering to pin the blame on each other.

When a Conversation Heats Up, Call a Time-out and Use "Reflective Coping"

Conventional thinking contends that telling other people off "clears the air" and makes you feel less angry. But, in truth, many times the opposite may be true. Studies report that venting anger tends to make people more hostile and destructive, not less.[25] A fifteen-year controlled study of husbands and wives by the University of Michigan School of Public Health measured the effects of expression of anger, supression, and "cool reflection." The researchers discovered that ineffectively managed anger was linked to a two and a half times greater risk of death from all causes.[26] The findings held true for both sexes and all age groups and education levels, regardless of whether the individuals smoked or had any other common risk factors for heart disease. "The key issue," says Dr. Ernest Harburg, one of the researchers, "is not the amount or degree of your anger, but *how you cope with it.*"

"Reflective anger-coping," explains Dr. Mara Julius, who headed the study, "not only promotes better problem solving but better health, and possibly longer life." And it affects our children, too. A recent study by researchers at the National Institute of Mental Health confirmed that young children are especially susceptible to psychological problems from angry exchanges they see or hear in the home.[27] This "background anger" of heated arguments clearly distressed the children studied, causing them to freeze in place, cry, cover their ears or eyes, or run away from the scene. Their reactions suggest that background anger may have a cumulative effect, perhaps even more detrimental than television violence.

Reflective coping means waiting until tempers have cooled to rationally discuss the conflict with the other person or to sort things out on your own. In general, reflective coping is the best choice because it enables you to avoid hostility traps, restores a sense of control over the situation, and helps resolve it. Studies show that those people who keep their cool—who acknowledged their anger but were not openly hostile, physically or verbally— feel better faster, solve problems more easily, and have superior health.[28]

Of course reflective coping does *not* mean ignoring your anger—since it's a signal worth listening to. "Our anger may be a message that we are being hurt, that our rights are being violated, that our needs or wants are not being adequately met, or simply telling us that something isn't right . . . ," says Harriet Goldhor Lerner, Ph.D., in *The Dance of Anger.* "Just as physical pain tells us to take our hand off the hot stove, the pain of our anger can motivate us."[29]

Aldous Huxley once remarked that it was a bit embarrassing to get to the end of his life and have no more profound advice than "Be a little kinder."[30] But what golden counsel that is. Indeed, one of the consummate ways to head off useless hostility and anger is to develop a more trusting heart, says Redford Williams, M.D., professor of psychiatry, associate professor of medicine, and director of the Behavioral Medicine Research Center at Duke University Medical Center.[31] His research suggests that when you begin to feel angry, it really pays to pause for an extra moment to gently laugh at yourself, forgive others, put yourself in the other person's shoes, use some logic, and in short, find ways to keep things from getting blown out of proportion. Ask, "Is my anger useful? Does it support my integrity and help me achieve my goals—or does it just defeat me?"

Agree with your partner that, at any time, either one of you can say, "This is not a good time to talk" or "I'm getting upset and I don't want to argue, so let's not talk about this right now," as long as you choose another discussion time soon and keep your word. Pick a time *later* to talk about what's bothering you, and separate *discussing* the problem—bringing an issue into the open by describing behaviors that are upsetting to you but without calling your partner abusive names or criticizing his or her character— from *solving* the problem. Stretch your awareness so you can understand—not change—your partner's position or feelings, and refrain from mind-reading or anticipating what your partner will say. Instead of rehashing the past, turn your attention toward the future.

Eat First, Then Talk

Don't forget biology. "You can avoid a lot of relationship conflicts if you both have had something to eat first," says psychiatrist William Nagler, M.D. "Half the time, having a full stomach will prevent major fights. Blood-sugar battles are often what you are really fighting. . . . When your blood sugar is low, things that normally wouldn't bother you seem like major events."[32]

Relate to Your Loved Ones Eye to Eye

One of the most important ways in which we affirm our connection to loved ones is eye to eye. No matter how old you become, you never cease to need unconditional, simple *valuing* in another's eyes—*and* in your own eyes. "These looks," says Ruthellen Josselson, Ph.D., author of *The Space Between Us*, "are far beyond words: eyes speak more profoundly than language the tenor of relatedness. They express, surely and absolutely, how much and in what way we matter to the Other. Words may lie; eyes cannot."[33] In short, *saying* "I love you" in words pales in contrast to the potential power of *expressing* "I love you" without any words, *eye to eye.*

The Golden Rule of Love is: Relate first, resolve second. It is impossible to resolve relationship concerns if either partner feels misunderstood, unappreciated, or ignored.

CLIFFORD NOTARIUS, PH.D., AND HOWARD MARKMAN, PH.D.

Set Clear Relationship Boundaries and Take Care of Emotional Safety

As noted in chapter 7, *we each have a right to boundaries of emotional and physical safety.* It's essential to openly discuss and acknowledge these rights to emotional and physical safety in relationships. These include:

The right to say no.
The right to set clear boundaries and have these respected by others.
The right not to have to justify these limits and boundaries.
The right to decide when and in what ways others get near to you and touch you.
The right to be free of abuse of any kind.
The right to walk away whenever you are being mistreated.

National statistics indicate that nearly 85 percent of all rapes are committed by acquaintances—attackers who know or recognize their victims.[34] This could be a family member, casual acquaintance, or date. With alertness and planning, you can significantly reduce the chances of being attacked by someone you're dating or by a new acquaintance. If a man asks for your phone number or address, don't reveal it right away. Perhaps give a work number instead or ask to call him. Don't be specific about where you live (and with whom) until you feel safe. On early dates, meet at a public place and take enough money to get a taxi home if need be. Avoid alcohol and drugs—which play a large role in many acquaintance rapes. Make certain someone else knows where you are going and with whom. At the first moment you have a feeling something isn't right, excuse yourself and leave. If it turns out that your hunch is wrong, a respectful person will understand later. Many of us are trained to be polite, but put yourself first and respect your feelings.

"If you're in a car and feel like you're being driven to a house or location against your will," warns Louise Rafkin, self-defense instructor and author of *Street Smarts*, "be creative. Ask to stop to use the bathroom or to get food. Once out of the car, get help immediately and ask someone to call the police. . . . If you don't want to date or continue seeing someone, be clear and firm about ending the relationship. Be explicit. People often hear only what they want to hear when they have an emotional attachment. Don't negotiate. After you have stated your wishes, end the conversation. Rejections can be firm without belittling the other person. Saying 'I'm sorry you feel differently. This is how I need things to be' should work."[35]

Enhance Your Verbal Safety Skills

Many of us unwittingly trigger arguments with our intimate partner. We do this through unawareness of certain statements and, as pointed out in chapters 6, 7, and 8, by taking verbal "bait" when others are angry. Take several evenings to read the books listed under "Safety Resources" at the end of this chapter. There are few better investments of your time and attention. The guidelines and practical examples in these books can make a significant difference in how you respond to, and guide, your daily conversations, resulting in a deeper sense of safety, less stress, and more lasting love.

At the Heart of Emotional Safety Is Empathy

Empathy is the ability to step aside from fixed views and old patterns and try to see and feel an experience through the other partner's eyes and heart. "Here is the bottom line of communication," observes George J. Thompson, Ph.D., former police officer and author of *Verbal Judo*. "Empathy absorbs tension. It works every time. I've even seen it save a life." What's one of the best empathetic statements, one that may allow you to interrupt most people without fear of bodily harm? According to Thompson, it's "Let me be sure I heard what you just said." Everything about that sentence conveys that you are sincerely trying to understand.

Be Alert for These Six Warning Signs of Disturbed, Abusive Men

Many abusive relationships could be avoided if women knew which signals to look for. When a man is considerate to others but mean to the woman in his life, this is often not temporary and is a sign that things may get worse. Having difficulties communicating with each other and handling day-to-day disagreements is normal to most relationships, but many disturbed men exhibit certain character flaws. A combination of some or all of the following behaviors, if repeated, are warning signs of a lack of emotional safety for a woman:

1. He has a charming personality to others but is cruel when he is alone with you.
2. He chronically lies about all kinds of things—money, jobs, past and present girlfriends, and even family background.
3. He denigrates or tears down most or virtually all of your contributions and accomplishments to make himself appear more successful.
4. He relentlessly criticizes—with tongue-lashings or veiled put-downs—your appearance or sexual performance, although he may later apologize.
5. He repeatedly ignores limits and boundaries or has a warped sense of right and wrong and tries to exert power over you by breaking rules and agreements.
6. He twists things so that you seem to take the blame for everything, and he may rarely or never give you genuine apologies, even for the most hurtful, intolerable behaviors.

SAFETY RESOURCES

• *We Can Work It Out: Making Sense of Marital Conflict* by Clifford Notarius, Ph.D., and Howard Markman, Ph.D. (Putnam, 1993). A well-proven approach to anger management in love relationships.

• *Why Marriages Succeed or Fail* by John Gottman, Ph.D. (Simon & Schuster, 1994). A variety of research-proven methods of anger management for couples.

• *Coping with the Stressed-Out People in Your Life* by Ronald G. Nathan, Ph.D., and Marian R. Stuart, Ph.D. (Ballantine, 1994). A sound, practical guide to defusing arguments in personal relationships.

Relationship Safety Skills

• *Sex, Power, and Boundaries: Understanding and Preventing Sexual Harassment* by Peter Rutter, M.D. (Bantam, 1996). An outstanding resource guide.

• *Street Smarts: A Personal Safety Guide for Women* by Louise Rafkin (HarperCollins, 1995). Filled with basic, thought-provoking advice from this columnist and self-defense instructor.

• *Lifemates: The Love Fitness Program for a Lasting Relationship* by Harold H. Bloomfield, M.D., and Sirah Vettese, Ph.D. (Signet, 1991). A practical program for emotional safety and intimacy.

Gender Talk

• *You Just Don't Understand: Women and Men in Conversation* by Deborah Tannen, Ph.D. (Ballantine, 1992). An insightful, well-written guide by a professor of linguistics at Georgetown University.

• *Men Are from Mars, Women Are from Venus* by John Gray, Ph.D. (HarperCollins, 1993). A best-seller filled with good common sense.

Domestic Safety

• The National Domestic Violence Hotline (800-799-7233). The first twenty-four-hour, toll-free national hot line that anyone suffering from physical abuse can call for help. Established in 1996 by the U.S. Department of Health & Human Services and staffed by trained, multilingual counselors. Battered individuals, their families, and friends can call for counseling. They can also be hooked up immediately with local law enforcement agencies and emergency shelters. The hot line provides referrals to more than two thousand local shelters, legal-aid offices, and health-care centers specializing in abuse victims.

• *Getting Free: You Can End Abuse and Take Back Your Life*, 2nd ed., by Ginny NiCarthy (Seattle: Seal Press, 1986). A book reported to be a lifeline for thousands of women since it was first published.

• *When Love Goes Wrong* by Ann Jones and Susan Schechter (HarperPerennial, 1992). An insightful guide for women who find themselves in relationships with controlling or abusive partners and don't know what to do.

• *Next Time She'll Be Dead: Battering & How to Stop It* by Ann Jones (Beacon Press, 1994). A battle cry to end the epidemic of violence against women and children. Covers its history, depth, far-reaching impact in America, and a host of practical solutions.

• *Defending Our Lives* by Susan Murphy-Milano (Anchor Books, 1996). A comprehensive guide to the options available to battered women by the founder of Project: Protect.

Chapter 10

HOME SAFE HOME

For most of us, home is the safest place we know. In fact, a significant part of our self-image and safety, or lack of safety, is tied to the physical environment where we live. Ask yourself, How do you feel when you come home? Safe and secure? Or is the place you inhabit no longer a safe haven for you and your loved ones?

We believe that basic, sensible home-security actions are called for in today's world, but that an extremist "fortress mentality" of locks, bars, dogs, and guns actually does little to increase *inner*— or *emotional*—safety and, instead, may contribute to a magnified state of hypervigilance, distress, and risk.

Imagine the safest possible home. What would be its characteristics? Surely not just external security, like a military camp, or bomb shelter. What would the safest home *feel* like when you walk in the door? When you fall asleep at night? What would give it that feeling of comforting safety?

To make your home safer, you might want more secure doors and windows, good outside lighting, and perhaps a large dog. But look deeper. What else would turn your home into a safe haven? Perhaps open landscaping or some added indoor lamps, cheerful colors, a window with a view, a balcony under the stars, pleasant music, the company of a good friend or pet, or the enticing, comforting smell of your favorite food in the kitchen?

Invest a few minutes creating a list of the qualities, or small changes, that might make your current home *feel* safer, starting right away, today. You may be surprised that many of the deepest safety features have little to do with alarm systems, guard dogs, or surveillance cameras.

To become more knowledgeable about home safety, we recommend reading one of the books in the resource section at the end of this chapter and spending a few evenings reviewing the various options for "hardening" the outer security of your home. Determine what makes the most sense for you. You might also be able to arrange for a free home-security inspection by contacting the crime prevention unit of your local police department. Most precincts will send an officer to your home to identify any doors, windows, or locks that need to be strengthened or secured.

Here are several of the obvious and not-so-obvious "home safe home" security-tightening measures:

- *Easily readable house numbers* so that police can locate your home in a hurry.
- A *wide-angle door viewer* or *peephole* in each exterior door.
- A hidden *security wall-vault* for storing valuables.
- *Solid-core wood or metal exterior doors and "safe room" doors* with stiff door frames and well-rated *dead-bolt locks* and *strike plates*.
- *Window locks* to windows and *security latches for sliding glass doors*.
- A *securely locking garage door* so that thieves and assailants cannot easily break in.
- *Full-coverage window shades or blinds* so that no one standing outside can see directly into your house at night.
- *Alarm system decals* and *Operation ID decals* (for marking valuables) displayed in prominent windows to discourage thieves.
- Trimming back shrubs to no taller than waist height and limiting trees around the perimeter of your house so there are *no dark hiding places* for an assailant.

- Illuminating each entrance area and walkway using *exterior floodlights with motion-detector switches* (so the lights turn on automatically when anyone walks up toward your house, apartment, or garage).
- Reliable *smoke detectors* in each zone of your home.
- A *large dog* as a family pet and deterrent to criminals. Studies indicate that homes with dogs are less likely to be targeted by burglars or assailants than homes without them.[1]

Consider Creating a "Safe Room"

It's shocking to realize that 37 percent of rapes occur at night between the hours of 6 P.M. and 6 A.M., usually in a woman's bedroom. Even though you may have an alarm system, another sensible strategy may be to make your bedroom into a "safe room." In doing this, the first priority would be to install a *solid-core door* and *strong door frame* with a top-rated (Medeco-brand, for example) *dead-bolt lock and hardened strike plate*. It also might be a good choice to mount a $29.95 Door Jammer security unit inside the door. The Door Jammer is easy to install and, when instantly activated by your foot, stops an intruder from entering your room unless the door is literally smashed down. The Door Jammer can also be used on exterior doors (see Defenders Network in "Safety Resources" at the end of this chapter). Next, purchase two *flashlights* with extra batteries and place them where they are easily accessible in the safe room. If possible, keep a handheld *cellular phone* from your car on a charger near your bed. Some security experts recommend this in case the phone lines to your house are cut by a burglar or assailant.

In her book *Not an Easy Target*, protection specialist Paxton Quigley recommends that, if you have young children, you make your youngest child's room the primary family safe room, because it can save time to bring everyone together in one child's room. "Let's say your husband is out of town and you're with your five-year-old daughter and nine-year-old son when someone breaks in. Here's what I'd do: I'd (take my cellular phone and) rush down the hallway, pull my son out of his bed, and run with him to my daughter's room, which is my family's primary safe room. I'd close the solid-core door, lock the dead bolt (and set the Door Jammer), then call 911 from a second (or cellular) phone line. I'd tell the police operator that my children and I are barricaded in the southeastern corner bedroom and that, when they arrive, I'll throw the front door keys down to them. For just such an occasion, I have an extra set of keys stored in a small yellow box in my daughter's room. (I have the keys in a yellow box so that they will be easily seen in the dark.) All this can be done in three minutes or less if you practice."[2]

Do You Need an Alarm System?

Many people believe that investing in an *electronic burglar alarm* will make them and their household members *feel* safer and sleep better at night. And it's true that research indicates that most robbers prefer to avoid homes that have them. A study in Portland, Oregon, showed that homes without alarms were *six times* more likely to be burglarized than homes with them.[3] The cost of alarm systems varies widely, and all homeowners with a burglar and fire alarm must be willing to cope with the irritation of false alarms. The truth is, even the best systems can malfunction or be beaten by criminals. In deciding on an alarm system, you might talk to local law enforcement agencies and get several qualified opinions as to the most cost-effective and potentially useful protection features in an alarm system for your home.

Establish a Basic Home Safety Plan, Then Put It Out of Mind

Take some time to review exactly what you would do if a criminal were to break into your home. If you live with others, discuss possible strategies and choose the best plan of action. Once this is accomplished, stop worrying and get on with your life.

SAFETY RESOURCES

• *House as a Mirror of Self: Exploring the Deeper Meaning of Home* by Clare Cooper Marcus (Conari, 1995). Practical examples for making a home *emotionally* safe.

• *Take Control: You Don't Have to Be a Victim of Crime* by Bob Portenier (Wichita, Kans.: Eagle and Beacon Publishing Co., 1994; available from Defenders Network, 800-800-1011). By a former convicted burglar, now president of Crimebusters, Inc. This book is filled with practical advice.

• *Not an Easy Target* by Paxton Quigley (Fireside, 1995). A simple, assertive guide by the personal security expert who has taught thousands of women how to protect themselves against attack.

• *Defenders Network, Inc.* (860 Cottage Hill Avenue, Mobile, AL 36693-3919; 800-800-1011; 334-661-1244; E-mail, defender@defend-net.com). A mail-order source for emergency safety tools such as door jammers, personal alarms, books, and videos.

Chapter 11

EMERGENCY SAFETY AWARENESS AND TOOLS

The readiness is all.

HAMLET

When your sense of danger rises, what are the most sensible options? When situations turn threatening or violent, what do the experts recommend? Will you actually be and feel safer if you arm yourself with protective weapons? For each of these areas, and more, this chapter offers a series of practical safety considerations and options for action.

PRIORITY 1: SAFETY AWARENESS AND PERSONAL FITNESS

Although a few of the following insights may seem obvious, because danger and crime are things many of us prefer not to think about, we neglect to plan ahead and end up in trouble. Our philosophy is to *become aware,* make *sensible plans,* and then *put an end to chronic worry* about safety. Here are several important considerations:

• *Maintain good physical conditioning and fitness.* Regular exercise builds muscle tone and endurance and sharpens the mind and senses. If you stay reasonably fit, trim, and limber, it also contributes to what, in chapter 2, we called "natural, confident movement." Human predators may often notice when a person seems to take good care of himself, and this may help imply that you can take care of yourself on the street. At the minimum, you might make it a goal to go for a brisk walk every day, adding a zigzag running pattern now and then, and perhaps do some mild muscle-toning exercises several times a week (see "Safety Resources" at the end of this chapter).

• *In general, wear comfortable clothing that does not restrict freedom of movement or your ability to run.* Choose comfortable shoes that are secure on your feet—if lace-ups, you might consider double-knotting them so they cannot easily come untied or trip you if you suddenly need to step aside or run from an assailant.

• *If you carry a purse, shoulder-strap models are usually best.* Walk with the flap side against your body and hold the base of the strap.

• *Whenever possible, walk with friends.* A study conducted by the San Francisco organization Community United Against Violence showed that walking with one other person reduced assault risk by 67 percent, and that two or more companions reduced it by 90 percent.[1] When it's not feasible to recruit friends to walk with you on errands or to and from a parking place, check other options. A number of police departments have established "senior escort services" and "parking escort services" to improve safety. It can also prove helpful to take a large dog with you, if you have such a pet. In many cases, the peace of mind that comes from having a dog outweighs the food and care required.

• *Make it a point to walk in well-lighted, populated areas.* The simple presence of bystanders deters many rapists and muggers.

• *If you are being followed on a busy street . . .* Cross the street and head in the opposite direction. Get immediate help, if needed. Walk up to someone, such as a shopkeeper or vendor, and begin to speak as if you were an acquaintance. If the person following you is not dissuaded and keeps getting too close to you, call attention to your situation so that others around you are aware of it, by continuing to move as you say assertively, "Stop following me. Leave me alone!" or "That man is bothering me. You are standing too close, move back!"

• *If you are being followed on a deserted street* . . . Go immediately for help, sensing the closest source of bright light and likely assistance. As Louise Rafkin, self-defense instructor and author of *Street Smarts*, suggests, "Are there storefront windows (with alarms) that could be broken? What can you do to make a scene and alert others? Don't lead an attacker to your home, especially if no one is home. In that case, you are safer on the street than you would be in your home or in an elevator."[2]

• *When you sense danger, walk in the street—on the left side, facing traffic—not on the sidewalk.* The shadows created by alleys, doorways, trees, and stairwells provide cover for assailants. When you sense danger and choose to walk in the street, where it is usually better lighted, with greater visibility and room to maneuver, it can increase your safety by, as some crime researchers call it, "putting the assailant onstage."[3]

• *Avoid alcohol—or use it sparingly.* Intoxication is a known risk factor for assault, disrupting wholeness of movement and impairing reaction time.

• *Whenever possible, avoid parking structures and park on the street.* The dilemma is that street parking increases the risk of car theft yet is often less risky for assault.

• *Remain especially alert while waiting for public transportation.* When waiting for trains, buses, taxis, and elevators, stay aware of the immediate area around you. Don't enter vehicles if you sense trouble. Trust your intuition.

• *Always have your keys in hand before you reach your car or door.* Pause for a moment or two as you near your car with keys in hand. Look underneath the vehicle and in the backseat to be certain no one is lying in wait. If anyone is loitering nearby who makes you uncomfortable, do not enter your car, home, or office; walk past and return later, with a friend. Even when everything seems clear, glance around before unlocking a door. Push-in robberies and rapes are increasingly common.

• *If it appears that a break-in has occurred, or that an intruder is in your home or place of work when you arrive, do not enter.* Examine the circumstances from a safe distance. If an unknown vehicle is parked on your property, note the make, model, and license number. Dial 911 and say, "Burglary in progress," which may get faster police response than a burglary that is already finished. Don't go inside until the police come or until you are certain the intruder has left. If you see him, take note of his escape route and description. Don't attempt to be a hero and chase after him. Cornered burglars are considered some of the most dangerous criminals.[4]

• *Consider a dog for companionship and protection.* Ohio State University researchers asked criminals what they would use to protect their own homes. The number one choice was a dog.[5] Even if you don't have a dog and don't choose to own one, consider placing a dog dish on your back porch and Beware of Dog sign on your garage or fence, along with security system stickers on doors and windows. These simple actions may deter some burglars or rapists.

• *Be security conscious when using automatic teller machines (ATMs).* At drive-up ATMs, keep your engine running, doors locked, and windows up at all times when waiting in line. When possible, leave room for a quick exit from line, should one become necessary. If an ATM is poorly lighted or obstructed from view, go to another (and report the problem to the financial institution that operates the ATM). Before unrolling your window to use the ATM, observe the entire area, and if you see anyone or anything suspicious, leave at once. Minimize the time spent at the ATM by having your card out and ready for use. Drive away immediately after completing the transaction. If anyone follows you, go immediately to a crowded, well-lighted area and call the police.

• *Deal assertively with obscene phone calls.* The obscene phone call is one of the most common acts of harassment directed at women. In one study, more than 80 percent of almost two thousand women interviewed by Canadian researchers reported that they

had received at least one obscene, threatening, or silently intimidating phone call. The typical obscene caller was an adult male—
apparently a stranger. But 10 percent of the women suspected
they knew the caller.[6] To deal with obscene phone calls: Hang up
immediately. Leave the phone off the hook. Get an unlisted number. Screen calls with a caller ID device or answering machine.
Arrange for call tracing. Report calls to the police and your phone
company.

• *Know what to do when faced with a snarling dog.* Although most
dogs are fairly predictable and can be friendly, a growling canine
can be a fearsome sight when it comes charging at you on the
sidewalk or in the park. In general, trying to elude a charging dog
by turning and running away or speeding off on a bicycle is risky,
often triggering a chase-and-attack intinct in the animal, and is
usually not recommended. Marc Paulhus is the vice president of
the Companion Animals Section of the Humane Society of the
United States. He explains, "Most dogs don't differentiate if it's a
car, truck, jogger, or bicycle that comes into their home territo-
ry. It's *movement* that makes a dog go for you, so the least amount
of running and aggravating you do, the better chance you have
that a dog eventually will leave you alone. Adopt a nonthreatening posture, then you won't be perceived as something to chase,
and the dog will lose interest."[7] Caution, not overreaction, is the
guideline here. Dogs are social creatures and will watch you for
cues. If a dog continues to approach you and is snarling or barking aggressively, Paulhus says to let it think it's in control. Slowly bring your arms up and cross them over your chest to protect
yourself, then remain very still. Once the dog has sniffed you and
its aggression is defused, back away slowly. Paulhus says outdoor
exercisers should carry a small stick for protection from dogs. "If
a dog attacks, the stick can be used as a target to distract the animal. As a last resort, you might have to use the stick to strike the
dog, preferably in the shoulder area or rump. Such a blow is not
likely to cause severe injury, but it will certainly cause a majority
of dogs to back off once you have established this dominance."
Red-pepper spray is recommended by some trainers (see upcom-

ing section of this chapter) or the Dazer by K-II Enterprises (see "Safety Resources" at the end of this chapter), a battery-operated, handheld device that deters aggressive dogs with the push of a button, emitting an unnatural, ultrasonic sound audible only to dogs. If you are unarmed and come under actual attack, you might try to "feed" the dog your jacket, umbrella, water bottle, purse, briefcase, or other object to bite instead of you. For further information, contact the Humane Society (see "Safety Resources").

• *In most cases, if a stranger comes to your door, don't pretend you're not home.* That's the advice of Louise Rafkin, self-defense instructor and author of *Street Smarts: A Personal Safety Guide for Women*, who points out that if you ignore the caller, you might find yourself face-to-face with a burglar. "If you are alone," she advises, "check the peephole and verify his or her identity and reason for being at your home. If you're still unsure, talk to the person through the door. Before answering, you might want to call out a phrase like 'John, I'll get it.' Be wary of 'emergencies.' If someone says he or she needs to make a call, do it for the person. Make the person wait outside while you call 911. Women are often used as fronts for this kind of break-in, because a woman is more likely to open a door to another woman. She may be working with a partner, hidden beside the house, or she may be casing your apartment for a future break-in. . . . Trust your gut feeling."[8]

• *If you're awakened by strange noises at night, rely on preplanned options.* All of us dread the thought of this situation. As discussed in chapter 10, "Home Safe Home," by taking sensible precautions—exterior lights with motion-detector switches, solid-core doors, good dead-bolt locks and strike plates, secure window locks, a dog in the yard or house—you make it less likely that a break-in will occur. Yet there is always a chance that a burglar, or rapist, might break in while you're home. In this case, your options include calling 911 and saying, "Burglary in progress," and giving your address, as you quickly gather up your loved ones and head to your designated safe room where you lock the dead bolt and Door Jammer. If you are alone and there is a safe exit point, you might choose to leave the house. You might also try to scare away the burglar—chances are, he's a teenager[9]—and if hallway lights flash on and off or someone shouts, "The police are on their way!" or a personal shriek alarm goes off, he may leave. Stay in the relative security of your "safe room"—where you can still try to scare away an intruder from behind the locked door. Use your bedroom phone or, better yet, your portable cellular phone, to stay in touch with police. Refer to chapter 10 for further details.

• *When you are away, make it appear that you're still at home.* Most of us have long heard that "lived-in" houses and apartments are less likely to be broken into than those appearing vacant, and it's true. After locking up, setting light timers, and making arrangements for newspaper, mail, and yard care, turn on a radio and consider hiring a trusted house sitter or ask a close friend to stop over periodically to check on things.

• *Use safety awareness when traveling.* When staying in a hotel, have a simple travel security plan. Most hotel guests are at a distinct safety disadvantage. Many people have access to your room. Two of the "emergency safety tools" (part three of this chapter) that protection specialist Paxton Quigley recommends for travel are (1) a small "door jammer" unit that securely wedges your door shut from the inside, and (2) a personal shriek alarm that can hang from the inside doorknob and will sound if someone manages to open the door, giving you warning and hopefully scaring the intruder away. If you're concerned about safety in your hotel, do your own security check before you settle in for the night. The door to your room should have a dead bolt lock and a peephole. The door to an adjoining room should also have a locked dead bolt. Windows that could be accessible from the outside should have a strong lock, and sliding glass doors should have a secure bar locking device. The hallways of the hotel should have no blind corners or dark foyers for an attacker to hide. Once in your room, never open the door to anyone, even a hotel employee, without first calling the front desk to confirm that someone was sent to your room. If you feel uneasy in a particular room, never hesitate to call the manager and ask to be switched to another floor.

• *Use safety skills against "road rage."* The lead story of a recent edition of the ABC television news program 20/20 was entitled "Road Rage."[10] A number of law enforcement officers and researchers were interviewed, and they confirmed what most of us have already realized: driving in daily traffic, always a safety risk, has in the past few years taken on an added dimension of danger and stress. Other recent studies confirm that an increasing number of motorists are driving aggressively, flagrantly disregarding common courtesy, traffic laws, and public safety.[11] They are speeding, tailgating, flashing headlights, honking, screaming profanities, running red lights, changing lanes without signaling, cutting so close to other vehicles that they almost ram them. At least fifteen hundred people are now killed or injured each year in the United States as a result of "minor" traffic disputes—congestion, merging, getting cut off, and so on—in which one of the drivers, a "road warrior," snaps from anger so explosive it pushes him over the edge. In many of these cases, potentially violent drivers are acting out unresolved conflicts elsewhere in their lives and displace their rage on other drivers. For some individuals, the car has become a provocative symbol of status, power, independence, and competitiveness. It seems that to road warriors, driving has turned into a forced form of crowding, of "fighting traffic," of waiting in line. Prof. Jack Levitt, an expert on violence, points out that the auto gives an illusion of privacy, of anonymity, even though a car is a powerful two-hundred-horsepower, three-thousand-pound weapon of steel that can go one hundred miles per hour. And more and more people are carrying firearms in their vehicles, which makes it all too easy to reach for a weapon in frustration, rather than in justifiable self-defense.

• *Keep your anger in check on the road.* One of the best defenses against road rage is to maintain sufficient emotional distance from other drivers. Remember they are people, too. Don't let rude drivers tick you off. Don't react by leaning on the horn or yelling. That will likely amplify the problem. Don't glare at offending drivers. Instead, stay alert and calm, and steer clear of the way of livid, anxious motorists, who seem to be more evident all the time. This is a technique long practiced by professional security drivers who are duty-bound to protect their passengers. They see everything around them but do not make eye contact with rude drivers. If another driver tries to provoke you, ignore it and remain calm, with no outburst of swearing or hand gesturing—it's simply too hard these days to predict the other driver's reaction.

• *Create a pleasant environment in your car.* Listen to music or radio programs that soothe rather than irritate or aggravate you.

The "What a . . ." Humor Technique

Whenever you find yourself on the streets or highways and feel a surge of anger or hostility, shift your attention. Ask yourself, "Are the other people driving slowly, or jammed in traffic, a deliberate affront to me?" Try to reframe the provocation and see things from the other person's view:

• *There's no need to get upset about this.*
• *Maybe he's angry about something else and is letting off steam.*
• *This could turn into a difficult situation, so stay calm.*

Finally, be sure you cope with any effects of antagonism. Relax tense muscles. Slow your breathing. Whenever possible, use humor. If someone has failed to signal and cut into the lane ahead of you during rush-hour traffic, you think, "What a clown!" Envision a huge bodyless clown face, red lips and nose pressed to the wheel, fumbling to steer down the road. Or, as suggested by psychologist Martin E. P. Seligman, Ph.D., if you say, "What an ass!" go ahead and visualize a pair of buttocks steering the car ahead.[12] *Decorate them with some feathers or glitter paint. Get into the image. Or visualize yourself as a bomb disposer. Your job is to slowly and cooly defuse the bomb of anger. Then move on with some kind of action without attacking. In conversations, you might rely on a short list of "defusing lines" tailored to reduce anger on the part of your spouse, boss, difficult coworkers, irritating neighbors, and children.*

For further anger-management options, see chapter 7.

• *Drive with your windows closed and doors locked.* This helps prevent an assailant from jumping in or snatching your purse at a light or stop sign. Once you get in your car, lock the doors and drive away. Don't waste time fishing for a CD or cassette tape, advises Helen Shatinsky, a crime prevention specialist with the New York City Police Department. "You can always do that later, when you're in a safe area."[13]

• *For women: Place a few props on the seat of your car.* If you keep a pair of men's basketball shoes and a baseball hat, or a man's tie and jacket, on the seat of your car, it can make criminals think your car is owned by a man. Self-defense instructor Nicole Reynolds of the San Diego–based Alternatives to Violence says to women, "When you're driving alone at night, tie back your hair, take off your earrings, and put on the baseball cap. Anyone who looks at you will assume you're a man."[14]

• *If you are being following in your car, don't go home.* Go to a police or fire station, a hospital emergency room, or another well-lighted and populated place. Once you arrive, if the pursuer is still following you, keep your doors locked and flash your lights and lean on the horn. Do not get out of your car to talk to an angry or violent person, even if it is an ex-spouse or friend. A number of people have been harmed or killed by abusive partners who have followed them in order to "talk."[15]

• *If you are outside your car and face an armed carjacker, give up your vehicle.* Remain calm and alert, assuring the carjacker with some statement such as "Okay, here are my keys." Drop the keys on the ground near the criminal and run in the other direction, using a zigzag pattern as discussed in chapter 6 and recommended by Hugh C. McDonald, former chief of the Detective Division of the Los Angeles County Sheriff's Department in his book *Survival.* As self-defense instructor Louise Rafkin observes, "If you have another set of keys on you—post office keys, unmarked office keys—and if there is help nearby, throw these other keys instead [at the carjacker] while you run to safety. By the time the carjacker figures out they aren't the right keys, you'll be safe."[16]

• *Prevent or resist an abduction attempt.* As noted in the scenarios in chapter 6, if you are approached by a man with a weapon and he orders you to go with him in your car or his, *don't.* He may try to assure you that if you go, you won't be hurt, but statistics indicate you will be far less likely to be fatally wounded if you flee, even from someone with a firearm, than if you accompany a criminal to a "secondary crime site." Some studies report that over 85 percent of all people abducted to secondary sites are seriously injured or killed.[17]

• *When buying your next car, consider security.* Many newer vehicles have keyless entry systems that automatically unlock the driver's door, trunk, hatchback, or all car doors from a distance, and "panic buttons" that set alarms wailing and lights flashing if you sense trouble as you approach your car.

• *Be wary of the "bump and rob."* It works like this: A car, usually with a driver and at least one passenger, rear-ends or bumps you in traffic. If you quickly pull off the road and get out to inspect the damage and exchange insurance information, either the driver or one of the passengers jumps into your car and drives off. Or worse, you are assaulted and robbed or raped. To help avoid such an occurrence, if you are bumped by another car, carefully look around without getting out. Be certain your doors are locked, and if *anything* about the other car or its occupants or the situation makes you feel uneasy, memorize or jot down the license number and make/model of the other car. Call 911 on your cellular phone, if you have one. Then signal the driver to follow you and drive to the nearest police station or a busy, safe, well-lighted area.

• *If you must get out of your car, take your keys with you and stay alert.*

• *When you come to a stop sign or signal, try to leave enough room to maneuver around other cars.* Stay watchful so you don't get hemmed in by other cars.

• *Keep all valuables out of sight in your car, and lock up, even in your own driveway or garage.* Many vehicle burglaries are the result of the robber's seeing something he wants inside your car. And some assailants would welcome the chance to hide in an unlocked car, waiting for the owner to return. Keeping valuables out of sight and locking up is prudent advice today no matter where you live.

• *Make certain all children wear appropriate-sized, federally approved auto safety seats.* Period.

• *If someone tried to force his way into your locked car, keep your hand on the horn to attract attention.* And then drive off if you can.

• *If you have a flat tire . . .* Call 911 on your cellular phone. If you do not have a cellular phone or sense that your breakdown happened in a dangerous area, drive slowly to the nearest safe place and seek help. This may ruin your wheel, but that's a small price to pay for your security and peace of mind.

• *Learn accident-avoidance techniques.* Safe, alert driving reduces your chance of a collision but can't entirely eliminate it. When another vehicle is hurtling toward you, you must react quickly and intelligently. To avoid one horrible accident, you may need to steer into another, less lethal crash. The rationale for accident evasion is to save lives. Here are the seven guidelines of the American Automobile Association (AAA) and National Safety Council (800-621-7615) as summarized in *American Health* magazine:

1. *Generally, veer to the right.* Too many drivers have it in their heads that cars belong only on the road—not lawns, sidewalks, or wide open spaces. But when a head-on collision is in the offing—and there are no pedestrians on the shoulder—make your car an off-road vehicle. Thousands of people have been killed or injured because they hesitated to leave the road and got hit head-on instead.

2. *Steer—don't skid—off the road.* Avoid hitting the brakes when you're on the softer surface; instead, emphasize steering your way out of trouble.

3. *If you have to hit another vehicle, hit one moving the same direction that you are moving.* If a car screeches to a halt in front of you and another car passes by on your right, hitting the moving vehicle on the right will produce less impact than slamming into the one that's stopped in front of you.

4. *If you have to hit a stationary object, try to hit a "softer" one.* Soft is a relative term here and includes bushes, small trees, wood-frame buildings, and even the fender of a parked car. *Hard* objects are massive and inflexible: for example, large boulders, brick walls, concrete abutments, and giant oak trees.

5. *If you have to hit a hard object (or soft one, for that matter) try to hit it with a glancing blow.* This reduces impact.

6. *No matter what, avoid hitting pedestrians, bicyclists, and motorcyclists.* This is a cardinal rule. If you hit these people, you will probably kill them.

7. *Try to never be involved in a head-on collision.* In most cases, you're better off being in almost any other type of crash.[18]

• *Put an end to stalking.* Experts project that 5 percent of the people in the United States—one out of every twenty of us—will be stalked at some time in their lives.[19] If you are being repeatedly harassed or followed, it's vitally important to contact your law enforcement agency and become informed about the antistalking laws in your area, which usually require, at a minimum, that you, the victim, *feel* threatened by the stalker's actions. Begin to document every incident, including the date, time, description of circumstances, vehicle license numbers, names of any witnesses, and any action taken by you. This documentation can begin to show a pattern of behavior that may warrant legal action to safeguard you from the stalker. Notify the police of each incident, requesting that they log your call, which may serve as important documentation later. If you know who the stalker is, you might have your attorney send a registered letter telling the stalker he or she must stop the behavior immediately, and that you will work closely with the police to secure an arrest if the problem continues. If the stalking continues, you may be able to have a judge issue a restraining order.

PRIORITY 2: YOUR VOICE

Studies have shown that when individuals are experiencing the heightened stress of an angry confrontation or imminent attack, they don't hear well. That is, they don't hear *what* is being said, only *how* it is being said.[20] Many assaults have been stopped with voice power alone. As stated in chapters 5 and 8, and in Dr. Deepak Chopra's foreword to this book, a battle scream that comes from deep within the very center of your being can startle or even intimidate your assailant, increase your power in protecting yourself, and may provide an extra moment or two for you to break free and escape.

Many women who "freeze" under attack have found themselves incapable of making any sound. Fortunately, this tendency can be overcome with some regular practice, and "voice power" and "verbal stunning" are features of some highly regarded defense programs for women (for a listing of these centers, contact SDE, P.O. Box 896, San Luis Obispo, CA 93406; 805-995-1224). Two studies, one funded by Brandeis University and the other by the National Institutes of Health, showed that the women in rape situations who were most likely to be raped were those who did not fight back.[21] Pauline Bart, Ph.D., a sociologist at the University of Illinois, interviewed ninety-four women who had been attacked: forty-three had been raped and fifty-one had avoided rape. The study indicated that, on average, the women who had avoided rape had used more and different strategies of resistance—fleeing, yelling, and fighting—than those who had been raped. The study also showed that the resisting women did not significantly increase their likelihood of serious injury by yelling or fighting back. Dr. Bart also found that most of the women who had remained passive and pleaded not to be harmed had, in fact, been raped. Of course, your own defensive approach must fit the circumstances and your abilities and choices.

Many of us are astonished to find how powerful our voices can be. In fact, voice conditioning is one of the best ways to break the "freeze" response. Once you yell, you breathe and this unfreezes your body. Some experts recommend what is called *verbal stunning*, in which you use loud, repetitive verbal commands—"Stop! Stay back!"—that are spoken as assertive ultimatums rather than passive pleading such as "Please don't hurt me" or "What do you want?"[22] Review the guidelines and options given in chapter 8.

Your voice is a safety tool in other respects, too. If an antagonist or would-be assailant *says* he has a weapon, but does not show it, and your intuition suggests there's a chance he doesn't have one, you might ask to see it. "This may seem unthinkable," says Judith Fein, Ph.D., author of *Are You a Target?*, "but many women get raped by men with nonexistent weapons." A study by Manachim Amir, one of the nation's leading authorities on sexual assault, estimates that rapists who claim to have weapons only display them about 20 percent of the time; that is, four out of five rapists might *not* have weapons.

PRIORITY 3: EMERGENCY SAFETY TOOLS

• *Should you train in "empty-hand" self-defense fighting?* As noted in chapter 5, if forceful self-defense responses are required, the most important thing is to have a *simple, preferred means of response* (with no intricate or complicated moves) that may give you an opening to resolve the situation or escape. The simple protective strikes recommended by various experts include an eye jab (full hand, angular, natural, sudden), an ear clap (with cupped-hand, circular-palm strike), a head butt (in which the top of your head is driven into the attacker's face), a forearm/elbow strike (usually delivered to the side of head/jaw or throat), a knee slam (to the groin), biting (the arm that is choking you or the hand clamped over your mouth), or a "power throw"/push/spin away (see upcoming section).

Once you've decided to learn to protect yourself with "empty-hand" martial arts, we believe it's essential to get the best possible training available. Before enrolling in a self-defense program, carefully and thoroughly check out the training approach. Ask if you can observe a class. Request written materials and interview current and former students. Does documentation exist for real-life assaults faced by students after they have completed the training? If yes, then what were the outcomes? What standards are used for instructor training? How are emotions dealt with in the classes? Do the instructors have crisis counseling skills as well as physical expertise? What measures are used to reduce the likelihood of injuries during training?

Mary Tesoro, author of *Options for Avoiding Assault*, suggests asking, "Are program goals fear-based (focused on hatred, competition, or vengeance), or are they empowerment based? How does the organization approach women's issues? Are women held in esteem, or are they considered victims to be saved by the instructors? Are professional standards and program policies in place for governing instructor-student relations? Ask how are mistakes handled in the learning process. Programs with the most effective training environments are those that embrace mistakes as *natural and necessary* elements of the learning process. . . . How a self-defense program views and handles mistakes not only influences how *well* students learn physical techniques, it will affect the degree to which 'shaming' is used as a teaching technique."[23]

Women might also check with local rape crisis centers and law enforcement agencies for their opinions about different self-defense programs.

• *Be prepared to use improvised safety tools.* An umbrella, cane, or walking stick may provide a slight—and we repeat, *slight*—defensive advantage through "visibility from a distance." This possible deterrent suggests to a would-be assailant that you're not an attractive target, especially if your "safety tool" is combined with a confident step that implies you don't need the device to help you walk. With training, these devices can be functional tools of protection, particularly against a snarling dog, as noted in part one of this chapter.

• *Pepper spray. Chemical tear gas* and, more specifically, *pepper sprays* are legal in most states. Pepper spray, which is made from hot-pepper extract, is a potent skin and eye irritant and makes breathing difficult. Many police departments now consider it more effective than tear gas, which will not stop drunken, drugged, or mentally unbalanced assailants or vicious dogs. Pepper spray usually will. It is sprayed from a hand-sized canister from a safe distance of at least several strides. These sprays apparently cause no permanent harm and, if sprayed correctly (which takes some practice), can temporarily disable many, or even most, unarmed attackers. It's important to note that pepper sprays, and all chemical sprays, are pressurized and may not be effective after the expiration date marked on the canister. Don't take sprays through airport checkpoints because you will be stopped and questioned. And, most important of all, do not let carrying a self-defense spray, or any other safety tool, lull you into a false sense of security. Effective spraying is not as simple as it may seem and requires some training in three steps: avoiding the line of attack, verbal stunning, and effective spraying technique. Ideally, a personal defense spray will be in your strong hand at all times when you might be at risk of an attack, suggest personal security specialists Tim Powers and Richard B. Isaacs, authors of *The Seven Steps to Personal Safety*. To make this more likely, they recommend purchasing a personal defense spray that is portable and fits easily in the palm of your hand, concealed from plain view, and with a key ring at the bottom for your keys. Mace-brand pepper sprays, for example, offer these features and use a simple flip-up top so that, even in the dark, you can better feel which way is the front. As you carry the personal defense spray, advise Powers and Isaacs, make certain that if you perceive a threat, you place your thumb on the spray's actuator button, ready to respond as necessary. It may be good practice to have the spray in your hand going to or coming from your car, coming toward the door when returning home, in elevators, in deserted public transportation exits, when walking or jogging, in parking lots, and any other place you might be at risk.[24]

• *Personal alarms, door jammers, and police whistles.* A *personal alarm,* or shriek alarm, is a pocket-sized device that emits an ear-shocking sound when triggered. As with police whistles, or with effective verbal stunning, a shriek alarm may be useful to break the "psychological holding mechanism" during the early confrontation stages. If used quickly and properly, any kind of noise alarm may—and, we repeat, *may*—distract an assailant, giving him an unexpected loss of control, drawing attention from bystanders or police, and hopefully providing you a brief chance to escape to safety. Some Neighborhood Watch groups use "whistle brigades," whereby members carry the same noisemakers and recognize its sound, quickly responding if they hear it. Another possible use for a shriek alarm, such as the palm-sized Personal Alarm from Defenders Network (see "Safety Resources" at the end of this chapter), which looks like a digital pager, is to hang it from the inside of your bedroom doorknob where it will sound if someone opens the door, awakening you and, hopefully, scaring off the intruder. The Sharper Image stores offer another shriek alarm, the SoundMate, which is ergonomically shaped like an egg roll and is grip activated.

Another simple safety tool is the Door Jammer (see "Safety Resources"), which can be installed on any solid-core bedroom door (a travel model slips beneath the door) and with a push of your foot locks or unlocks the doorway by wedging the door securely closed.

• *Power throwing.* This is one of the most innovative considerations for keeping yourself safe. If an attack seems imminent and you have no other means of protection, you might consider the sudden surprise and distraction effect of what has been called power throwing.[25] Even the well-regarded P.O.L.O. (Protecting Our Loved Ones) training programs for children (see chapter 12) teach throwing things as a deterrent to attackers. The P.O.L.O. instructors have students practice with tennis balls, but in real life they could pick up rocks, dirt, sand, or throw whatever they already have in their hands (such as a book, bottle of juice, pocket coins, a can of soda, shopping bag, or jacket). The technique— which requires practice—is to use *surprise*, the unexpected suddenness of standing relaxed and alert and then, without any warning, throwing and fleeing. The P.O.L.O. program teaches voice stunning while throwing the first object at the face of an assailant, then throwing a second object at the body and perhaps holding on to a third object as a reserve while you flee. This technique can capitalize on the two+ responses concept we discussed in chapters 5 and 6, in which you respond suddenly and with at least two actions—such as an unexpected voice command or battle scream *and* a power throw *as you simultaneously* feign a run in one direction, then flee in another.

• *Mini-batons.* One of the more popular personal protection tools is the mini-baton, or Kubaton, a device designed by a martial arts instructor, Shihan Tahuyuki Kubota. This mini-baton is a solid-plastic, ribbed dowel three and a half inches long with a key chain attached to one end. It is used by the police, prison guards, and other security personnel. However, it takes *many weeks of serious training* with a mini-baton to learn to effectively execute wrist and neck-lock takedowns and slashing attacks at an assailant's face and eyes. Without training, the mini-baton might serve as a visual deterrent when carried in your hand and may also make your keys easy to find in your purse or pocket. However, it's essential to realize that strikes or slashes to the face or other vulnerable areas not only require considerable skill and commitment, they can also cause great bodily harm. From a legal perspective, force that can cause great bodily harm or death is considered deadly force. "Because of this," explain Powers and Isaacs, "civilian use of the defensive mini-baton is at the same level of force as other impact weapons, and much higher on the force continuum than personal defense sprays or empty-hand techniques. The only justification of using defensive force of this magnitude (with a mini-baton) on another person is if you face the imminent likelihood of death or grave bodily harm from that person! Even though the use of a defensive mini-baton is a viable option to stop a violent attack . . . the personal defense spray should still be your primary emergency safety tool."[26]

• *Firearms for protection? It's an individual choice and serious responsibility.* Most of us would agree that, when in the right hands and used in a safe and legal manner, a firearm can be an effective deterrent to crime and may provide *distance defense.* However, owning a gun is a tremendous responsibility. Firearms are dangerous, lethal weapons that deserve constant respect, awareness, and safe care. This includes storing the weapon in a secure place, preferably a locking gun-vault or gun-safe where children and teenagers cannot gain access to it; taking instruction classes from qualified professionals; and then undergoing regular, ongoing practice. If you are unable to devote this time and attention to firearms safety, owning a gun may end up making you be and feel *less* safe, rather than more secure.

Should you own a firearm for protecting yourself and loved ones? Expert opinions are passionately split, and research statistics are similarly contradictory. Yet one thing that few would disagree with is that, without proper training, firearms are almost certainly more of a safety risk than a protective aid. In contrast, pepper spray can be relatively safe and easy to use. A firearm is not and requires considerable training. If you do decide to own a gun and choose to carefully use it as a safeguard, one absolutely essential point is to never, *ever*, point or shoot at anything you cannot clearly identify as an attacker who intends—and is capable of and in the process of—putting your life in extreme danger. As noted in chapter 5, this means that, according to the law and common sense, three criteria must be present to determine the judicious use of deadly force in personal defense:

Ability: The aggressor must have the apparent physical ability to seriously harm you.
Opportunity: The aggressor must be close enough to you to use his/her force.
Jeopardy: The aggressor must be acting in such a manner that a reasonable and careful person would believe the aggressor was about to attack an innocent person (you or someone else). In this case, the attacker is saying, "I'm going to attack you," *and* is big and strong enough to do it *and* is clearly moving forward to do it.

• *Unarmed against a handgun?* What about a situation of the gravest extreme, when it appears certain that you are about to be shot and killed? Is there any last-ditch defensive strategy you might try when facing the attack of an armed assailant? According to Hugh C. McDonald, former chief of the Detective Division of the Los Angeles County Sheriff's Department, "If a man is standing close to you, with a gun pointed at your chest . . . keep your eyes riveted on the gun and twist very slowly either to the right or left, talking all the time to the gunman. You will find that to twist your body just a few inches, twisting at the hips and not moving your feet, will take you out of line with the barrel opening so that if the weapon discharges, the bullet will miss you. . . . Remember to keep your eyes on the gun barrel. The man holding the gun will probably move it slightly. . . . [Move] as smoothly as you can. . . . It's up to you to calm him down. If you fail and he pulls the trigger, drop as though you were struck by the bullet; drop and lie perfectly still. . . . I know the steps outlined here may seem complicated and difficult. Believe me, they are not. They are simple, easy to master, and highly effective."[27]

SAFETY RESOURCES

Personal Fitness

• *Tactical Aerobics* by Tim Powers (Defenders Network, Inc., 860 Cottage Hill Avenue, Mobile, AL 36693-3919; 800-800-1011; 334-661-1244; E-mail, defender@defend-net.com). A fitness training video by a defensive authority and former police chief.
• *Health and Fitness Excellence* by Robert K. Cooper, Ph.D. (Houghton Mifflin, 1990). A comprehensive action plan for staying healthy and fit.
• *The Power of 5* by Harold H. Bloomfield, M.D., and Robert K. Cooper, Ph.D. (Rodale Books, 1995). Includes simple, practical health and fitness advice from experts worldwide.

Street Smarts

• *Crime Free* by Michael Castleman (Fireside, 1984). A highly recommended modern classic in the field.

• *Not an Easy Target* by Paxton Quigley (Fireside, 1995). An assertive self-protection guide for women.

• *Stalked: Breaking the Silence on the Crime of Stalking in America* by Melita Schaum and Karen Parrish (Pocket Books, 1995). Resource guide to a growing problem.

• *A Life Without Fear: A Guide to Preventing Sexual Assault* by Laura C. Martin (Rutledge Hill Press, 1992). This book began when the author's sister was raped and draws together a variety of strategies to reduce the risk of an attack.

• *Street Smarts: A Personal Safety Guide for Women* by Louise Rafkin (HarperCollins, 1995). A clear, concise set of tips for women written by a columnist and self-defense instructor.

• *Stopping Rape: Successful Survival Strategies* by Pauline B. Bart and Patricia H. O'Brien (Pergamon Press, 1985). A scholarly book filled with moving insights on women who successfully fought back against being raped.

Defensive Fighting Skills—with and without Weapons

• *Options for Avoiding Assault: A Guide to Assertiveness, Boundaries, and De-Escalation for Violent Confrontations* by Mary Tesoro, 1994 (an international publication of the nonprofit organization Personal Safety Options, P.O. Box 986, San Luis Obispo, CA 93406; 805-995-1224). This is an outstanding book, written primarily for women.

• *The Seven Steps to Personal Safety* by Tim Powers and Richard B. Isaacs (New York: The Center for Personal Defense Studies, 1993; available from Defenders Network, 800-800-1011). A straightforward approach to personal protection written by a former police chief and security expert.

• *Not an Easy Target* by Paxton Quigley (Fireside, 1995). A tough-minded self-protection guide for women.

• *Her Wits About Her: Self-Defense Success Stories by Women,* edited by Denise Caignon and Gail Groves (HarperPerennial, 1987). A memorable book on women who successfully defended themselves against violent attacks.

• *Protecting Children from Danger: Building Self-Reliance & Emergency Skills without Fear* by Bob Bishop and Matt Thomas (North Atlantic Books, 1993). An outstanding guidebook by two highly qualified protection specialists.

• *Model Mugging for Children* (Matt Thomas, Model Mugging Program, 859 N. Hollywood Way, Suite 127, Burbank, CA 91505). Based on years of teaching realistic self-defense to men and women, this program is taught by certified instructors for children and provides lessons in defense against adult "assailants" wearing protective gear.

• *Street Safe* and *Street Safe II* by Paul Vanuk (available from TRS, 2945 S. Mooney Boulevard, Visalia, CA 93277; 209-732-5317). Two video programs on basic, no-frills empty-hand techniques for self-protection.

Emergency Safety Tools

• *Defenders Network, Inc.* (860 Cottage Hill Avenue, Mobile, AL 36693-3919; 800-800-1011; 334-661-1244; E-mail, defender@defend-net.com). A mail-order source for emergency safety tools such as Mace-brand pepper spray, mini-batons, door jammers, personal alarms, books, and videos.

• *The Door Jammer* (Intertrade Marketing, 2145 Resort Drive, #204, P.O. Box 5164, Steamboat Springs, CO 80477; 800-800-1011).

• *The Seven Steps to Personal Safety* by Tim Powers and Richard B. Isaacs (New York: The Center for Personal Defense Studies, 1993; available from Defenders Network, 800-800-1011). Practical instruction for using personal defense sprays and mini-batons.

• *MSI* (800-446-6223). Makers of Mace and Mace-brand pepper spray.

• *Cap-Stun* (800-882-7011). Supplies pepper spray to more than two thousand U.S. police departments and markets a retail version for the public.

• *Citizens Against Crime* (800-466-1010). Markets a chemical-pepper combination spray with an ultraviolet dye that temporarily marks an attacker for police identification.

• *Quorum PAAL Personal Attack Alarm* (602-951-6990). A shriek alarm the size of a pager, with a pin-operated siren as loud as many burglar alarms.

• *SoundMate Personal Siren* (800-882-5778 or from the Sharper Image, 800-344-4444). This shriek alarm is grip-activated and looks like an innocuous plastic egg roll, but its 120-decibel screech is terrifyingly earsplitting and disorienting.

• *Dazer* (K-II Enterprises, 800-262-3963). A battery-operated, handheld device that deters aggressive dogs with the push of a button, emitting an unnatural, ultrasonic sound audible only to dogs.

• *Humane Society of the United States* (2100 L Street, NW, Washington, DC 20037; 202-452-1100). Information on dogs as protective pets and preventing dog attacks.

Chapter 12

TEACHING YOUR KIDS INNER SAFETY

Our children live in a more threatening world than most of us, as parents, can fathom. While we adults have the opportunity to head off to work and the ability to choose our social circle, children can't easily avoid crossing paths with teenage gangsters, wanna-bes, and every type of unsavory or dangerous element of junior society in schools, malls, amusement parks, and on city streets.

Los Angeles psychologist Rick Shuman, Ph.D., has witnessed the wreckage. In a recent feature article in *L.A. Magazine* entitled "Growing Up Scared," he says, "It really doesn't matter in what part of town a child lives—they're all shackled by psychological demons. Yet, the violence—sometimes just the threat of it—filters into the kids' psyches. For kids there's a profound feeling of vulnerability. They believe nobody can protect them. And when kids are victimized, they are no longer able to trust; they see the world as a menacing place. . . . They begin to hold their breath, waiting for the next bad event to happen. Many wind up in a state of hyperarousal. That means they are constantly on alert and in a chronic state of fear. Mundane sights and sounds are perceived as dangerous. . . . Those who walk around in this kind of stress disorder are far more likely to be violent or suicidal down the road."[1]

One of the most important realizations is that, by and large, *safety is instilled at home.* This is where life's central "safe haven" should be. And home is also where much violence, or numbness to violence, actually begins and gets embedded in mind and heart. That's the conclusion of many specialists who address the issue of violence in our society. According to Deborah Prothrow-Stith, M.D., former Massachusetts commissioner of public health, and dean of the Harvard School of Public Health, "I believe that if all the children born in America learned at home how to manage anger and aggression nonviolently, our homicide and assault rates would decline by 50 percent—maybe even 75 percent. The destructive lessons parents teach when they are physically and psychologically abusive to their children and when they allow their children to be physically or psychologically abusive to others, in conjunction with our society's glorification of violence, the ready availability of guns, and the drug culture, are an explosive combination that set our children up to be the perpetrators and the victims of violence."[2]

To begin with, when you start to explain safety rules to your young children, ages three to teens, make it a point to do it in a safe, supportive, nonparanoid manner, and avoid overly detailing terrifying situations. Your goal is not to frighten your child into safety—which, in many cases, is impossible—but rather to help your child become stronger, and more alert and confident, which will help him or her appear less vulnerable and less likely to be targeted for an attack. If, on the other hand, you scare your child, you may inadvertently trigger increased fearfulness and vulnerability to attack.

• *Do all you can to ensure that your home is a genuine safe haven for your children.* It is a parental obligation to do everything possible to provide a truly safe space in the home for each child. To do this effectively, you will need to learn what, exactly, helps each of your children feel the most secure. To review some of the basics on this subject, refer to our discussion in chapter 10.

• *Begin promoting emotional safety for infants and continue this until adulthood.* Healthy emotional development depends on reciprocation by parents and is harmed by indifference or clashing responses. It's the pattern of interactions that count. Early life experiences, for example, help form the brain's "calm-down" circuit, as Daniel Goleman, Ph.D., describes it in *Emotional Intelligence.* One father gently soothes his crying infant, another drops him into his crib; one mother hugs the toddler who just skinned her knee, another screams, "It's your own stupid fault!" The first responses are attuned to the child's distress and need of emotional support; the others are dramatically out of emotional sync. Between the ages of ten and eighteen months, a cluster of cells in the rational prefrontal cortex is busy connecting the emotional regions of the brain. These circuits appear to grow into some form of control switch, able to calm agitation by infusing reason into emotion.[3] Maybe it's parental soothing that strengthens this circuit and the neural connections that form it, so that the child learns to calm down. Stress and constant danger also re-form emotion circuits, centered in the amygdala, an almond-shaped, small structure in the brain whose function is to scan incoming sights and sounds for emotional content. Impulses from the eyes and ears reach the amygdala before the rational, thought-producing neocortex. Over time, unsafe or painful experiences trigger the amygdala to flood the circuits with neurochemicals of fear or hypervigilance. As a result, the cortex falls behind in development and has trouble assimilating such complex information as language.

It's up to each of us as parents to help our children express and cope with dangers and fears. Listen to your child's fears in a calm manner, without belittling or shaming them, or somehow implying that it's unnatural or babyish to have fears. Respect your child's fears, and do whatever you can to help protect him or her, in part by creating a "safe space" for discussing these fears and then by teaching appropriate actions. As psychologist Bruno Bettelheim has said, small children are frequently unable to express their everyday fears in words and can only do it by talking about fear of the dark or of some animal or some anxiety about the body. Be patient and understanding.

• *Do everything you can to ensure that your neighborhood is safe for children.* In many communities, parents now take pledges assuring other parents and kids that their home is free of dangers such as guns and other weapons, that visiting children will be supervised at all times, and that in the case of older kids, alcohol and other drugs will not be served or allowed in the home. It's essential that we watch out for each other's children and get more comfortable talking about such safety issues as children's fears, conflict resolution, media violence, anger management, all forms of abuse, community dangers, and gun safety. You may also find it helpful to form, or join, a Neighborhood Watch and a Child Watch group. Neighborhood Watch includes law enforcement officials, business owners, religious leaders, parents, and others joining together to strengthen neighborhood spirit and safety. The Child Watch program, which is coordinated by the Children's Defense Fund (see "Safety Resources" at the end of this chapter), enables community leaders to see for themselves how life is for children in their local neighborhoods.

• *Keep things very simple for children under three.* The big rule here is "Never go anywhere without asking Mommy, or Daddy, first," says James Garbarino, Ph.D., a leading violence researcher and director of the Family Life Studies Center at Cornell University in Ithaca, New York.[4] Use repetition and role-playing to help your toddler or preschooler understand that this one rule applies to *anyone*, whether it's her best friend or the stranger who invites her to pet a kitten or puppy.

• *Choose child care with extra care.* To minimize the risk of sexual, emotional, or physical abuse by caregivers, it's crucial to meet with all people who may have contact with your child, such as family members—husbands and sons, in particular—of care providers, and bus drivers and janitors. Fortunately, the National Child Protection Act, passed in December 1993, provides safeguards for families by making available to child-care organizations FBI records, if any, of a job applicant's history of child abuse *before* that person is allowed to be around children again. For more information, call NCMEC (see "Safety Resources"). If you are hiring a caregiver to work in your home, be certain to talk with more than one set of parents who have already used the caregiver, says Lewis Leavitt, M.D., professor of pediatrics at the University of Wisconsin Medical School in Madison.[5] Be sure to search for someone mature and responsible who listens and responds well to your child and appears relaxed, confident, and happy to be with him.

• *Safety is built on trust and open communication.* Dr. Garbarino points out that children get their first sense of community and trust from interactions *within* the family. Certain words and phrases in everyday life may help your child feel that the world is generally a good place to be:

> Let's talk about it. Tell me more.
> Sure I'm disappointed, but as long as you did your best, that's what's most important.
> I'm sorry I got upset.
> Maybe you're right. Let me think about it.
> That must have been difficult for you.
> Great job!
> I don't like how you're acting right now, but I care about you and love you.
> How do you think we can solve this problem?
> What do you think you would do differently the next time?
> I have faith in you to do your best and do the right thing.
> I hope you feel you can tell me anything.

• *Watch the way you vent anger.* Some families use verbal insults and humiliation in an attempt to get children to behave. Kids treated this way may close off their feelings, vowing that they will never be hurt by anyone again. Parents who try to shape behavior through shame may end up with a child who spends a lifetime tormenting others. It pays to remember that coarsening of language may be the first step toward coarsening behavior. A good family rule might be that anyone who speaks hurtfully to another person must make a donation to charity that goes into a "grouch box."

• *Teach your child by word of mouth and personal example to be cooperative, empathetic, and nonviolent.* A psychological void common to those who commit mean-spirited crimes—rape, muggings, child molestation, and family violence—is an inability to feel empathy. The inability to feel their victims' distress, fear, or pain allows them to tell themselves lies that encourage the violence. Children need warm, ongoing support from adults to develop foundations of empathy at a young age and, by late childhood, the advanced levels of empathy required to clearly sense another person's distress, such as feelings for the plight of the poor, the oppressed, the outcast, the battered.

In addition, how children cope with violence, and images of violence, is directly connected to their parents' coping strategies. According to Richard Weissbourd, Ph.D., who teaches at Harvard University's Kennedy School of Government and at its Graduate School of Education and is the author of *The Vulnerable Child,* "children are less likely to be scarred by violence when they are able to talk to an adult shortly after their exposure to it, when they have ongoing opportunities to discuss their fears, and when adults are able to give violence some meaning that is logical." To function effectively in adulthood, all children need to believe that there is at least some justice in the world, and that there is a reasonable moral order maintained by caring, trusted adults. It is up to each of us to provide this.

• *Pay attention to setting and enforcing reasonable limits.* Being too lenient with children can be as harmful to healthy development as being too strict. A parent's ability to set and keep reasonable limits may be at least as important in preventing and controlling violence as providing a home filled with caring, respect, and love.

• *Protect your child against media violence.* Over time, the incessant violent images on television and in movies can have a numbing effect. For some children, TV is "like a loaded gun in your house," warns Laurie Humphries, a child psychologist at the University of Kentucky in Lexington. "Even nonviolent kids absorb the expectation that shouting always leads to shooting, and that conflicts always lead to violence," says Dr. Garbarino. TV violence is made to look glamorous rather than gory. Images of violence can also be influential in a child's violent behavior as an adult. A University of Michigan study under the direction of Leonard Eron, Ph.D., a professor of psychology, followed the viewing habits of 875 eight-year-old boys and girls for one year in upstate New York. Over time, the study found that the more frequently the boys watched TV, the more serious were the crimes for which they were convicted by age thirty. Twenty-two years later, the more frequent viewers were also more likely to have abused their wives. Recent studies by psychologist L. Rowell Huesmann, Ph.D., of the University of Michigan, Ann Arbor, indicate that girls, too, emulate aggression seen on TV.

For these and other reasons, take control of your child's TV viewing. Plan a viewing strategy, choosing shows that best fit a set time limit—perhaps a maximum of one to two hours a day— and meet standards for nonviolence as newly endorsed by the television industry and the government. Make it a point not to use TV as background noise, and turn off the set when the news comes on, especially if you have very young children who are watching. View certain shows together and openly discuss what you see: "I didn't like the way that man talked to his wife and child just now, did you?" It's up to you to pay attention and run interference, since many children get confused about what's real on TV and what isn't, unable to wholly understand the difference. In addition, there can be lasting value in a home collection of videotapes of shows such as *Sesame Street,* since young children love to watch great programming over and over again.

• *Say no to violent play.* It's usually not realistic to put an outright ban on imaginary gunplay, since this can make such actions all the more attractive to a child. But be observant. If your youngster does natural pointing and pretend shooting with his finger and seems to sort out the good guys from the bad guys while playing and imagining, that may be a normal and acceptable thing. But if the gunplay seems very aggressive, it may need to be toned down, or if it persists uncontrollably, talk to a counselor.

• *Keep your home a healthy place for developing minds and bodies.* This includes ready access to wholesome, nutritious food, regular physical activity, plenty of sleep, and careful avoidance of such toxic contaminants as lead (which appears in some water sources from old pipe fittings and in the air from peeling lead-based wall paint, especially in older homes). The main problem is that lead has been linked in a recent study in the *Journal of the American Medical Association* to delinquency and antisocial behavior.

• *Use safety seats in cars and helmets and safety rules for bike riders.* Use age- and size-appropriate federally approved child-restraint safety seats whenever your child is in a motor vehicle, and insist that bicycle safety rules be followed and protective helmets be worn.

• *Make certain each child knows how to dial 911.* Keep your home address next to each phone so that in an emergency your child can tell the 911 operator where you live. Hugh C. McDonald, former chief of the Detective Division of the Los Angeles County Sheriff's Department, recommends posting emergency numbers in easily readable strips taped directly onto each telephone in your home and office.[6] All older children should memorize your address and phone number and have the pocket change to make a call home.

• *Set clear rules about opening doors.* Look first, never open to strangers. Decide as a family who is all right to allow to enter.

• *Be strict about safe phone use.* Kids should never say that their parents are not home. It may be a good idea to advise them to say, "My mom (or dad) can't come to the phone right now. Who's calling?"

• *Trust your child's feelings.* Most kids have good instincts and clear emotional reactions to family members, acquaintances, and strangers. If there is a fear of someone, parents should pay attention to this. Never deny or belittle a child's feelings. To be safe, each child must learn to trust his or her gut feelings.

• *Teach your children safe emotional and physical boundaries.* Use the insights presented in chapter 7 to help your kids understand what "safe distances" are when people approach them.

• *Teach children that it's not just "scary men" who could harm them.* Most young victims are harmed by people they know. An abuser or abductor could be a well-dressed or casually attired man or woman, even a doctor, priest, or neighbor. Children must understand that adults don't naturally ask children for any kind of help—whether for directions or to find a lost pet. Teach your child to be extra-alert and to stay away from any adult—including a woman or elderly person—who approaches offering anything or asking for help. The lure might be candy or "Come help me find my lost dog, Shorty" or a lost kitten or a nice woman who claims she's helping because Mommy was in an accident.

• *If a car slows down and someone asks directions . . .* Your child should know not to approach the car—and to back away.

• *Curbside safety.* Make it a rule that no child steps out from the curb into the street without holding the hand of a parent.

• *Never force a child to kiss or hug anyone, even a relative.* Trust the child's instincts, and teach them they always have the right to say no to hugs or touches from strangers and acquaintances.

• *Be clear about what touches are never okay from anyone.* Let them know it is illegal for any adult or other child to touch their "private parts"—the places covered by bathing suits—even during games. Let them know about the few exceptions to this guideline: supervised visits to the physician and bath time for small kids.

• *Have your child walk with at least one other friend.* When you give your child permission to visit a neighbor or to go on a short walk, he or she is generally safer if accompanied by at least one other friend or an older sibling. Children should learn to avoid taking shortcuts through alleys, deserted streets, parking lots, or fields.

If someone seems to be following your child, he or she should know to go into a store or business and ask the owner for help.

• *Teach your children how to deal with dogs.* When kids have problems with dogs, it's usually because they are scared or overfriendly. Ideally, children under seven or eight should not be allowed to be alone with a dog. Most kids are bitten by a dog they know. Once a child has your permission to approach a dog, he or she should know that a head-on approach may make a dog nervous, so it's better to move slowly to the dog's side and hold out an open hand, for sniffing. Pet the shoulder or under the chin, not on the top of the head. If a dog is running toward a child and barking, the best advice for the child may be to stand still and place something between the child's body and the dog, such as homework, a knapsack, lunch box, or bicycle. If a dog seems to come too close, the child might face the animal and back away slowly, avoiding eye contact and not smiling (some dogs think a smiling person is baring teeth and wants a fight). Or huddle down on the ground so you look like a log, rather than prey. To do this, have your child make fists and hold them up to their ears (since fingers and ears are easy for an animal to bite). Hopefully, the dog will quickly lose interest and leave.

• *Consider arranging for your child to learn self-protection skills.* When properly taught, training in the martial arts can be a valuable means of developing a child's confidence, strength, safety awareness, fitness, and agility. See the guidelines in chapter 11 on selecting a qualified, caring, nonviolence-oriented instructor.

• *Teach gun safety at an early age.* Children should learn early on to stay away from firearms and to steer clear of people with firearms, including other kids. Talk openly about gun violence on the news and on television.

• *Never leave a child alone in a vehicle.* It's an invitation to trouble.

• *Have a plan if separated or lost.* According to former convicted felon Bob Portenier, president of Crimebusters, Inc., and author of *Take Control,* if your child becomes separated from you in a shopping mall, or on the beach or in a park, make sure your child knows to go directly to a store, concession stand, or lifeguard station, and to not approach just "any adult" at random.

• *Make sure your child has a plan for running to safety.* Children should know that it is not safe to simply run from danger to "any adult" nearby. And it's not a safe idea to run home if no parent is there. Develop a plan for which "safe houses"—places where trustworthy adults are likely to be home—are in your neighborhood.

• *Ask "What if . . . ?" questions.* In *How to Raise a Street-Smart Child,* Grace Hechinger suggests a series of questions for young children:
WHAT IF . . .

1. We are separated in a shopping center, at the movies, at the beach?
2. You are lost in a department store, in the park, at a parade?
3. A stranger offers you candy or presents to leave the playground?
4. A stranger wanted you to get in his car?
5. A stranger started fussing with your clothing?
6. Someone you did not know asked your name and phone number?

• *Encourage children to use their voices for "safety power."* Instead of yelling "Help!"—which sometimes does not draw immediate attention because people think it's just kids playing—teach your

When You Argue in Front of the Children . . .

The truth is, at one time or another we all have heated disagreements in front of our children. Research suggests that when that happens, it's important to go through a visible resolution in front of your children. Children who view films of adults arguing are much less disturbed when the argument ends with a clear resolution in the spirit of friendship.[7] When arguments happen—and children are near enough to see or hear—make it a point to resolve the conflict, *clearly and* in front of your children.

children to shout "Help! Fire! Help!" Help them understand that adults are afraid of fire and will quickly come to the rescue. "Stop! No! Leave me alone!" is a verbal shout that should be given *before* an attacker closes within range of abducting a child. If the child *is* grabbed, then it's time to yell, "Help! Fire! Help!" again and add, "He's not my father! She's not my mother!"

• *No! Go! Yell! Tell!* Louise Rafkin recommends four defensive steps for children:

1. Say, "*No!*"
2. *Go!* Run away!
3. *Yell* loudly, "Help! Fire! Help!"
4. *Tell* a parent or someone trustworthy what happened and describe who bothered you.

• *Stay in touch with your child's world.* Always make a mental note of what your child wears each day, along with a running list of your child's friends and their family phone numbers. Initiate a safety policy at your child's school if one is not already in use. Example: Parents must be notified if a child doesn't arrive at school without previous notification, and children are allowed to leave school early only with a parent or with written parental permission given to another adult provided this adult can show proper identification. In addition, it's a good idea to keep a current identification folder for each member of the family, including height, weight, hair and eye color, dental records, a recent color photograph, professional fingerprints, and hand and palm prints. For assistance, contact Ident-a-Kid Services of America (see "Safety Resources").

• *Become an activist to ensure that in your home and in local schools all children learn to nonviolently manage conflict and anger.* When children learn to assert their needs and opinions without trampling on the rights of other people, when they learn to express their angry feelings without losing control or hurting others, they have mastered skills that enhance their lives and the life of the community. There is no better place than school, where diverse groups of people congregate, to learn these lessons.

Effective conflict resolution and anger-management programs for kids share some central themes:

- That conflict is a common part of everyday human interaction.
- That violence is not inevitable; there are choices.
- That when people take the time to explore their open and hidden biases or prejudices, they can learn how to get along with (and enjoy) people whose backgrounds are different.
- That most disputes do not have a winner or loser. Win/win is the ideal way to resolve most disagreements and conflicts.
- That children and adults who learn how to assert themselves nonviolently can avoid becoming bullies or victims.
- That the self-esteem of children will be enhanced if they learn to build nonviolent, nonhostile relationships with their peers.

SAFETY RESOURCES

Nonviolent Management of Conflict and Anger

- *Viewing Violence: How Media Violence Affects Your Child's and Adolescent's Development* by Madeline Levine Pluto (Doubleday, 1996). A thoroughly referenced guide to one of the most important issues for every family.
- Educators for Social Responsibility (ESR) (National), 23 Garden Street, Cambridge, MA 02138 (1-800-370-2515; 617-492-1764). ESR is a national nonprofit organization promoting children's ethical and social development through its leadership in conflict resolution, violence prevention, intergroup relations, and character education. It supports schools, teachers, and parents with professional development programs and instructional materials.

For readers looking for activities to implement the ideas in our book in the classroom, ESR offers curricula and other practical guides, including the following.

• *Teaching Young Children in Violent Times: Building a Peaceable Classroom* by Diane E. Levin, Ph.D. A practical guide designed for teachers from pre-school to grade three.

• *Elementary Perspectives: Teaching Concepts of Peace and Conflict* by William J. Kreidler. Activities for teachers and students, K–8, for exploring peace, justice, and the value of conflict and its resolution.

• *Conflict Resolution in the Middle School: A Curriculum and Teaching Guide* by William J. Kreidler. More than 150 activities to help middle school students effectively handle conflict at this developmental stage.

• *Making Choices about Conflict, Security, and Peacemaking* by Carol Miller Lieber. A two-volume high-school curriculum that explores the roots of everyday interpersonal conflicts and their relationship to local and international conflicts.

• Resolving Conflict Creatively (RCCP) National Center, 163 Third Avenue, #103, New York, NY 10003 (212-387-0225 phone; 212-387-0510 fax). RCCP, an initiative of Educators for Social Responsibility, is a pioneering school-based conflict resolution and intergroup relations program that provides a model for preventing violence and creating caring learning communities.

• *Deadly Consequences: How Violence Is Destroying Our Teenage Population and a Plan to Begin Solving the Problem* by Deborah Prothrow-Stith, M.D., with Michaele Weissman (HarperPerennial, 1991). One of the most valuable books of the past decade.

• *Emotional Intelligence* by Daniel Goleman, Ph.D. (Bantam, 1995). Contains a review of many successful conflict-resolution and anger-management programs for children.

• *Teaching the Skills of Conflict Resolution: Activities and Strategies for Counselors and Teachers* by David Cowan, Suanna Palomares, and Dianne Schilling (Palomares Publications, 1993; 619-698-2437). A clearly designed program for children in grades K–8.

• *Peace Patrol: Creating a New Generation of Problem Solvers and Peace-makers* by Eden Steele (Palomares Publications, 1994; 619-698-2437). Organizational guide: grades K–8.

• *Not in Front of the Children . . . How to Talk to Your Child About Tough Family Matters* by Lawrence Balter, Ph.D. (Penguin, 1993). A sensible guide from a well-known child psychologist.

• *The Optimistic Child* by Martin E. P. Seligman, Ph.D. (Houghton Mifflin, 1995). Dr. Seligman is professor of psychology at the University of Pennsylvania. This is a sensible program that helps parents safeguard their children against pessimism and depression and contribute to each child's lifelong safety and resilence.

• *The Enchante Children's Book Series* (415-529-2100). A collection of brightly illustrated books promoting *emotional literacy*—the ability to recognize, value, and appropriately guide and express emotions.

• *MegaSkills,* rev. ed., by Dorothy Rich (Houghton Mifflin, 1992). A widely praised guidebook with activities for children, parents, teachers, and others on confidence, motivation, effort, responsibility, initiative, perseverance, caring, teamwork, common sense, and problem solving.

• *Waging Peace in Our Schools* by Linda Lantieri and Janet Patti (Beacon, 1996). A model of emotional intelligence in schools.

General Safety for Kids

• *The Vulnerable Child: What Really Hurts America's Children and What We Can Do About It* by Richard Weissbourd, Ph.D. (Addison-Wesley, 1996). A scholarly and unforgettable discussion of the emerging risks faced by children and a series of practical options for solving them.

• *"Get Street Smart: A Kid's Guide to Stranger Dangers"* (Capstone Entertainment, 4685 S. Highland Drive, Suite 206, Salt Lake City, UT 84117; 800-636-2002). An entertaining collection of guidelines for children presented on videotape, audiocassette, and in activity booklets, a parents' guide, a poster, and colorful stickers.

• *Protecting Children from Danger: Building Self-Reliance & Emergency Skills without Fear* by Bob Bishop and Matt Thomas (North Atlantic Books, 1993). An outstanding book by two highly qualified protection specialists.

• *Model Mugging for Children* (Matt Thomas, Model Mugging Program, 859 N. Hollywood Way, Suite 127, Burbank, CA 91505). Based on years of teaching realistic self-defense to men and women, this program for children provides instruction in defense against adult "assailants" wearing protective gear. We believe that skills of realistic self-defense for children should be learned from well-trained, certified instructors who are chosen with care.

• *Home Organizer for Medical Emergencies*. A free guide from the American College of Emergency Physicians (800-446-9144; http://www.acep.org)

• *The Safety Zone* (Hanover, PA 17333-0019; 800-999-3030). A mail-order catalog of products aimed at promoting children's safety and family safety.

• *National Crime Prevention Council* (1700 K Street, NW, 2nd Floor, Washington, DC 20006-3817; 202-466-6272). Offers a full range of materials and resources about safety, including the Take a Bite Out of Crime series for children.

• *Safefit: Seatbelts for Kids* (800-370-5959). A simple, valuable safety aid.

• *National Center for Missing & Exploited Children* (NCMEC, 2101 Wilson Boulevard, Suite 550, Arlington, VA 22201-3052; 800-THE-LOST). Offers a toll-free hot line and pamphlets on child protection.

• *Ident-a-Kid Services of America* (2810 Scherer Drive, Suite 100, St. Petersburg, FL 33716; 813-577-4646). Identification assistance in preventing child abductions.

• *National Committee for the Prevention of Child Abuse* (332 S. Michigan Avenue, Suite 1610, Chicago, IL 60604; 800-55NCPCA). Information on local prevention groups.

• *Children's Defense Fund* (25 E Street, NW, Washington, DC 20001). Coordinates the Child Watch program.

• *National Foundation to Improve Television* (60 State Street, Suite

3400, Boston, MA 02109; 617-523-6353). Provides information on protecting children from TV violence.

• *P.O.L.O.* (Protecting Our Loved Ones, Bob Bishop, director; P.O. Box 150058, San Rafael, CA 94915; 415-453-9774; in Canada, 613-395-3639). Provides child protection and kidnap protection services, audiovisual materials, safety and security equipment, and a variety of other special services and products.

Chapter 13

SAFETY RESOURCES FOR
TEENAGERS AND COLLEGE
STUDENTS

It is our opinion that every teenager and college student should read a variety of safety resources, including those on the nonviolent management of conflict and anger. Here are several added areas of safety concern about teenage and campus security:

• *Do not tolerate any kind of sexual harassment or violent behavior.* Violence in teenage and college-age relationships has emerged as a serious problem. No one should tolerate abusive behavior of any kind. Demeaning insults, lewd taunts, or striking another person are all attempts to dominate or control, and they are always wrong. Parents should give immediate support to a child who has been harassed or attacked, rather than shaming or condemning them for going out with the "wrong" people. All teens should be primed to immediately and safely leave the scene of potentially violent situations, such as fights, dangerous parties, and crime activities.

• *Protect yourself from sexual attacks.* A recent survey indicated that one out of every four college women have survived a rape or rape attempt, and nearly 85 percent of these women knew their attackers.[1] You have the right to question any stranger in your residence building or hall, asking, "Whom are you here to see?" which makes the person know you are aware of his presence. If the stranger has no bona fide explanation or in any way appears threatening or nervous, get help immediately from your dorm mates, resident manager, police, or campus security. Be certain you lock your door even if you're leaving only for a few minutes. If you need to study in offices, laboratories, or other isolated areas of the campus, try to do it with trusted friends rather than alone, and follow the safety procedures noted in chapter 14 on workplace security—checking, for example, to see that all access doors are locked. If you still feel uncomfortable, notify the campus police where you will be studying, ask about police escort services for walking after dark across campus, and consider carrying pepper spray (and practice so you know how to use it effectively) and making good use of a portable Door Jammer and personal alarm. These and other "emergency safety tools" are described in chapter 11.

• *Be adamant about firearms safety.* It's imperative that teenagers and college students steer clear of firearms and tell a trusted adult about any situation that feels dangerous, even if you are told by the armed individuals not to tell. If a teenager is too frightened to tell, parents should let them know that it's okay to do so anonymously, such as by writing a letter or note and then mailing or delivering it to someone who can deal with the potentially dangerous situation.

• *Abstain from sex or, if appropriate, practice safe sex.* Intimate relationships depend *at all times* on a genuine sense of safety and trust. This requires that you and your partner be honest and clear with each other every time you are making sensual contact—not just in body but in your minds and shared words—about what pleases and what displeases or hurts. This requires sharpening your skills in listening to your inner signals. Limits can be gently set but must be firmly respected. A sense of safety also depends on the feeling that we, women and men, each create for ourselves by refusing to be involved with a partner who breaches our trust or attempts to hurt us. If a young man or woman is old enough for sex, and if it's appropriate—depending on age, family values, religious constraints, and other factors—then the guidelines for safe sex take on special importance. The latest medical guidelines should be readily available from your physician or from school health service departments.

SAFETY RESOURCES

• *Options for Avoiding Assault: A Guide to Assertiveness, Boundaries, and De-Escalation for Violent Confrontations* by Mary Tesoro, 1994 (an international publication of the nonprofit organization Personal Safety Options, P.O. Box 986, San Luis Obispo, CA 93406; 805-995-1224). This is an outstanding book, written primarily for women.

• *The Seven Steps to Personal Safety* by Tim Powers and Richard B. Isaacs (New York: The Center for Personal Defense Studies, 1993; available from Defenders Network, 800-800-1011). A straightforward, practical approach to personal protection written by a former police chief and security expert.

• *Not an Easy Target* by Paxton Quigley (Fireside, 1995). A tough-minded self-protection guide for women.

• *The National Victim Center* (800-FYI-CALL) offers a "College Security Questionnaire for Parents and Students" and an information packet on preventing campus crime.

• *Safe Schools* (Jeff Marschner, John F. Kennedy High School, 6715 Gloria Drive, Sacramento, CA 95831; 916-433-5236). Parents on Campus was established by parents to promote campus safety through the stabilizing influence of a positive parent presence on campus every day. Teams of parents, walking the halls in pairs, serve as deterrent to negative behavior. Parents also learn firsthand what high school is like today—and students see vivid proof that campus safety and their education are high priorities.

Nonviolent Management of Conflict and Anger

• *Deadly Consequences: How Violence Is Destroying Our Teenage Population and a Plan to Begin Solving the Problem* by Deborah Prothrow-Stith, M.D., with Michaele Weissman (HarperPerennial, 1991). A scholarly plan to rebuild safety in America.

• *Emotional Intelligence* by Daniel Goleman, Ph.D. (Bantam, 1995). Memorable insights into the many ways that recognizing, valuing, and managing emotions is essential to a safe, successful life.

Chapter 14

FEELING SAFER AT WORK

In recent years, increased violence has been spreading through our places of work and business. Physical assaults, threats, verbal abuse, and other forms of violence are on the rise. And evidence from medical science indicates that even threats and harassment can leave us emotionally injured and chronically distressed. According to the U.S. Department of Justice Crime Victimization Survey (released in 1994), an estimated 1 million crimes are committed each year at work. The Northwestern National Life Insurance Survey (for the year ending June 30, 1993) reported that one out of every four employees was harassed (16 million workers), threatened (6 million workers), or attacked (2 million workers). A 1994 Gallup Poll Survey indicated that two out of three employees did not feel secure at work. In all, workers and managers who have experienced an increased sense of danger, or the fear of violence, are firmly dedicated to seeing the fear and violence end and must work together to create safer, more secure job sites.

According to Joseph A. Kinney, founder and director of the National Safe Workplace Institute and author of *Violence at Work,* "The violence that we are now experiencing in our workplaces has its roots in several sources. The entertainment media, for example, have depicted the use of guns and violence in glamorous fashion and have made criminals into heroes, turning standards upside down. We are also a society that has developed a high attachment to work. For many, success at work has become equivalent to success in life. Moreover, there has been a steady decline, especially among men, in the anchors that serve to stabilize us in life—family, church, and community, among others. When we get in trouble, we reach for these anchors to pull us through crisis. If they are not there, we will struggle and some of us will fail." Kinney suggests an organizational model to identify and curb workplace violence:

1. Identify vulnerabilities.
2. Develop early-intervention systems.
3. Prepare a threat protocol.
4. Establish a method for assessing threats.
5. Organize to manage complex threats and provide protective services.
6. Develop feedback mechanisms to assess performance and detect high-risk individuals.

A person who threatens a worker or manager is a safety hazard who must immediately and effectively be dealt with. Although most threats do not result in violence, management must respond as if violence were a real possibility, whether the threat is *direct* ("I'm going to kill you"), *conditional* ("If you report me, I will hurt you"), or *veiled* (subtle threat messages and body language). The primary responsibility for workplace safety rests with the employer and announced—and adhered to—policies and procedures of the organization. Here are several basic action steps you might take as an individual:

• *Maintain clear physical and emotional boundaries in the workplace and prevent sexual harassment.* One of the pillars of personal safety is establishing and maintaining borders of comfort between you and other people. Some of your coworkers may, in fact, become good friends over time, and you will not feel unsafe when they approach you. Other people, however, can be distressing or threatening by their nearness. Follow the guidelines in chapters 7 and 8 for keeping these people at a safe distance.

• *Do whatever you can to create a safer space for yourself at work.* Refer to the preceding chapters and make a personal list of the steps you might take to make your work area safer. These actions might include repositioning your work station or desk so that you have a clearer vision of people approaching you; alerting security personnel to beef up security at exists, doorways, or stairwells; improving the lighting in remote or darkened hallways and storage rooms; and reviewing your verbal skills to more assertively put an end to perceived harassment and more effectively defuse anger and resolve conflicts. Other workplace considerations include:

• *Don't engage in workplace conversations that make you uncomfortable.* Excuse yourself and walk away. If necessary, say, "I'm not comfortable discussing this."

• *Be firm and confident, and do not permit any kind of sexual harassment.* Sexual harassment—defined as any unwelcome sexual contact, whether physical, emotional, or verbal, that is a term or condition of employment or that creates an intimidating, hostile, or offensive workplace—is illegal and is a form of violence. Sexual harassment is often a precursor to assault, rape, or murder in the workplace. Workers and managers have the right to a safe and secure workplace that is free from unwanted advances and implied or actual threats related to those advances. A harasser can be a boss, employee, coworker, customer, client, supplier, or stranger. If you feel you are being harassed, trust your instincts and take action. Firmly tell the offender to stop. Begin a written record of the offensive behavior, noting the date, time, witnesses (if any), and description of each incident. Keep this document at home. Tell a third party and gather support. Consider informing the offender in writing about the offensive behavior. If the harassment continues, pursue legal action (see "Safety Resources" at the end of this chapter).

• *You can keep your personal life private.* You are under no obligation at work to reveal anything about your personal life, marital status, values, beliefs, or sexual preference to employers, potential employers, or anyone else in a workplace. If asked, reply that you would prefer to keep your personal life private.

• *Be alert for anger and hostility—and de-escalate arguments wherever this is appropriate.* High-stress jobs generate a heightened potential for violence. Watch for signs of unusual or threatening behavior in coworkers, employees, bosses, customers, or suppliers that might lead to obsession or violence. Many workplace offenders show erratic mood swings and sullen or paranoid behaviors prior to making attacks. Trust your gut feelings and get help—from coworkers, security, and the police—if you sense there is a threat of violence. Make certain your company or organization has clear plans for dealing with violent or erratic behavior (see "Safety Resources"). Try to maintain an avenue of escape from your work area so that you can leave at the very first sign of impending violence, even if this seems premature. Don't take chances. Use the guidelines in chapters 7 and 8 for dealing with angry people. If it seems appropriate, you might say, "Calm down. I'll talk with you."

• *Use "safety sense" when working late or shift work.* One of the important things here is to be certain that others—a trusted coworker, friend, or building security personnel—know where you are. If you work alone, consider bringing a handheld cellular phone with you so if you hear troubling noises or a threatening person you can immediately call 911 no matter where you are. Check all entrances and exits to make certain they are locked, and if feasible and acceptable to your employer, you might also secure doors with a personal alarm and Door Jammer. Keep the work areas well lighted. If possible, try not to work at night in an area that can readily be viewed from outside through a window.

SAFETY RESOURCES

Preventing Workplace Violence

• *The National Safe Workplace Institute* (3009 Bishops Ridge Court, Monroe, NC 28110; 704-289-6061). Offers books and programs.

• *Violence at Work: How to Make Your Company Safer for Employees & Customers* by Joseph A. Kinney (Prentice Hall, 1995). A thorough and comprehensive guidebook from the founder and executive director of the National Safe Workplace Institute. Highly recommended.

• *Ticking Bombs: Defusing Violence in the Workplace* by Michael Mantell with Steve Albrecht (Irwin, 1994). Covers the issues of prevention, response, and recovery and offers unique techniques developed for the safest possible interventions.

• *The Nonviolent Crisis Intervention Video Series* (National Crisis Prevention Institute, Inc., 3315-K North 124th Street, Brookfield, WI 53005; 800-558-8976). A video series and catalog of resources for the safe management of disruptive and assaultive individuals.

• *Taking Charge of Organizational Conflict: A Guide to Handling the Demands of Human Interaction* by David Cowan (Palomares Publications, 1994). A guide for educators.

Ending Sexual Harassment

• *9 to 5, the National Association of Working Women* (800-522-0925). A national hot line. If you are being harassed, call for free advice.

• *Sex, Power, and Boundaries: Understanding and Preventing Sexual Harassment* by Peter Rutter, M.D. (Bantam, 1996). An excellent resource and action guide.

• *The Nine to Five Guide to Combating Sexual Harassment* by Ellen Bravo and Ellen Cassedy (Wiley Books, 1992). An excellent source of candid advice on harassment in the workplace.

• *Sexual Harassment on the Job: What It Is and How to Stop It* by

William Petrocelli and Barbara Kate Repa (Nolo Press, 950 Parker Street, Berkeley, CA 94710, 1992). A guidebook written by two attorneys.

Emergency Safety Tools

• *Defenders Network, Inc.* (860 Cottage Hill Avenue, Mobile, AL 36693-3919; 800-800-1011; 334-661-1244; E-mail, defender@defend-net.com). A mail-order source for emergency safety tools such as Mace-brand pepper spray, door jammers, and personal alarms.

Chapter 15

HEALING THE EMOTIONAL WOUNDS OF VIOLENCE

The last of the human freedoms is to choose one's attitude
in any given set of circumstances, to choose one's own way.

VIKTOR FRANKL, M.D., Holocaust survivor

Despite the best safety precautions, a traumatic assault can strike
suddenly. And its emotional pain can last for months, or even
years. No matter how healthy you are, grief from a traumatic
attack can cause profound distress that's as painful as any experience life brings. However, difficult as it is, grieving can't be avoided or hurried. It's natural healing that takes time and patience.

After an attack, grief usually runs a long and tortuous route of
emotions—sadness, hopelessness, fears, anxiety, sleep disorders,
loss of appetite, crying, deep occupation with objects and loca-
tions associated with the attack and the person or job that was
lost, and crushed hopes or dreams of that person or experience.
Yet all of these emotions and thoughts are normal, healthy
responses, says Camille Lloyd, Ph.D., a professor of clinical psychiatry at the University of Texas Medical Center at Houston.[1]
It's important to recognize this since self-doubt about coping can
contribute to depression. And grieving signifies how deeply
we've been able to care about ourselves, another person, or an
experience.

Coping with the aftermath of violence, and the associated

pain, shame, loss, and heightened sense of vulnerability, is inherently turbulent and complex. One of the well-referenced models of recovery centers on several basic steps:

1. Establish a "safe space" within yourself and your environment.
2. Experience grieving, including remembrance and mourning.
3. Reconnect with "normal" everyday life with an increased awareness of safety.

1. ESTABLISH A "SAFE SPACE" WITHIN YOURSELF AND YOUR ENVIRONMENT

Recovering from a violent assault first requires the establishment, or reestablishment, of safety, says Judith Lewis Herman, M.D., an associate clinical professor of psychiatry at Harvard Medical School and director of training at the Victims of Violence Program at Cambridge Hospital, and the author of *Trauma and Recovery: The Aftermath of Violence.* "The first task of recovery is to establish the survivor's safety," explains Dr. Herman. "This takes precedence over all others, for no other therapeutic work can possibly succeed if safety has not been adequately secured. No other therapeutic work should even be attempted until a reasonable degree of safety has been achieved."[2]

Survivors often feel unsafe in their bodies. Their emotions and thinking feel out of control. They also feel unsafe in relation to other people. These posttraumatic stresses can be treated in a variety of ways, such as with medication to reduce hyperactivity and hyperarousal, and behavioral therapies such as medication, relaxation, and vigorous exercise, to help manage stress. Psychological trauma can be addressed with cognitive and behavioral approaches, such as the recognition and naming of symptoms, daily logs to chart symptoms and adaptive responses, the identification and implementation of manageable "homework" assignments, and specific, comprehensive safety plans—at home and when traveling outside the home. The traumatized person needs a guaranteed *safe refuge*, either at home or in a secured shelter. The damage to safety in relationships must be addressed with progressive interpersonal strategies, such as the gradual development of a trusting relationship in psychotherapy or counseling, and social strategies that mobilize the survivor's natural support system of family and friends. She may seek to surround herself with caring, protective people at all times or may want to isolate herself completely, at least for a while. The task of reestablishing safety is especially complex when the survivor is still involved in a relationship that has been abusive in the past. The potential for violence should always be considered, even if the survivor insists she is no longer afraid.

Establishing a safe environment requires more than just the mobilization of caring people. It requires the assessment of continued threat and exactly what precautions are sensible or necessary.

2. EXPERIENCE GRIEVING, INCLUDING REMEMBRANCE AND MOURNING

One may not reach the dawn save by the path of the night.

KAHLIL GIBRAN

In the second phase of recovery from a traumatic attack, the survivor needs to find ways to tell the story of the trauma, completely, in depth and with detail. This work, as Dr. Herman observes, actually transforms the traumatic memory, so that it can be integrated into the survivor's life story.

Each of us experiences grief differently, but certain emotions are common. Denial, anger, and symptoms of depression (loss of appetite, sleep problems, and difficulty accomplishing daily activities) are stages that we each pass through. And it's important to recognize that every mourning takes time. It's never easy to fully acknowledge, for example, the deep value of a dream or self-image that has been lost, or of a loved one who has died. Sometimes it takes many months to pass through the acute stage of grieving.

• *Find strength in simple daily rituals.* According to Steven Wolin, M.D., a psychiatrist at George Washington University, "Resiliency is the capacity to rise above adversity and forge lasting strengths in the struggle. . . . Even in the face of serious trouble, there are things families can do with protecting, cherishing, altering, and strengthening family rituals. In the face of trouble, families can evaluate, alter, and improve family rituals, adopt new ones, and revive old ones."[3]

Over time, these daily rituals might include some of the basics such as regular meals, between-meal snacks, drinking plenty of water, getting enough rest, and reducing tensions with whatever seems appealing—a warm bath, sipping a favorite tea, listening to music, watching positive television programs or movies, and in general, finding sensible ways to comfort your mind and body. Whenever possible, immerse yourself in activities that provide an outlet for your physical and emotional tensions at the same time they begin to relax you and gradually strengthen your inner resources. Examples are music, sports, walking, movies, yard work or gardening, and hobbies.

• *Express your grief and anger through daily journaling.* There is growing evidence—from studies involving thousands of people of all ages and backgrounds—that a significant emotional uplift and healing effect can come from spending as little as five to fifteen minutes a day for several days writing in a private journal about whatever issues and experiences are getting you down.[4]

"We encourage individuals to write for themselves [keeping the words anonymous and confidential] as opposed to writing for someone else," say two leading researchers in the field, James W. Pennebaker, Ph.D., and Martha E. Francis, Ph.D., of the department of psychology at Southern Methodist University in Dallas. "The benefits of writing lie in the act of letting go and expressing those deepest thoughts and feelings surrounding a personal upheaval. . . . By setting aside [up to] fifteen to twenty minutes a day for several days to write down their deepest thoughts and feelings surrounding disturbing issues, individuals may gain new understanding and insight about their personal lives and, at the same time, foster their own physical health."[5] A similar benefit may come from talking, at the right time and in clear, honest ways, with a trusted friend.

• *Seek times of solace, and draw help from family and friends.* In general, survivors of traumatic attack should be encouraged to turn to others for support, but considerable care must be taken to ensure that they choose people they can truly trust. Family members, friends, lovers, and close friends may be of immense help, or they may interfere with recovery or be dangerous themselves. A careful evaluation must be made of each important relationship in a traumatized person's life, assessing each as a source of potential protection, emotional support, practical help, and also as a possible source of danger.

Identify whatever feels best to you for finding solace during times of grief. For some of us, spending time outdoors in a natural setting is uplifting. For others, hurts are resolved best by browsing through photo albums or old letters. Express your feelings of grief—this may mean talking about your grief with loved ones, close friends, and perhaps your family physician or counselor. In chapter 7, we discussed several ways to safely confide in others. You might also find it beneficial to talk with those who have experienced similar losses—by joining an organized support group (see "Safety Resources" at the end of this chapter).

Notice whenever you feel like blaming yourself for the trauma you are coping with. "If unchecked," explains psychologist Julius Segal, Ph.D., author of *Winning Life's Toughest Battles*, "our natural tendency to blame ourselves for our suffering becomes unreasonable and immobilizing. The danger is especially great because our readiness to indict ourselves is often reinforced by the attitudes of people around us."[6] Therefore, be certain to assure your loved ones and friends that it's all right for you to take time to work through this—and that it's not helpful for them to sympathize or inadvertently accentuate your feelings of self-blame by saying things like "Oh, you poor thing—it's just been one problem after another!" or "You've spent long enough feeling sorry for yourself" or "It's time to get on with your life" or "You'll get over it soon."

Know when and how to get professional help for recovery from traumatic assault. In many, even most cases of recovery from a traumatic assault, professional counseling is vital. How much is your distress adversely affecting your personal life, your family, or your work? Is your grief getting in the way of your ability to function? It can be very important to seek help from a psychologist, psychiatrist, or other qualified counselor:

1. For psychiatrists, the American Psychiatric Association (1400 K. Street, NW, Washington, DC 20005; 202-682-6142). The APA will provide information brochures on a variety of mental health topics and one explaining how to select a therapist. Callers are referred to the local district office where you will talk with a psychiatrist. The nature of each caller's problem is assessed, and a referral is then made to one or more practitioners in your area. An effort is made to match the caller with a therapist who has experience with the caller's problem or issue.

2. For psychologists, the American Psychological Association (1200 17th St., NW, Washington, DC 20036; 202-336-5500). The APA will refer a caller to the state branch office where the caller's name and number are taken. A referral coordinator returns the call and can provide a list of qualified psychologists and mental-health centers in the caller's local area.

3. For clinical social workers, the National Association of Social Workers (7981 Eastern Ave., Silver Spring, MD 20910; 202-408-8600). Provides callers with the names of members in its Clinical Registry and makes referrals to members in the caller's local area.

4. For marriage and family therapists, the American Association of Marriage and Family Therapy (1717 K. Street NW,

Suite 407, Washington, DC 20006; 202-452-0109). Makes referrals to members in caller's local area.

TAKE A "DEPRESSION TEST"—AND GET HELP IF YOU NEED IT

Everyone feels sad or hopeless from time to time, although even during a down mood—sometimes referred to as common, everyday depression—most of us still feel some control over our emotions and realize that the sad feelings will eventually pass. But people with serious depression—often referred to as major depression or clinical depression—may feel that "a terrible heaviness and hopelessness has descended that they are powerless to prevent or resist, and that it will go on and on. The intensity of despair that some people can feel in serious depression goes far beyond the lows of normal life. It destroys the person's ability to continue in life's usual roles and can lead to utter confusion, mental paralysis, or the brink of suicide," say researchers.[7]

Just because you may feel blue, therefore, does not mean you are suffering from a serious, or clinical, depression. Your feelings may be a normal, even healthy, reaction to a loss—at home or work. A key distinction is this: While the unhappiness of daily life or adjustment to a loss comes and goes, the unhappiness of serious depression stays on. With normal unhappiness, for example, going for a walk or to the movies may cheer you up, at least temporarily. With clinical depression, even your favorite comedy movie or a walk through a beautiful park will leave you unmoved. Will your family members or friends recognize if you're seriously depressed? In many cases, no, they won't. They may try to coax you into feeling better, but nothing they do will seem to help. All joy in life seems gone—and, day after day, it does not return.

"People are now recognizing clinical depression as an illness and not a character flaw," says Robert Hirschfield, M.D., chief of the Mood, Anxiety, and Personality Disorders Research Branch of the National Institute of Mental Health in Rockville, Maryland.[8] One significant shift in public attitudes about severe clinical depression—which affects an estimated 15 million Americans—is that it is a disease that is, at least in part, biologically based. Evidence suggests that many of us—perhaps 5 percent of Americans—may have an inherited vulnerability to depression, which may be triggered by environmental stresses or psychological distress. Fortunately, more than 80 percent of all cases of depression can be successfully treated.[9]

If you discover, or even suspect, that you may have some form of serious depression, you should immediately seek professional help.

Signs of Depression

According to the DEPRESSION Awareness, Recognition, and Treatment (D/ART) Program of the National Institute of Mental Health, symptoms of depression can include:

- Persistent sad or "empty" mood.
- Loss of interest or pleasure in ordinary activities, including sex.
- Decreased energy, fatigue, being "slowed down."
- Sleep disturbances (insomnia, early-morning waking or over-sleeping).
- Eating disturbances (loss of appetite and weight, or weight gain).
- Difficulty concentrating, remembering, or making decisions.
- Feelings of guilt, worthlessness and helplessness.
- Thoughts of death or suicide; suicide attempts.
- Irritability.
- Excessive crying.
- Chronic aches and pains that don't respond to treatment.
- Decreased productivity.
- Safety problems; accidents.

- Alcohol or drug abuse.
- Moral problems.
- Lack of cooperation.

A thorough diagnosis is needed if four or more of these symptoms persist for more than two weeks or are interfering with work or family life. Consult a qualified mental health professional (psychologist or psychiatrist) for a thorough diagnosis.

3. RECONNECT WITH "NORMAL" EVERYDAY LIFE WITH AN INCREASED AWARENESS OF SAFETY

Having established safety and come to terms with the traumatic past, the survivor must then face the task of creating a future. Her sense of self and relationships may have been forever altered by the attack, and now a new self must emerge. By this stage of recovery, a survivor is often keenly aware of continued vulnerability to threats, or perceived threats, and reminders of the past attack. She understands that her traumatic memory will tend to exaggerate normal responses to danger. Some survivors choose to actively face and engage these fears. For some, instruction in physical protection skills (where the organization and instructor are carefully chosen, as discussed in chapter 11) becomes a means of fitness conditioning and mental-emotional recovery.

Dr. Herman points out that the simple statement "I know I have myself" could "stand as the emblem of the third and final stage of recovery. The survivor has gained the ability to create and maintain boundaries, and to distinguish between trusting others where that trust is warranted, and withholding trust where it is not. The survivor no longer feels possessed by her traumatic past; she is in possession of herself. She has some understanding of the person she used to be and of the damage done to that person by the traumatic event. Her task is now to become the person she wants to be. In the process she draws upon those aspects of herself that she most values from the time before the trauma, from the experience of the trauma itself, and from the period of recovery. Integrating all these elements, she creates a new self, both ideally and in actuality."[10]

We also want to mention that one of us (Harold) has personally experienced and recommends the Hoffman Quadrinity Process (800-506-5253). This is an intensive residential program that lasts several days and uses a combination of approaches to promote healing and inner safety.

Researchers have also discovered that, in many cases, the pain we feel and the losses we sustain become more bearable and the recovery fuller when we adopt a mission of caring.[11] This service can be volunteer work, and often the best is with children, suggests Dr. Segal. Self-sacrifice and thinking about others during an extended time of personal grief may seem irrelevant or even unhealthy, but it is neither. In the face of a crisis, one of the most courageous and healing steps is to practice empathy and compassion for other people in need. Once we've given ourselves a brief time to begin to come to grips with our own loss, then helping others "is eventually the best thing we can do for ourselves."[12]

SAFETY RESOURCES

• *The National Victim Center* (800-394-2255) offers a toll-free information line with access to more than five thousand victim-assistance programs nationwide.

• *National Organization for Victim Assistance* (NOVA, 1757 Park Road, NW, Washington, DC 2010; 800-TRY-NOVA (879-6682) or 202-232-6682). A private, nonprofit organization that provides information and referrals for victims of crime. Most states offer funding for emergency medical care, lost wages, counseling, and many other services. Callers can receive information about local victim-assistance programs and services from the twenty-four-hour, toll-free number. Crisis counselors are available during daytime working hours.

- *National Victim Resource Center* (Box 6000, Rockville, MD 20850; 800-627-6872). Provides access to various state compensation programs and offers more than seven thousand victim-related books and articles that address issues of child abuse (physical and sexual), domestic violence, victim-witness programs, and general victim services.

- *"Rape Crisis Hotline"* or *"Rape Counseling Center"*—see the yellow pages in your phone book.

- Human Options: Alternatives for Abused Women and Their Children (P.O. Box 9376, Newport Beach, CA 92658; 714-737-5242; Hotline 714-854-3554). One model of a community resource.

- *The National Clearing House on Marital and Date Rape* (2325 Oak St., Berkeley, CA 94708; 510-524-1582). Provides information and referral.

- *Aftermath: Survive and Overcome Trauma* by Mariann Hybels-Steer, Ph.D. (Fireside, 1995). Written as a practical guide for those who have faced a sudden and potentially life-threatening event, such as a mugging, rape, accident, robbery, or fire.

- *Trauma and Recovery: The Aftermath of Violence—from Domestic Abuse to Political Terror* by Judith Lewis Herman, M.D. (Basic Books, 1992). An outstanding scholarly and insightful work by an associate clinical professor of psychiatry at Harvard Medical School and director of training at the Victims of Violence Program at Cambridge Hospital. Highly recommended.

- *Consumer's Guide to Psychotherapy* by Jack Engler, Ph.D., and Daniel Goleman, Ph.D. (Touchstone, 1992). An authoritative reference for making informed choices about all types of psychotherapy.

- *The Grief Recovery Institute* (800-445-4808). Offers telephone counseling from 9 A.M. to 5 P.M. Pacific time, Monday through Friday, and makes referrals to affiliated outreach programs.

- *How to Heal Depression* by Harold H. Bloomfield, M.D. and Peter McWilliams (Prelude, 1994). A simple user-friendly guide.

• *How to Survive the Loss of a Love* by Melba Colgrove, Ph.D., Harold H. Bloomfield, M.D., and Peter McWilliams (Prelude, 1991). A practical, reassuring self-help book on coping with loss and enriching your life.

• *Making Peace With Your Parents* (Ballantine, 1983) and *Making Peace With Yourself* (Ballantine, 1985) by Harold H. Bloomfield, M.D., with Leonard Felder, Ph.D. Clear advice on healing the hurts in life's important relationships.

• *Opening Up: The Healing Power of Confiding in Others* by James W. Pennebaker, Ph.D. (Morrow, 1990). Documents the health benefits of self-disclosure—through private writing or, at the right time, through conversations with others.

• *Staying on Top When Your World Turns Upside Down* by Kathryn D. Cramer, Ph.D. (Viking, 1990). An action plan developed by a well-known health psychologist and founder of the Stress Center at St. Louis University.

Chapter 16

BUILDING A SAFER WORLD

All it takes for evil to triumph is for enough good people to do nothing.

EDMUND BURKE

Personal safety awareness and self-protection skills are, in the final analysis, only part of the way to be and feel safe. The rest of the effort must center on reaching out to others and building a safer world. "Everyone radiates an influence in society that is either stressful or coherent," says Jay B. Marcus in *The Crime Vaccine: How to End the Crime Epidemic*, "and the society has a *collective consciousness* and *collective stress* level that is based on the functioning of its individual members."

How willing are you to develop your own emotional safety and practice anger management in your dealings with others? Or to promote nonviolent conflict resolution? Do you demonstrate and teach tolerance? As Helen Keller warned us, "No loss by flood and lightning, no destruction of cities and temples by hostile forces, has deprived man of so many noble lives and impulses as those which his intolerance has destroyed."

In what specific ways might you reach out to help others be safer? The word *mentor* derives from the Greek roots meaning "counsel," "remember," and "endure." Prof. Uri Bronfenbrenner of

Cornell University describes mentoring as a one-to-one developmental relationship between two individuals: "A mentor is an
experienced person who seeks to further the development of
character and competence in another person." This guidance may
take many forms, including instruction, demonstration, and
encouragement. Furthermore, this relationship is distinguished by
"a special bond of mutual commitment" and "an emotional character of respect, loyalty, and identification."[1] How many adults in
America are *mentors of safety* outside their limited circle of family
and friends? The answer: far too few of us.

In the midnineteenth century, Alexis de Tocqueville comment-
ed that American life tends to isolate citizens within the solitude
of their own hearts. There is a yearning for connection, for people to help show us the way to succeed in life. Over the past
decade, a converging body of research strongly suggests that, for
greater personal and societal safety, relationships truly matter,
and bonds with caring adults make a vital difference, not only in
the lives and work of other adults, but also in the lives of vulnerable children and teens as they try to navigate their way toward
adulthood.

As a prominent article in the *Harvard Business Review* recently
stated, "Everyone who makes it has a mentor." Norman Brown,
president of the Kellogg Foundation, says that "the greatest need
of young people is not another program, but another caring, loving human being" as a mentor or role model. The benefits of
mentoring include the legacy we leave, referring to developmental psychologist Erik Erikson's words: "I am what survives of me.
We are facing a widespread and debilitating crisis. What's lacking
is . . . a generativity that will promote positive values in the lives
of the next generation."

Every effort matters; yet, as James Garbarino, Ph.D., a leading
violence researcher and director of the Family Life Studies Center at Cornell University in Ithaca, New York, reminds us, there
are no quick fixes for the poverty, deprivation, and despair confronting many young people. "Much as we would like to make the
world new for them through some magical program, this aspira-

tion is for the most part out of reach. We must console ourselves with helping them survive emotionally."

What safety issues do you care most deeply about? How can you encourage others to care deeply about them, too? Are you willing to face the challenge this entails? In the words of the ancient teacher Hillel in the first century A.D., "If I am not for myself, who will be for me? And if I am only for myself, what am I? And if not now—when?"

Take the larger view of safety. An estimated 70 percent of all violent crimes are committed by 6 percent of the violent criminals. The truth is, any individual who is eliminated from, or kept from joining, this group makes a significant difference. In light of this, we believe that for long-term personal safety and the security and well-being of our neighborhoods, workplaces, and communities, it's essential that each of us make a *personal social commitment* to deal with the range of core issues that foster danger and violence. For example, we must reduce the glorification of violence in the movies and on television and replace the view that violence is an effective problem-solving method with nonviolent conflict resolution and anger-management education. In addition, there must be stronger victims' rights and deterrents to violence, including some form of mandatory sentencing for violent crimes, sexual predators, habitual criminals, and for crimes against children.

At the heart of the safety issue are the children of the world. The stuff of our own nightmares has become common reality for children today. It is a crisis. And *all* children deserve trustworthy, courageous adults to make the world safer for them. To provide friendship and havens for learning and living. To teach lasting values and open up new opportunities. Think about it: If other parents' children are hostile, alienated, and unsafe, then ultimately *your* children are not safe either.

Moreover, the children of America cannot afford to wait as we adults wage great ideological battles about health, education, safety, and justice. We have a difficult time understanding how our nation and its government can continue, in so many instances, to spend money on piecemeal programs that do little or nothing to prevent violence, dependency, or despair and that leave so many people unsafe and unprotected. It is time, for example, to subsidize high-quality child care—because we *all* benefit. And to provide some effective form of universal health care; to offer nutritional services for poor children; and to provide safe after-school programs for the children of working parents.

What can you do? Begin today to share your concerns about safety with friends, coworkers, neighbors, people you see regularly at churches and other organizations, and elected officials. Consider supporting a variety of volunteer projects in your area aimed toward preventing danger and abuse and promoting antiviolence.

Caring for persons, the more able and the less able serving each other, is the rock upon which a good society is built.

ROBERT K. GREENLEAF, lecturer at the Harvard Business School

According to Robert Vanourek in *Reflections on Leadership*, "The true leader cares about the people. The leader places the well-being of the followers ahead of himself or herself. So, enlightened leadership is service, not self-gratification. And why does a leader care? Because he or she knows the potential that is there in each of us. He or she respects those untapped powers and feelings. . . . The leader wants to empower people, to unlock those hidden potentials. People intuitively sense that. They aren't foolish. They can't be tricked for long. They know in their hearts that a true leader is worthy of their trust. So they commit, voluntarily. With their mind and their body and their heart. Great victories are won in the hearts of people."[2]

We must come together to make our communities and world a safer place. We must come together—across generations, races, religions, gender, and other distinctions of all kinds—in a way that affirms our peaceful interdependence, acknowledging, in Martin Luther King Jr.'s words, that "we are caught in an inescapable network of mutuality, tied to a single garment of destiny."

All that we have left, it appears, is ourselves. Working alone and together, fighting safety battles on a wide front, holding evil at bay long enough to create a better, safer future. The choice is ours. Let us hope that, years from now, we will be able to look back and know that it was today—in these dark times of anger and violence—that we finally began to see, and seize, the opportunity to build a safe world for one and thus all.

SAFETY RESOURCES

• *The Kindness of Strangers: Adult Mentors, Urban Youth, and the New Voluntarism* by Marc Freedman (Josey-Bass, 1993). A book that provides wise reflections and useful information on the myths and realities of the mentoring movement.

• *National Association of Town Watch* (P.O. Box 303, Wynnewood, PA 19096; 215-649-7055). Helps to organize and coordinate Neighborhood Watch groups and activities.

• *The Crime Vaccine: How to End the Crime Epidemic* by Jay B. Marcus (Baton Rouge, La.: Claitor's Publishing Co.; available from the Natural Law Party, 51 W. Washington Street, Suite 100, Fairfield, IA 52556; 515-472-2040). This is a well-referenced and compelling work, incorporating approaches proven in a series of independent scientific studies to promote stress reduction and dramatically reduce violence and crime.

• *Points of Light Foundation* (1737 H Street, NW, Washington, DC 20006; 202-223-9186). Helps connect you with volunteer projects in your local area.

• *Healthy Families America* (Leslie Mitchel, National Committee to Prevent Child Abuse, 332 S. Michigan Avenue, Suite 1600, Chicago, IL 60604; 312-663-3520). This is a nationwide initiative to establish a universal, voluntary *home visitor* system for all new parents. The idea behind Healthy Families America is to intervene with families at risk for child abuse or neglect at the earliest possible moment—at the moment the child is born. Trained workers approach families in the hospital or prenatally to determine those who are overburdened. Those identified as being under stress and who are interested in receiving support are offered the service of a home visitor. If the parent enrolls in the three-to-five-year program, an HFA home visitor visits the home regularly, depending on the needs of the family. The HFA vision is that new parents will receive some services, with those at greatest risk receiving intensive support.

• *Everybody's Children: Child Care as a Public Problem* by William T. Gormley Jr., Ph.D. (Washington, DC: The Brookings Institution, 1995). Gormley is a professor of government and public policy at Georgetown University, and this is a clear, accessible call for attention and action on a dilemma that has far-reaching implications for the safety of all Americans.

• *Amnesty International* (322 Eighth Avenue, New York, NY 10001). The nonprofit organization that fights to end violence and free prisoners of conscience around the world.

• *Fist Stick Knife Gun: A Personal History of Violence in America* by Geoffrey Canada (Beacon Press, 1995). A modern classic on our culture of violence, a deeply personal story and a beacon of light and hope for humanity's future. Geoffrey Canada is the president of the Rheedlen Centers for Children and Families in New York City.

• *Teaching Tolerance: A Project of the Southern Poverty Law Center* (P.O. Box 548, Montgomery, AL 36177-9621). An Oscar-winning video plus books and teaching kits that show practical ways to end the bigotry and prejudice that afflict America.

• *Volunteers of America* (800-899-0089).

• *Youth Employment and Empowerment Program* (Kathleen Millard, project coordinator, 421 S.W. Fifth Avenue, 2nd Floor, Portland, OR 97204; 503-248-3476). This program utilizes the combined resources and talents of the entire community, including youth, community service agencies, government, and business to offer gang-involved and at-risk youth realistic alternatives to gang lifestyles by creating meaningful employment and business opportunities leading to economic self-sufficiency; and to provide those youth with preemployment training and on-the-job support services to enhance success through a relationship model.

• *Bethesda Day Treatment Center* (Dominic Herbst, director, P.O. Box 270, Central Oak Heights, West Milton, PA 17886-0270; 503-248-5184). The Bethesda Program is one of the most comprehensive and community-intensive treatment programs for juvenile offenders in the United States. All treatment is conducted in the home and community of the youth and may exceed fifty-five hours of intervention each week. Every form of counseling is available, including group and individual therapy, parental and family sessions, and drug and alcohol counseling. All treatment is values oriented and designed to defuse family conflict in an effort to help troubled youth adjust to mainstream society. Bethesda has a national vision to replicate its programs in many other cities.

• *Truth in Sentencing* (Gov. Fife Symington, Executive Office, 1700 W. Washington, Phoenix, AZ 85007; 602-542-1415). Statistics indicate that a small percentage of criminals commit the vast majority of crimes. "If you do the crime, you have to do the time" had become an old, often inaccurate cliché. But in Arizona, convicted criminals are now required to serve at least 85 percent of their sentences. Truth in Sentencing became Arizona law on January 1, 1994, at the urging of the governor. It eliminates parole, work furlough, and all other forms of early release.

• *Guilty: The Collapse of Criminal Justice* by Judge Harold J. Rothwax (Random House, 1996). Rothwax has been known in legal circles for his sharp mind, candor, and tough rulings during twenty-five years as a judge on the New York Supreme Court. In this carefully thought out work, he puts the American legal system on trial. Filled with shocking insights and suggestions for action.

• *The Spirit of Community: The Reinvention of American Society* by Amitai Etzioni, Ph.D. (Touchstone, 1993). Etzioni is a professor at George Washington University and a former White House adviser. He explains why the critical institutions of our country are in crisis and shows what we can do to restore them with a new and balanced social contract—one that both protects individual rights and serves and protects the needs of our society.

Notes

Chapter 1: Safety Is the #1 Human Need

1. D. Levy, "USA Almost Flunks Violence Report Card." *USA Today* (June 12, 1996): 1D.
2. R. J. Gelles and M. A. Straus, *Intimate Violence* (New York: Simon & Schuster, 1988), 18.
3. P. H. Robinson, "Moral Credibility and Crime," *Atlantic Monthly*, March, 1995, 72–78.
4. A. Stone, "If You're Afraid, You're a Victim of Crime," *USA Today,* December 9, 1994, 4A.
5. R. S. Eliot, *From Stress to Strength* (New York: Bantam, 1994); R. Williams and V. Williams, *Anger Kills* (New York: Times Books, 1993).
6. R. Sapolsky, "Glucocorticoids and Hippocampal Damage," *Trends in Neurosciences* 10 (1987); U.S. Department of Health and Human Services, *Special Report on Aging,* NIH No. 80-2135 (August 1980); S. J. Troell, "Cerebral Atrophy in Young Torture Victims," *New England Journal of Medicine* 307, no. 21 (November 18, 1982): 1341; "Research on Stress Hormones: Powerful Agents in Health and Disease," *Salk Institute Newsletter* (summer 1986): 2–3. A. Winter and R. Winter, *Build Your Brain Power* (New York: St. Martin's Press, 1986), 153.
7. L. J. Siegel, *Criminology* (St. Paul: West Publishing Co., 1995), 192.
8. S. Brownlee. "The biology of soul murder." U.S. News & World Report (November 11, 1996): 71–72, and R. Kotulak, *Inside the Brain* (Kansas City, Mo.: Andrews and McMeel, 1996).

9. See, for example: B. Kerr, *Sky Burial: An Eyewitness Account of China's Brutal Crackdown in Tibet* (Chicago: The Noble Press, 1993); P. K. Kelly, G. Bastian, and P. Aiello, eds., *The Anguish of Tibet* (Berkeley, Calif.: Parallax Press, 1991); and L. Feignon, *Demystifying Tibet* (Chicago: Ivan R. Dee, 1996); or contact the International Campaign for Tibet: (202) 785-1515.

10. Eliot, *From Stress to Strength*, J. D. Spence, American Heart Association Conference Reports, *USA Today*, January 26, 1996, D1.

11. A. de Tocqueville, *Democracy in America*, vol. 2 (Cambridge: Sever and Francis, 1863), 119–23.

12. J. B. Marcus, *The Crime Vaccine: How to End the Crime Epidemic* (Baton Rouge, LA: Claitor's Publishing Division, 1996).

13. Ibid., 24.

14. T. Todorov, *Facing the Extreme: Moral Life in the Concentration Camps* (New York: Metropolitan Books, 1996), 296.

15. C. L. Hays, "Fall Kills Woman Trying to Help a Friend's Child," *New York Times*, May 15, 1991, B3.

16. L. R. Huesmann, University of Michigan study. Cited in M. Elias, "Girls Emulate Aggression Seen in TV Heroines," *USA Today*, January 30, 1996, D1.

17. C. Derber, *The Wilding of America: How Greed and Violence Are Eroding Our Nation's Character* (New York: St. Martin's Press, 1996).

18. W. Wade, "Prevention Urged for Teen Violence," *Ann Arbor News*, January 20, 1996, 1.

19. P. Moynihan, "Toward a Post-Industrial Social Policy," *The Public Interest*, (Fall 1989).

20. A. Manning, "Kids Get an Early Education in Fear," *USA Today*, December 7, 1995, D1.

21. R. Price, "Child Safety Still Is Not a Guarantee," *USA Today*, February 6, 1996, A1–2.

Chapter 2: The Moment of Choice

1. D. Grossman, *On Killing: The Psychological Cost of Learning to Kill in War & Society* (Boston: Little, Brown, 1995).

2. B. Bettelheim, *The Informed Heart* (New York: Bettelheim Foundation, 1960).

3. J. Kabat-Zinn, *Full Catastrophe Living* (New York: Delacorte, 1990), 264–66.

4. Ibid., 269.

5. M. Castleman, *Crime Free* (New York: Fireside Books, 1984); B. Grayson and M. Stein, "Attracting Assault: Victims' Nonverbal Cues," *Journal of Communication* (winter 1981), 74.

6. S. H. Elgin, *The Gentle Art of Verbal Self-Defense* (New York: Prentice Hall Press, 1980), 3–4.

7. R. Cailliet, *The Rejuvenation Strategy* (New York: Doubleday, 1987).

8. Grayson and Stein, "Attracting Assault," 74.

9. S. H. Elgin, *Staying Well with the Gentle Art of Verbal Self-Defense* (New York: Prentice Hall Press, 1990), 74–75; Castleman, *Crime Free.*

10. Castleman, *Crime Free,* 64.

11. R. E. Thayer, *The Biopsychology of Mood and Arousal* (New York: Oxford University Press, 1989).

12. L. C. Martin, *A Life Without Fear* (Nashville, Tenn.: Rutledge Hill Press, 1992), 31.

13. C. R. Stroebel, *QR: The Quieting Reflex* (New York: Berkley, 1983); R. G. Nathan, T. E. Staats, and P. J. Rosch, *The Doctors' Guide to Instant Stress Relief* (New York: Ballantine, 1987); K. Sedlacek, *The Sedlacek Technique* (New York: McGraw-Hill, 1989).

14. A. Ziv, and R. Israel, "Effects of Bombardment on the Manifest Anxiety Level of Children Living in Kibbutzim," *Journal of Clinical Psychology* 40 (1973): 287–91.

15. R. Weissbourd, *The Vulnerable Child* (Reading, MA: Addison-Wesley, 1996), 7.

16. Canada, *Fist Stick Knife Gun.*

Chapter 3: Safety Intelligence Principle #1

1. *New York Times,* November 11, 1994.

2. E. J. Langer, *Mindfulness* (Reading, MA: Addison-Wesley, 1989).

3. Stroebel, *QR;* Nathan, Staats, and Rosch, *Doctors' Guide.*

4. Winter and Winter, *Build Your Brain Power,* 90.

5. P. Jaret, "Mind: Why Practice Makes Perfect," *Hippocrates,* November/ December 1987, 90–91; T. Salthouse, *Scientific American,* February 1984.

6. Jaret, "Mind."

7. M. Csikszentmihalyi and I. S. Csikszentmihalyi, eds., *Optimal Experience: Psychological Studies of Flow in Consciousness* (New York: Cambridge University Press, 1988); M. Csikszentmihalyi, *Flow: The Psychology of Optimal Experience* (New York: Harper and Row, 1989); Jaret, "Mind"; M. Teich and G. Dodeles, "Mind Control: How to Get It, How to Use It, How to Keep It," *Omni,* October 1987, 53–60.

8. M. G. Fischman, *Journal of Motor Behavior* 16 (1984): 405–23; P. M. Fitts and J. R. Peterson, *Journal of Experimental Psychology* 67 (1964): 103–12; A. G. Greenwald and H. G. Schulman, *Journal of Experimental Psychology* 101 (1973): 70–76; S. W. Keele, "Motor Control," in L. Kaufman, J. Thomas, and K. Boff, eds., *Handbook of Perception and Performance* (New York: Wiley, 1986); K. M. Newell et al., *Journal of Motor Behavior* 12 (1980): 47–56; J. T. Quinn and D. E. Sherwood, *Journal of Motor Behavior* 15 (1983): 163–78; D. A. Rosenbaum, *Journal of Experimental Psychology* 109 (1980): 444–74;

R. A. Schmidt, *Psychological Bulletin* 70 (1968): 631–46; R. A. Schmidt, *Motor Control and Learning, a Behavioral Analysis* (Champaign, Ill.: Human Kinetics, 1988).

9. R. Leehotz, "Tiny Structure in Brain May Be Key to Recognizing Fear," *New York Times*, December 15, 1994, A1, A32.

10. E. B. Bolles, *A Second Way of Knowing: The Riddle of Human Perception* (New York: Prentice Hall Press, 1991), 152–53.

11. D. M. Wegner, *White Bears and Other Unwanted Thoughts* (New York: Viking, 1989), 73.

12. J. M. Rippe, *Fit for Success* (New York: Prentice Hall Press, 1989), 114.

13. C. Garfield, *Peak Performance* (New York: Warner, 1984), 95; Csikszentmihalyi, *Flow;* Csikszentmihalyi and Csikszentmihalyi, *Optimal Experience.*

14. A. R. Damasio, *Descartes' Error: Emotion, Reason, and the Human Brain* (Grosset/Putnam, 1994), 171–80.

15. J. Kramer, *The Passionate Mind* (Berkeley, Calif.: Celestial Arts, 1974); T. Crum, *The Magic of Conflict* (New York: Simon & Schuster, 1987), 114.

16. S. H. Elgin, *Success with the Gentle Art of Verbal Self-Defense* (New York: Prentice Hall Press, 1989), 46.

17. D. Hingsburger, "Learning How to Face That Stressful Situation," *Management Solutions* 33, no. 2 (1988): 41–45.

18. S. E. Duclos et al., "Emotion-Specific Effects of Facial Expressions and Postures on Emotional Experience," *Journal of Personality and Social Psychology* 57, no. 1 (1989): 100–108; J. H. Riskind and C. C. Gotay, "Physical Posture: Could It Have Regulatory or Biofeedback Effects on Motivation and Emotion?" *Motivation and Emotion* 6, no. 3 (1982): 273–98; G. E. Weisfeld and J. M. Beresford, "Erectness of Posture as an Indicator of Dominance or Success in Humans," *Motivation and Emotion* 6, no. 2 (1982): 113–31; V. Bhatnager et al., "Posture, Postural Discomfort, and Performance," *Human Factors* 27, no. 2 (April 1985): 189–99.

19. Stroebel, *QR.*

20. Adapted from T. Crum, *The Magic of Conflict* (New York: Simon & Schuster, 1987), 156; and Kabat-Zinn, *Full Catastrophe Living* (New York: Delacorte, 1990), 373–74.

21. E. deBono, *De-Conflicting Conflict* (London: Penguin, 1978, 1993).

Chapter 4: Safety Intelligence Principle #2

1. K. Quinn, *Everyday Self-Defense* (London: Thorsons/HarperCollins, 1993), 19.

2. D. Goleman, *Emotional Intelligence* (New York: Bantam, 1995), 36.

3. R. S. Lazarus, *Passion and Reason: Making Sense of Our Emotions* (New York: Oxford University Press, 1994).

4. H. C. McDonald, *Survival* (New York: Ballantine, 1982), 80.

5. H. E. Marano, "Big. Bad. Bully," *Psychology Today*, September/October 1995, 50–58.

Chapter 5: Safety Intelligence Principle #3

1. Our thinking on this subject has been greatly influenced by the work of Terry Dobson and Victor Miller, authors of *Aikido: Giving In to Get Your Way* (New York: Delacorte, 1992) as they use circles, squares, and triangles to represent the various basic forms of conflict and response options. Tom Crum, author of *The Magic of Conflict*, also uses this theme effectively.

2. Dobson and Miller, *Aikido in Everyday Life*, 88–89.

3. Fischman, *Journal of Motor Behavior* 16: 405–23; Fitts and Peterson, *Journal of Experimental Psychology* 67: 103–12; Greenwald and Schulman, *Journal of Experimental Psychology* 101: 70–76; W. E. Hick, *Quarterly Journal of Experimental Psychology* 4 (1952), 11–26; R. Hyman, *Journal of Experimental Psychology* 45 (1953), 188–96; Keele, "Motor Control"; J. Merkel, cited in R. S. Woodsworth, *Experimental Psychology* 2 (1938): 73–127; Newell et al., *Journal of Motor Behavior* 12: 47–56; Quinn and Sherwood, *Journal of Motor Behavior* 15: 163–78; Rosenbaum, *Journal of Experimental Psychology* 109: 444–74; A. F. Sanders in G. E. Stelmach and J. Requin, *Tutorials in Motor Behavior* (Amsterdam: North-Holland, 1980); Schmidt, *Psychological Bulletin* 70: 631–46; Schmidt, *Motor Control and Learning*.

4. A. Mindell, *The Leader as Martial Artist* (San Francisco: HarperCollins, 1994), 34–35.

5. *U.S. News & World Report*, February 21, 1994.

6. S. Pinker, *The Language Instinct: How the Mind Creates Language* (New York: Morrow, 1994).

7. Ibid.

8. Sedlacek, *The Sedlacek Technique*, 13.

Chapter 6: Eight Scenarios

1. Dobson and Miller, *Aikido in Everyday Life*, 237.

2. Wegner, *White Bears*.

3. R. Driscoll, *Mental Shielding* (Knoxville, Tenn.: Frontiers Press [615-690-0962], 1994).

4. W. Ury, *Getting Past No* (New York: Bantam, 1991), 37.

5. Ibid., 40.

6. Driscoll, *Mental Shielding*.

7. Ibid., 15.

8. Adapted from a story in Crum, *The Magic of Conflict*, 38–47.

9. D. Tannen, *You Just Don't Understand: Women and Men in Conversation* (New York: Morrow, 1991); Pinker, *The Language Instinct*.

10. R. Fisher and W. Ury, *Getting to Yes* (Boston: Houghton Mifflin, 1981).

11. Elgin, *Success with the Gentle Art of Verbal Self-Defense;* J. L. Thompson, *Verbal Judo* (New York: Quill, 1993).

12. Castleman, *Crime Free;* Tesoro, *Options for Avoiding Assault,* 69.

13. Damasio, *Descartes' Error,* 224–27.

14. R. Josselson, *The Space Between Us* (San Francisco: Josey-Bass, 1992), 99.

15. J. J. Bittenbinder, interview on *Primetime Live,* ABC News, 1993.

16. McDonald, *Survival,* 18.

Chapter 7: Emotional Safety

1. J. O. Prochaska, J. C. Norcross, and C. G. DiClemente, *Changing for Good* (New York: Morrow, 1994); M. E. P. Seligman, *What You Can Change and What You Can't* (New York: Knopf, 1994).

2. J. E. Loehr, *Toughness Training for Life* (New York: Penguin/Plume, 1993).

3. J. Wolpe, *Life Without Fear* (Oakland, Calif.: New Harbinger Publications, 1988), 3–6.

4. S. Jeffers, *Feel the Fear and Do It Anyway* (San Diego: Harcourt Brace, 1987), 4.

5. Thayer, *Biopsychology of Mood and Arousal;* Damasio, *Descartes' Error;* R. E. Thayer, P. J. Takahashi, and J. A. Pauli, "Multidimensional Arousal States, Diurnal Rhythms, Cognitive and Social Processes, and Extraversion," *Personality and Individual Differences* 9 (1988): 15–24; R. S. Lazarus, *Emotion and Adaptation* (New York: Oxford University Press, 1991); J-D. Vincent, *The Biology of Emotions* (Cambridge, MA: Basil Blackwell, 1990); J. A. Gray, ed., *Psychobiological Aspects of Relationships Between Emotions and Cognition* (Hillsdale, N.J.: Erlbaum, 1990).

6. Thayer, *Biopsychology of Mood and Arousal.*

7. Ibid.

8. Csikszentmihalyi, *Flow.*

9. Thayer, *Biopsychology of Mood and Arousal.*

10. L. Lamberg, *Bodyrhythms* (New York: Morrow, 1994), 8.

11. M. Moore-Ede, *The Twenty-Four-Hour Society* (Reading, Mass.: Addison-Wesley, 1993).

12. M. D. Chafetz, *Smart for Life* (New York: Penguin, 1992); Thayer, *Biopsychology of Mood and Arousal;* E. L. Rossi, *The 20-Minute Break* (Los Angeles: Tarcher, 1991); Moore-Ede, *Twenty-Four-Hour Society.*

13. Rossi, *20-Minute Break,* 93.

14. Castleman, *Crime Free;* Grayson and Stein, "Attracting Assault," 74.

15. F. Bartolome and P. Evans, *Must Success Cost So Much?* (New York: Basic Books, 1988); B. O'Reilly, "Why Grade 'A' Executives Get an 'F' as Parents," *Fortune,* January 1, 1990, 36–46; B. O'Reilly, "Is Your Company Asking Too Much?" *Fortune,* March 12, 1990, 38–46.

16. Rossi, *20-Minute Break*, 122–23.

17. P. J. Jones, C. A. Leitch, and R. A. Pederson, "Meal-Frequency Effects on Plasma Hormone Concentrations and Cholesterol Synthesis in Humans," *American Journal of Clinical Nutrition* 57, no. 6 (1993): 868–74; E. Grandjean, *Fitting the Task*, 3rd ed. (New York: Taylor, 1991), 213.

18. D. A. Jenkins et al. "Nibbling Versus Gorging: Metabolic Advantages of Increased Meal Frequency," *New England Journal of Medicine* 321, no. 4 (October 5, 1989): 929–34.

19. Jones, Leitch, and Pederson, "Meal-Frequency Effects," 868–74; S. L. Edelstein et al., "Increased Meal Frequency Associated with Decreased Cholesterol Concentrations," *American Journal of Clinical Nutrition* 55 (1992): 664–69.

20. Moore-Ede, *Twenty-Four-Hour Society*, 55.

21. "Breathing Linked to Personality," *Psychology Today*, July 1983, 109; Teich and Dodeles, "Mind Control."

22. S. S. Hendler, *The Oxygen Breakthrough* (New York: Simon and Schuster, 1989), 7, 8, 94.

23. Stroebel, QR; C. F. Stroebel, M. R. Ford, P. Strong, and B. L. Szarek, "Quieting Response Training: Five-Year Evaluation of a Clinical Biofeedback Practice" (Hartford, Conn.: Institute for Living, 1985).

24. J. E. Loehr and P. J. McLaughlin, *Mentally Tough* (New York: Evans, 1986).

25. Damasio, *Descartes' Error*.

26. Wegner, *White Bears*.

27. Damasio, *Descartes' Error*.

28. G. Hendricks and K. Hendricks, *At the Speed of Life* (New York: Bantam, 1993), 104.

29. Ibid.

30. R. K. Wallace (1970) "Physiological Effects of Transcendental Meditation." *Science*, 167, 1751–1754.

31. R. K. Wallace and H. Benson (1972) "The Physiology of Meditation." *Scientific American*, 226, 84–90.

32. M. C. Dillbeck and D. W. Orme-Johnson (1987) "Physiological Differences between Transcendental Meditation and Rest." *American Psychologist*, 42, 879–881.

33. K. R. Eppley, A. I. Abrams, and J. Shear (1989) "Differential Effects of Relaxation Techniques on Trait Anxiety: a Meta-analysis." *Journal of Clinical Psychology*, 45, 957–974.

34. Teich and Dodeles, "Mind Control"; E. E. Miller, *Software for the Mind* (Berkeley, Calif.: Celestial Arts, 1987); T. M. Otero, "Altering Your Inner Limits," in A. A. Sheikh, ed., *Anthology of Imagery Techniques* (American Imagery Institute, P.O. Box 13453, Milwaukee, WI 53213; 1986), 289–311. See also K. H. Pribram, *Brain and Perception* (Hillsdale, N.J.: Erlbaum, 1991); K. H. Pribram, *Languages of the Brain* (New York:

Brandon House, 1981). Variations of anchoring have been adapted from the "systematic desensitization" approach of Joseph Wolpe, M.D.—J. Wolpe, *Psychotherapy by Reciprocal Inhibition* (Stanford, Calif.: Stanford University Press, 1958); J. Wolpe, *The Practice of Behavior Therapy,* 2nd ed. (New York: Pergamin Press, 1973); Wolpe, *Life Without Fear;* Wegner, *White Bears.*

35. Teich and Dodeles, "Mind Control," 56.
36. Wolpe, *Life Without Fear.*
37. A. Katherine, *Boundaries: Where You End and I Begin* (Park Ridge, Ill.: Parkside, 1991), 86.
38. R. Williams and V. Williams, *Anger Kills* (New York: Times Books, 1993).
39. Ibid.
40. R. S. Lazarus, *Emotion and Adaptation* (Oxford: Oxford University Press, 1991), 222.
41. Williams and Williams, *Anger Kills;* R. S. Eliot, *From Stress to Strength* (New York: Bantam, 1994); R. S. Eliot and D. Breo, *Is It Worth Dying For?* (New York: Bantam, 1989); C. Tavris, *Anger: The Misunderstood Emotion* (New York: Simon and Schuster, 1982).
42. "Marital Conflict Can Be Hazardous to Your Health," *Mental Medicine Update* 2 no. 3 (winter 1993/94): 2.
43. M. Watsom et al., *Psychological Medicine* 21 (1991): 51–57; M. E. P. Seligman, *Learned Optimism* (New York: Knopf, 1991), 167–78.
44. C. Peterson and L. M. Bossio, *Health & Optimism* (New York: Free Press, 1991), 53.
45. A. T. Beck, *Cognitive Therapy and Emotional Disorders* (New York: New American Library, 1979); M. McKay, M. Davis, and P. Fanning, *Thoughts & Feelings: The Art of Cognitive Stress Intervention* (Richmond, Calif.: New Harbinger Publications, 1981); D. Burns, *Feeling Good: The New Mood Therapy* (New York: Signet, 1981).
46. R. S. Eliot and D. L. Breo, *Is It Worth Dying For?* rev. ed. (New York: Bantam, 1991), 95–96.
47. J. K. Kiecolt-Glaser et al., "Negative Behavior During Marital Conflict Is Associated with Immunological Down-Regulation," *Psychosomatic Medicine* 55 (1993): 395–409.
48. Seligman, *What You Can Change,* 130.
49. T. W. Smith et al., "Cynical Hostility at Home and Work: Psychosocial Vulnerability Across Domains," *Journal of Research in Personality* 22 (December 1988): 524–48.
50. Seligman, *What You Can Change,* 127–28.
51. H. Markman and C. Notarius, *We Can Work It Out: Making Sense of Marital Conflict* (New York: Putnam, 1993).
52. Seligman, *What You Can Change,* 120.

53. L. Berkowitz, "Experimental Investigations of Hostility Catharsis," *Journal of Consulting and Clinical Psychology* 35 (1970): 1–7; Tavris, *Anger;* Seligman, *What You Can Change,* 130.

54. D. Ornish, Dr. *Dean Ornish's Program for Reversing Heart Disease* (New York: Random House, 1991); Eliot and Breo, *Is It Worth Dying For?* rev. ed.; R. William, *The Trusting Heart* (New York: Times Books, 1989); R. Ornstein and C. Swencionis, *The Healing Brain: A Scientific Reader* (New York: Guildford, 1991).

55. Ornish, *Reversing Heart Disease;* L. Scherwitz et al., "Self-Involvement and Coronary Heart Disease Incidence in the Multiple Risk Intervention Trial," *Psychosomatic Medicine* 48 (1986): 187–99; L. Scherwitz et al., "Speech Characteristics and Behavior-Type Assessment in the Multiple Risk Intervention Trial (MR FIT) Structured Interviews," *Journal of Behavioral Medicine* 10, no. 2 (1987): 173–95.

56. D. Ornish, "The Healing Power of Love," *Prevention,* February 1991, 60–66.

57. Ibid., 65–66.

58. R. G. Nathan and M. R. Stuart, *Coping with the Stressed-Out People in Your Life* (New York: Ballantine, 1994), 150.

59. Example is adapted from L. Powell and C. Thoreson, "Modifying the Type A Patter: A Small Groups Treatment Approach," in J. A. Blumenthal and D. C. McKee, eds., *Applications in Behavioral Medicine and Health Psychology: A Clinician's Source Book* (Sarasota, Fla.: Professional Resource Exhange, 1987), 171–207.

60. "Exercise and Mental Health," *University of Texas Health Science Center Lifetime Health Letter* 5, no. 3 (March 1993): 7.

61. Ibid.

62. Williams and Williams, *Anger Kills,* 82–83.

63. A. Freeman and R. DeWolf, *The 10 Dumbest Mistakes Smart People Make* (New York: HarperCollins, 1992); R. Suarez, R. C. Mills, and D. Stewart, *Sanity, Insanity, and Common Sense* (New York: Fawcett, 1987); G. Emery, "Rapid Cognitive Therapy of Anxiety," research monograph (Los Angeles Center for Cognitive Therapy, 630 S. Wilton Place, Los Angeles, Calif. 90005; 1987), 39–52; G. Emery and J. Campbell, *Rapid Relief from Emotional Distress* (New York: Fawcett, 1986).

64. Freeman and DeWolf, *The 10 Dumbest Mistakes.*

65. Vincent, *Biology of Emotions;* Lazarus, *Emotion and Adaptation;* J. G. Thompson, *The Psychobiology of Emotions* (New York: Plenum Press, 1988); Gray, *Psychobiological Aspects of Relationships.*

66. R. C. Miller and J. S. Berman, "The Efficacy of Cognitive Behavior Therapies: A Quantitative Review of the Research Evidence," *Psychological Bulletin* 94 (1983): 39–53; A. Beck, *Cognitive Therapy and the Emotional Disorders* (New York: International Universities Press, 1976); A. Beck and G. Emery

with L. Greenberg, *Anxiety Disorders and Phobias* (New York: Basic Books, 1985); Burns, *Feeling Good;* McKay, Davis, and Fanning, *Thoughts & Feelings.*

67. M. E. P. Seligman in "Mind Over Illness: Do Optimists Live Longer?" *American Health,* November 1986, 50–53.

68. Adapted from C. Olson, "When and How to Intervene," *Self,* November 1994, 185.

69. Ibid.

Chapter 8: De-escalating Hostility

1. M. Tesoro, *Options for Avoiding Assault* (San Luis Obispo, Calif.: SDE News, 1994), 73–74.

2. M. Deutsch, "Conflicts: Productive and Destructive," *Journal of Social Issues* 25 (1969): 7–41.

3. J. Katz, *Seductions to Crime* (New York: Basic Books, 1988).

4. S. M. Retzinger, *Violent Emotions* (Newbury Park, Calif.: Sage, 1991).

5. Nathan and Stuart, *Coping with the Stressed-Out People,* 33–34.

6. Retzinger, *Violent Emotions.*

7. Ibid.

8. Adapted from "Components of Verbal Communication," *Self-Defense and Empowerment News* 9, no. 1 (winter-spring 1996): 10–11.

9. Sedlacek, *The Sedlacek Technique,* 13.

10. M. Tesoro, *Options for Avoiding Assault,* 73–74.

Chapter 9: Making Your Relationships Safer

1. S. Peterson, "Fighting Fair Keeps Marriages Strong." *USA Today,* February 20, 1992, 6D.

2. M. J. Renick, S. L. Blumberg, and H. J. Markman, "The Prevention and Relationship Enhancement Program (PREP)—an Empirically Based Preventive Intervention Program for Couples," *Family Relations* 41, no. 2 (April 1992): 141–47; J. M. Gottman and L. J. Krokoff, "Marital Interactions and Satisfaction: A Longitudinal View," *Journal of Consulting and Clinical Psychology* 57, no. 1 (February 1989): 47–52.

3. J. Gottman, *Why Marriages Succeed or Fail* (New York: Simon & Schuster, 1994), 181–82.

4. Pinker, *The Language Instinct.*

5. Gottman and Krokoff, "Marital Interactions."

6. Renick, Blumberg, and Markman, "Prevention"; and H. J. Markman quoted in Blau, "Can We Talk?" *American Health,* December 1990, 45.

7. Gottman, *Why Marriages Succeed or Fail,* 110.

8. Ibid.

9. Thayer, *Biopsychology of Mood and Arousal.*

10. D. Gelman, "The Thoughts That Wound," *Newsweek*, January 9, 1989, 46–48.

11. Gottman, *Why Marriages Succeed or Fail*; Notarius and Markman, *We Can Work It Out*.

12. Gottman and Krokoff, "Marital Interactions"; R. W. Levenson and J. M. Gottman, "Physiological and Affective Predictors of Change in Relationship Satisfaction," *Journal of Personality and Social Psychology* 49, no. 10 (July 1985): 85–94; J. M. Gottman and R. W. Levenson, "Assessing the Role of Emotion in Marriage," *Behavioral Assessment* 8, no. 1 (1986): 31–48.

13. J. Gray, *Men Are From Mars, Women Are From Venus* (New York: HarperCollins, 1992), 67–68.

14. Levenson and Gottman, "Physiological and Affective Predictors."

15. Gottman, *Why Marriages Succeed or Fail*, 153.

16. Gray, *Men Are From Mars*, 68.

17. Blau, "Can We Talk?" 41.

18. Gottman and Krokoff, "Marital Interactions."

19. Blau, "Can We Talk?" 42.

20. Gray, *Men Are From Mars*, 86.

21. Ibid., 88.

22. Markman and Notarius, *We Can Work It Out*.

23. S. E. Crohan, "Marital Happiness and Spousal Consensus on Beliefs About Marital Conflict: A Longitudinal Investigation," *Journal of Social and Personal Relationships* 9, no. 1 (February 1992): 89–102.

24. D. C. Delis, *The Passion Paradox* (New York: Bantam, 1990), 143–44.

25. S. Feshbach, "The Catharsis Hypothesis and Some Consequences of Interaction with Aggression," *Journal of Personality* 24 (1956): 449–62; L. Berkowitz, "Experimental Investigations of the Hostility Catharsis," *Journal of Consulting and Clinical Psychology* 35 (1970): 1–7; Tavris, *Anger*.

26. M. Julius et al., "Anger-Coping Types, Blood Pressure, and All-Cause Mortality: A Follow-up in Tecumseh, Michigan (1971–1983)," *American Journal of Epidemiology* 124, no. 2 (1986): 220–33.

27. E. M. Cummings et al., *Developmental Psychology* 21, no. 3 (1985).

28. Julius et al., "Anger-Coping Types."

29. H. G. Lerner, *The Dance of Anger* (New York: Harper and Row, 1985), 1.

30. "Kindness Week," *Brain-Mind Bulletin*, June 1991, 3.

31. R. Williams, *The Trusting Heart* (New York: Times Books, 1989), xiii, 11.

32. W. Nagler, *The Dirty Half Dozen: Six Radical Rules to Make Relationships Last* (New York: Warner, 1991), 47.

33. Josselson, *The Space Between Us*, 99.

34. L. Rafkin, *Street Smarts* (New York: HarperCollins, 1995), 97.

35. Ibid., 98.

Chapter 10: Home Safe Home

1. P. Quigley, *Not an Easy Target* (New York: Fireside, 1995), 59.
2. Ibid., 54.
3. Castleman, *Crime Free*, 107–8.

Chapter 11: Emergency Safety Awareness and Tools

1. Castleman, *Crime Free*, 67.
2. Rafkin, *Street Smarts*, 39.
3. Castleman, *Crime Free*, 69.
4. Ibid., 112–13.
5. D. Prufer, "How to Protect Yourself," *Self*, August 1994.
6. "Obscene Phone Calls Common for Women," *The Menninger Letter* 3, no. 6 (June 1995), 1.
7. G. S. Couzens, "Close Encounters of the Canine Kind," *Heartbeat/Fitness*, July/August 1992, 19–22.
8. Rafkin, *Street Smarts*, 25.
9. Castleman, *Crime Free*, 113.
10. T. Jarriel, "Road Rage," 20/20—*ABC Television Newsmagazine*, February 2, 1996.
11. W. J. Cook. "Mad Driver's Disease." *US News & World Report* (November 11, 1996) 574–76.
12. Seligman, *What You Can Change*, 132.
13. Prufer, "How to Protect Yourself."
14. Prufer, "How to Protect Yourself."
15. Rafkin, *Street Smarts*, 73.
16. Ibid., 74.
17. Ibid., 76.
18. J. Blyskal, "Crash Course," *American Health*, January/February 1993, 77.
19. M. Puente, "Legislators Tackling the Terror of Stalking," *USA Today*, July 21, 1992, 9A; Quigley, *Not an Easy Target*, 95.
20. T. Powers and R. B. Isaacs, *The Seven Steps to Personal Safety* (New York: Center for Personal Defense Studies, 1993), 80.
21. P. B. Bart and P. H. O'Brien, *Stopping Rape: Successful Survival Strategies* (Oxford: Pergamon Press, 1985); J. Fein, *Exploding the Myths of Self-Defense* (Sebastopol, Calif.: Torrance Publishing, 1993).
22. Powers and Isaacs, *Seven Steps to Personal Safety*, 80.
23. Tesoro, *Options for Avoiding Assault*, 111.
24. Powers and Isaacs, *Seven Steps to Personal Safety*, 80.
25. B. Taylor, "Power Throwing" (Tactical Response Solutions, 2945 S. Mooney Boulevard, Visalia, Calif. 93277; 1994); see also B. Bishop and

M. Thomas, *Protecting Children from Danger* (Berkeley, Calif.: North Atlantic Books, 1993), 152–53.

26. Powers and Isaacs, *Seven Steps to Personal Safety*, 76.

27. McDonald, *Survival*, 62–63.

Chapter 12: Teaching Your Kids Inner Safety

1. S. Greengard and C. M. Solomon, "Growing Up Scared," *L.A. Magazine*, July 1995, 50–61.

2. D. Prothrow-Stith with M. Weissman, *Deadly Consequences* (New York: HarperPerennial, 1991), 145.

3. S. Begley, "Your Child's Brain," *Newsweek*, February 19, 1996, 55–58.

4. N. Rubin, "A Safer World at Home," *Child*, October 1994, 128–42.

5. Ibid.

6. McDonald, *Survival*, 121.

7. Seligman, *What You Can Change*.

Chapter 13: Safety Resources for Teenagers and College Students

1. Rafkin, *Street Smarts*, 108.

Chapter 15: Healing the Emotional Wounds of Violence

1. "Coping With Grief," *University of Texas Lifetime Health Letter* 4, no. 5 (May 1992): 1–6.

2. J. L. Herman, *Trauma and Recovery* (New York: Basic Books, 1992), 159–60.

3. "How to Survive (Practically) Anything," *Psychology Today*, January/February 1992, 35–39.

4. M. E. Francis and J. W. Pennebaker, "Talking and Writing as Illness Prevention," *Medicine, Exercise, Nutrition, and Health* 1, no. 2 (January/February 1992): 27–33; J. W. Pennebaker, *Opening Up: The Healing Power of Confiding in Others* (New York: Morrow, 1990).

5. Francis and Pennebaker, "Talking and Writing."

6. J. Segal, *Winning Life's Toughest Battles: Roots of Human Resilience* (New York: McGraw-Hill, 1986), 80–81.

7. Engler, J., and Goleman, D. *The Consumer's Guide to Psychotherapy* (New York: Fireside, 1993): 461.

8. Hirschfield, R., quoted in "Beating Depression." *U. S. News & World Report* (March 5, 1990): 49.

9. "Depression: Lifting the Cloud." *Johns Hopkins Medical Letter: Health after 50* 2 (9)(Nov. 1990): 4–5.

10. Herman, *Trauma and Recovery*, 202.

11. Segal, *Winning Life's Toughest Battles*, 109–10.

12. Ibid., 105.

Chapter 16: Building a Safer World

1. S. F. Hamilton, *Apprenticeship for Adulthood* (New York: Free Press, 1990), 156.

2. L. C. Spears, *Reflections on Leadership* (New York: Wiley, 1995), 300.

ACKNOWLEDGMENTS

Harold wishes to lovingly acknowledge his wife, Sirah Vettese, and express much love and appreciation to Shazara, Damien, and Michael for their support. All love and gratitude to his dear mother, Fridil, departed father Max, and to Nora and Gus. He also expresses heartfelt appreciation to Deepak and Rita Chopra, Bobby Colomby, Mary Conn, Ken and Karen Druck, Mike and Donna Fletcher, Dana Plant, John and Bonnie Gray, Hoffman Quadrinity Process Teachers, Raz and Liza Ingrasci, Norman and Lyn Lear, Peter McWilliams, Jack Pursel, Vince and Laura Regalbuto, Ayman and Rowan Sawaf, and to Amanresorts for my writing environment, especially the staff of the Amandari and Amankila Hotels of Bali. Special gratitude to Lazaris and Maharishi Mahesh Yogi.

Robert wishes to express his love and appreciation to his wife and family, and his debt of gratitude to his teachers and mentors through the years in the United States, Europe, Tibet, and other parts of the world.

We express our deep and mutual appreciation to Stephanie Tade, our literary agent, and to Don Cleary and Jane Rotrosen.

We wish to acknowledge the shared vision and strong support we have received at Crown Publishers from Ann Patty, Carol Taylor, Jane Cavolina, Jim Walsh, Steve Boldt, Susan Hood, Brian Belfiglio, and Suzanne Wickham.

We also wish to acknowledge the contributions of the following men and women whose teachings and writings on health, safety, and psychology have influenced our thoughts and perspectives: Arnold A. Lazarus, Pauline B. Bart, Bob Bishop, James D. Brewer, Denise Caignon, Geoffrey Canada, Michael Castleman, Thomas F. Crum, Charles Derber, Terry Dobson, Ronald S. Dong, Richard Driscoll, Bob Duggan, Judith Fein, Margaret T. Gordon, Dave Grossman, Gail Groves, Grace Hechinger, Judith Lewis Herman, Richard B. Isaacs, Susan Jeffers, Ann Jones, Joseph A. Kinney, Samantha Koumanelis, Madeline Levine, Jay B. Marcus, Laura C. Martin, Hugh C. McDonald, Susan Murphy-Milano, Victor Miller, Arnold Mindell, Ronald Nathan, Patricia H. O'Brien, Esther M. Orioli, Tim Powers, Deborah Prothrow-Stith, Paxton Quigley, Khalegh Quinn, Louise Rafkin, Suzanne M. Retzinger, Stephanie Riger, Harold J. Rothwax, Elizabeth Starko, Marian R. Stuart, Mary Tesoro, Matt Thomas, George J. Thompson, Karen Trocki, Richard Weissbourd, and Joseph Wolpe.

Index

ABOUT THE AUTHORS

Harold H. Bloomfield, M.D., is a renowned psychiatrist, and a leading psychological educator of our time. Dr. Bloomfield has been at the forefront of many important self-help movements worldwide for twenty-five years. His first book, *TM—Transcendental Meditation* was an international best-seller on the *New York Times* list for many months. His two other best-sellers, *How to Survive the Loss of a Love* and *How to Heal Depression*, have become self-help classics. His other books, *Making Peace With Your Parents*, *Making Peace With Yourself*, *Lifemates*, and *Making Peace with Your Stepfamily*, introduced personal and family peacemaking to millions of people. His books have sold over six million copies and have been translated into twenty-four languages.

In recognition of his ground-breaking book, *The Holistic Way to Health and Happiness*, Dr. Bloomfield received the American Holistic Health Association's Lifetime Achievement Award. He frequently appears on national television and in other media and is adjunct professor of psychology at the Union Graduate School.

For further information regarding consultations, lectures, and seminars, please contact: Harold H. Bloomfield, M.D., 1337 Camino Del Mar, Del Mar, California 92014. Office: (619) 481-9950.

Robert K. Cooper is an independent scholar who has spent a number of years researching health sciences, leadership, conflict management, and personal and interpersonal effectiveness under pressure. He earned his doctorate in health and psychology, and served in the U.S. Marine Corps during the Vietnam era. His background includes work as an executive security and protection specialist, and he has been active for many years in human rights movements worldwide. He lives with his wife and family in the Midwest.